5/04

Mercy, Mercy Me

Mercy, Mercy Me

The Art, Loves and Demons of Marvin Gaye

Michael Eric Dyson

BASIC
CIVITAS
BOOKS

A MEMBER OF THE PERSEUS BOOKS GROUP

NEW YORK

Published by Basic Civitas Books, A Member of the Perseus Books Group

Books published by Basic Civitas are available at special discounts for bulk purchases in the United States by corporations, institutions, and other organizations. For more information, please contact the Special Markets Department at the Perseus Books Group, 11 Cambridge Center, Cambridge MA 02142, or call (617) 252-5298, (800) 255-1514 or e-mail special.markets@perseusbooks.com.

Designed by Lovedog Studio

Title page photograph © David Corio / RETNA

Library of Congress Cataloging-in-Publication Data
Dyson, Michael Eric.
  Mercy, mercy me : the art, loves and demons of Marvin Gaye / Michael Eric Dyson.
    p. cm.
  Includes bibliographical references and index.
  ISBN 0-465-01769-X (alk. paper)
  1. Gaye, Marvin. 2. Singers—United States—Biography. I. Title.
ML420.G305D97 2004
782.421644'092—dc22
                                        2004002411

04 05 06 / 10 9 8 7 6 5 4 3 2 1

To
Mr. Otis Burdette
*Teacher, friend and oratorical coach
in whose classroom I delivered my
first speech after listening to Marvin;*

Captain Stanley Perkins
*Los Angeles Fire Department
Gourmet cook, splendid dresser,
graceful dancer and American hero*

And to
Rochester Dyson and
Irene Dyson
*(1915-2002)
Beloved Uncle and Aunt and Wonderful
Examples of Strength and Courage*

Contents

"Ain't Nothing Like the Real Thing"

Marvin Gaye's Meaning

Every year, Fran Bell, a prominent community activist in Chicago, takes the day off from work on April 2 to celebrate Marvin Gaye's birthday. She began the practice nearly a decade ago when a friend who knew of her love for the legendary singer opened a compilation of his music for Bell to hear. "'He's so great, we should make his birthday a national holiday,'" Bell recalls her friend saying. "And from that point on, I said, 'You know what? That's exactly what I'm going to do.' He takes off as well, and we call each other on that day, just to celebrate the greatness of Marvin."

While Gaye's birthday is far from a national holiday, his impact on the lives of millions in several generations across the globe is undeniable. But the nature of his influence and the scope of his achievements may be lost on young people not yet born when this world famous icon met a violent death. There are a few biographies—especially David Ritz's path clearing work, *Divided Soul* and Steve Turner's more recent *Trouble Man*—that examine Gaye's life in rich detail.

Mercy, Mercy Me is not a biography of the singer. It is instead a work of biocriticism: an analysis of Gaye's art, loves, and demons that turns to elements of his life to illustrate his genius and to detail his struggles and failures. Joining my work on other historic personalities—including Malcolm X, Martin Luther King, Jr., and Tupac Shakur—this book assesses the cultural and intellectual importance of a great figure who helped to shape and define the times in which he lived. Marvin Gaye's music provides a powerful glimpse into the swirling currents of history and race that indelibly stamp the sixties and seventies.

Marvin's voice continues to call for freedom in the social and sexual realms, as his pioneering recordings document the struggle to be at once politically aware and erotically enlightened. And his demons and tragic death illumine the pitfalls of drug addiction and brutal forms of corporal punishment and alleged sexual abuse to which he was subject. Above all, Marvin Gaye's legacy warrants a fresh interpretation of his music, his passions and his life-and-death struggles, for a generation unfamiliar with the times and themes that shaped his monumental art.

I want to thank Liz Maguire, my faithful and fearless editor, whose unflagging belief in this project helped it see the light of day. I also want to thank Megan Hustad for her diligence and support. Thanks also to Matty Goldberg for creating the discography. I am grateful to Christine Marra for her expert management in producing the book, and to Marco Pavia for his incredible editorial skills and close reading.

I also thank Walter Licht, an associate dean at Penn, who, after seeing the documentary "Standing in the Shadows of

Motown," exulted in Marvin Gaye's genius and said that I ought to write a book about him. Well, here it is, Walter. Thanks for the encouragement. I thank my wonderful colleagues at Penn—including Tukufu Zuberi, Gale Garrison, Onyx Finney, Carol Davis, Ann Mather, Marie Hudson and many more—for their crucial support and love. I also thank Daniel Quon (for this book and the *Michael Eric Dyson Reader*), Paul Farber (a budding journalist) and Marc Hill (a rising scholar) for their timely research. I also thank Pastor Dr. Alyn Waller (and his lovely wife Ellyn), in whose church office I put the finishing touches on revisions to this book.

———

I also want to thank all the wonderful folk, many of them legends in their own right, who took time to talk to me for this book: Q-Tip; Janie Bardford; Claudette Robinson (my lovely friend; thanks for the Marvin compliment!); Kim Weston (my dining buddy); Rona Elliot; Elaine Jesmer; Leon Ware (serious genius); Arsenio Hall; Brenda Holloway; Pete Moore; Art Stewart; Ron Brewington (big ups for all your help); Gary Harris; Irene Gaye; R Kelly; Georgia Ward; Harry Weinger; Martha Reeves; Johnny Bristol; Bobby Rogers; Hank Dixon; Freddie Gorman; Gladys Horton; Obie Benson; Weldon McDougal; Kitty Sears; Ivy Jo Hunter; Ludie Montgomery; Dave Simmons; Louvain Demps and Fran Bell (a beautiful and singing sister). I also thank Suzanne DePasse for her always generous spirit—and her brilliance and beauty over the years. And to Jan Gaye, the bright and beautiful widow of Marvin Gaye, I am grateful for that long, late-night phone call when you shared your heart. Although you didn't allow me to interview you for this book, I still appreciate your openness and honesty. And to Nona Gaye, Marvin's gifted and beautiful daughter, thank you for your sweet spirit when we talked.

As always, I thank my family: my brilliant and beautiful mother Addie, my brothers Anthony, Everette, Gregory, and Brian, and their families; and my children, Michael Eric Dyson, II, Maisha, Mwata—and my other son Cory. Finally, thanks to Rev. Marcia Louise Dyson, my brilliant, beautiful and bold wife who took time from revising her novel, *Don't Call Me Angel*, to read and critique this book.

"What's Going On"
Marvin, Motown, and Me

When I was twelve years old, I gave my first speech in public as part of a Detroit oratorical contest. I was a bit nervous, so I lingered longer than usual before heading to a small classroom in my junior high school to do verbal battle. As I sat in my father's car in the school parking lot, the melodic strains of an instant classic spilled from the radio, calming and inspiring me at the same time.

"Mother, mother, there's too many of you crying," pleaded the sweet and poignant tenor. "Brother, brother, brother, there's far too many of you dying." The singer insisted that "only love can conquer hate," and that we'd have to "find a way, to bring some lovin' here today," as he demanded to know "what's going on."

On that spring day in 1971, as war raged and races clashed, I fixed on Marvin Gaye's political anthem and made it personal: I transformed the tune into a musical talisman to ward off fear and failure. When I proved victorious in my speechmaking,

"What's Going On," and the album that contained it, became a harbinger of blessing. It encouraged me to soldier on against trouble. I turned to Gaye time and again over the years to provide inspiration and hope whenever I faced crisis. He has done the same for millions across the globe.

Black Detroit took special pride in Gaye's monumental achievement. We were only three years past the bloodiest riots in the nation's history. The black population had swollen to almost half of the population from less than ten percent in 1940. That was due in large part to the mass migration of blacks to Detroit in the forties and fifties from Arkansas, Mississippi, Louisiana, Georgia, and the Carolinas. Henry Ford drew blacks by the bushels with the promise of a decent wage for hard work and by hiring them when few others would.

Ford's assembly line influenced the son of a black transplant from the Georgia cotton fields. That boy, born in 1929, was named Berry Gordy, and he would in 1959 establish Motown Records Corporation, which became one of the most successful black businesses in the nation. Gordy modeled his company's philosophy of producing records on Ford's methods of producing cars. Motown also shaped the musical tastes of millions of Americans with its bright melodies, upbeat lyrics, and crossover ambitions. It wanted to sell the beauty and brilliance of the black voice to white America. Motown broke down many racial barriers with its massive artistic achievements, even as it embodied both the triumphs and troubles of the American dream and capitalism.

Marvin Gaye was dubbed the Prince of Motown for his great voice, good looks—and his undeniable musical genius. He benefited from Motown's system of assigning producers to its artists, creating memorable music and several classics along the way. But no artist as gifted and independent as Marvin could long tolerate a mechanical approach that prohibited its artists from writing or producing for themselves. He bristled at the company's severe restrictions and finally broke out to create some of the most distinguished albums in the history of American music. Not only did he set a standard for musical achievement that has never been exceeded, but he inspired other artists with his extraordinary example, most notably his label mate and protégé Stevie Wonder.

Along with his success came problems—broken marriages, drugs, paranoia, sexual dysfunction, domestic violence, stories of childhood abuse, and finally, murder at the hands of his father. In the midst of his troubles, Marvin spoke from his heart and bore witness to the triumph of artistic creativity over debilitating personal setbacks. He also wrestled in his music to reconcile his spiritual heritage as the son of a Pentecostal preacher and the erotic legacy of sensual expression that he pioneered.

Marvin's music spoke to me at every stage of my life. Besides his landmark *What's Going On*, I thrilled to his 1973 classic *Let's Get It On* as a sexually curious and inexperienced teen. I garnered invaluable erotic encouragement and romantic inspiration from his underestimated 1976 classic, *I Want You*. I danced at many a house party and disco to Marvin's feral 1977 jam "Got To Give It Up." As I faced my first divorce in 1979, Marvin's 1978 LP *Here, My Dear* offered zestful and acute insight into a relationship's ups and downs, its stages of coalescence and erosion. Despite his anger at Motown for putting out 1981's *In Our Lifetime*, this overlooked masterpiece helped me to negotiate the tensions of being a young minister who sought to balance spiritual aspiration and sensual appreciation. And his final big hit, 1983's "Sexual Healing," inspired me to claim the benefit of unashamed sexual health.

When it was announced that he was killed on April Fool's day in 1984, the day before his 45th birthday, I was a college student who thought—even desperately wished—that it was a cruel joke. Of course, it was all too tragically true. Since that time, I have constantly turned to Marvin's music to lift my spirits and to travel with him over the vast landscape of human experience that he traversed. Now, twenty years after his death, and in the 65th year of his birth, I offer this consideration of his great art, his profound loves and his restless demons. This book, written at the same age Marvin would have been had he lived a single day more, is a small gesture of my gratitude for his towering gift—and as a way to critically engage his legacy and to learn from his mistakes. Like any of us, Marvin could skillfully avoid the truth about himself and others. But more often than not, and much more often than most of us, he could be dispassionately self-critical. He was able to train his high intelligence on himself and the world around him to enlightening effect. I hope this book in its own small way can do the same.

CHAPTER ONE

"Stubborn Kind of Fellow"

The Search for a Style

The best-selling Motown artist of all time, Marvin Gaye also transcended the boundaries of rhythm and blues as no other performer has ever done. In 2003, his seminal album *What's Going On* took the number six spot on *Rolling Stone's* "500 Greatest Albums"—nestled between the Beatles' *Rubber Soul* and the Rolling Stones' *Exile on Main Street*. Gaye was the only black artist to crack the top ten from that bastion of white rock and roll.

Twenty years after his death, how can we better understand the true achievements of this genius, the loves that inspired him, and the demons that haunted him until his untimely end?

The world into which Gaye was born in Washington, D.C.—much like the world in which his music would resonate—was torn by racial conflict. The *Washington Post* that appeared on April 2, 1939, the day of Gaye's birth, printed a brief article about the upcoming congress of the Daughters of the American Revolution—which had just barred opera star

Marian Anderson from performing at Constitution Hall. The paper noted that the group still anticipated being received at the White House despite the "late unpleasantness" of the Anderson snub.[1] The *Post* also included an essay by Louis M. Jiggitts, vice chairman of the Democratic National Committee. In "The South's Problems," printed on the op-ed page, Jiggitts claimed that the relationship "between the races throughout the South is not one of tension: on the contrary, it is one of friendliness, justice, and humanity."[2] Jiggitts argued that regardless of "attempts to prove otherwise, the Negro in the South is not unhappy, but on the whole is more contented than many of those who live in other sections of the Nation."[3] Despite his dishonest sentiments, Jiggitts managed to capture the plight of many blacks, including Gaye's family, when he wrote that poverty "stalks the streets of our greatest cities" and "rears its ugly head in our Nation's Capital."[4]

These same forces of poverty and racial conflict shaped the young Gaye's life. Marvin was the second of four children born to Rev. Marvin P. Gay, Sr., and his wife, Alberta Gay, in a Washington, D.C. housing project. (Marvin added the "e" when he began to sing professionally, to avoid his surname's association with homosexuality.) Marvin's father was a strict Pentecostal pastor who believed in firm discipline and severe corporal punishment to keep his children—including older sister Jeanne, younger siblings Frankie and Zeola—in line. Marvin got the worse of the beatings administered to Rev. Gay's brood: he was rebellious, outspoken, and deeply resentful of his tough treatment at the hands of his father. Alberta often got on her knees and prayed with Jeanne that Rev. Gay would stop beating Marvin. But the beatings continued, often with Rev. Gay increasing the psychological terror by making Marvin wait an hour or more after telling him he would be whipped. As it turned out, Marvin was also a gifted musician and singer who began performing in his father's church at the tender age of two. Since Rev. Gay earned very little as a pastor, his wife was the family's chief breadwinner, working as a domestic in Maryland and Virginia.[5] Nevertheless, he physically and psychologically abused his wife and children.

As they got older, the Gay children were prohibited from enjoying too much camaraderie with the neighborhood children, largely a function of Pentecostal religious practices—for instance, they subscribed to a branch of faith that worshipped on Saturday. Still, Marvin managed to forge relations with a few friends, some of whom would later join him in his local musical adventures in doo-wop groups as a teen. He excelled with his musical gifts, gaining confidence in his vocal abilities and in his skill on the piano and drums. Marvin entered talent contests at junior high school, singing not his father's religious music, but the sweet strains of popular singers like Johnny Ray. He listened to black musical greats such as Jesse Belvin and Nat King Cole, while also admiring the likes of Perry Como and Frank Sinatra. Marvin's early ambition to sing popular standards—rather than R & B—began during this time.

When Marvin entered Cardozo High School, he met other teens who loved music and formed a group that included Reese Palmer, Sondra Lattisaw, James Hopps, Vernon Christian, and Leon MacMickens.[6] As the DC Tones, they sang doo-wop, a fact that greatly displeased Rev. Gay, who looked with disdain on the "boogie-woogie" music. Marvin had become a tall, handsome youth who was polite and painfully shy. He desired to participate in athletics, but his father didn't allow his children a great deal of freedom on the streets. Still, Marvin managed to sneak to matinee shows at the Howard Theater to see black stars like Clyde McPhatter, Jackie Wilson, the Spaniels, the Dells, the Platters, and James Brown. Marvin was awed by their fame and freedom and vowed to be bigger than them all.[7]

As Marvin experienced growing tension at home—his father's merciless beatings began to let up, only to increase the psychic terror he imposed —he realized he would never fulfill his artistic potential if he remained in his father's vicious orbit. At 17, a year before graduation, Marvin dropped out of school and joined the Air Force. But the military proved to be as equally disastrous as it was chafing under the brutality of his father. Marvin didn't adapt well to authority, and found himself constantly challenging his superiors. He joined the military in Virginia and underwent basic training in San Antonio, Texas, before going to Cheyenne, Wyoming for further training. He was soon sent to Kansas to peel potatoes for Food Supply, which increased his feelings of humiliation. He began to frequent the nightclubs in the area, and had his first sexual experience at a local black whorehouse. In the meantime, Marvin reported late to duty several times, and otherwise bucked the authority of his commanders. He was arrested one night by the Military Police for being in an "unauthorized area." Finally, after an abysmal record of "continually absent[ing] himself without permission," Marvin was given an honorable discharge less than a year after he joined the Air Force.[8]

Marvin returned to Washington and his family, but he only stayed a few days. He could no longer abide his father's controlling and abusive behavior, and moved in with a female friend,

"Peasie" Adams, who was married and living in a nearby apartment. His old friend Reese Palmer from the DC Tones was busy organizing another group, assembled from local singers, and invited Marvin to join them. Their group was named the Marquees. Soon after forming in 1957, they had a meeting with famed singer Bo Didley, who was dating a mutual friend. Didley introduced the Marquees to the Okeh label, a subsidiary of Columbia Records. Palmer had written a song, "Wyatt Earp," and on the strength of his composition, the group was offered a contract from Columbia. Since Marvin was under 21, he needed a guardian's approval to sign the contract. Rev. Gay refused, and forbade his wife from signing, too. Not to be deterred, Reese Palmer forged Rev. Gay's signature, and the Marquees were under contract.

"Wyatt Earp" failed to become a hit, and the group had to seek employment to support their music. Marvin became a caddy for local golf-courses, and took on a second job with Palmer at a Washington commissary, where the duo was eventually fired for singing on the job. In the People's Drug Store, Marvin encountered racism in public for the first time since his days in the military—he was kicked out because it served whites. Although his life in the black ghetto had been shaped by white supremacy, this was Marvin's first face-to-face encounter with the institution of bigotry.

But fate smiled on Marvin and his comrades when they met up with the Moonglows, a famed doo-wop group that came to town for a week-long engagement at the Howard Theater. Marvin managed his way backstage and pleaded with Moonglows leader Harvey Fuqua to listen to the Marquees. As soon as he heard them, Fuqua was convinced of their talent, and Marvin's timing couldn't have been better—the Moonglows were torn by internal discord and were on the verge of breaking up. When the group disbanded, Fuqua hired the Marquees to form the new group Harvey and the Moonglows.[9]

Marvin moved with his musical mates to Chicago, where Harvey rehearsed the group and sharpened their musical instincts and deepened their harmonic vocabularies. It was while he toured and rehearsed that Marvin honed and shaped his trademark background harmonies. After putting them through their paces, Harvey taught the group the Moonglows' old songs, and led his new charges on tours across the nation. Marvin got his first taste of real freedom, and even began to smoke pot and enjoy sex with women he'd meet on the road. One night, the group was busted for possessing drugs, which—along with the change in popular musical tastes in R & B from doo-wop to a harder sound—lead very shortly to their demise. But Harvey, as before, was angling to take Marvin, the most vocally gifted of the group, and use him to land even bigger contacts. Fuqua had already been hired by Leonard Chess, of Chess Records, to help Anna Records, a Detroit label it had been distributing.[10] Anna Records was owned by Billy Davis and his girlfriend Gwen Gordy. The label was named after Gwen's sister Anna. One of Davis's writing partners was Berry Gordy, who started Motown Records in 1959 with an $800 loan from his family.

Harvey and the Moonglows' last shows occurred in 1959 at Detroit's Twenty Grand Club. Fuqua invited Billy Davis and Gwen and Berry Gordy to watch the Moonglows perform. Berry Gordy had already written some hits—including "Reet Peteet" for Jackie Wilson—and Fuqua was strategizing to lure the dynamic songwriter with his musical bait, Marvin Gaye. That night, Marvin met Anna Gordy, who eventually became his first wife, even though she was 17 years his senior. Marvin and Anna shared a passionate, stormy, and complex relationship. At times, their love turned violent, and they engaged in some very public spats and even physically fought each other. Both also were guilty of infidelity, even as they continued to proclaim a strong love.

Later, at the first Christmas party for Tamla, a Motown label, Berry was urged by Gwen (who would later marry Fuqua) to meet the young man whose phenomenal gifts were already creating a buzz. Marvin played "Mr. Sandman" for Gordy, who was immediately impressed by the young singer. In his autobiography, *To Be Loved*, Gordy determined right there that he wanted Marvin on his label, but he didn't tell him immediately. He didn't know how they'd get along, and he had to keep the upper hand. Eventually Fuqua, without Marvin's knowledge, sold his interest in Gaye to Gordy. Marvin was now a Motown artist. And it was at Motown that Marvin's incredible musical talents, as a collaborator and as a soloist, would flourish.

———

To understand Marvin Gaye's majestic achievements, one must grasp a seeming contradiction: he produced his best music in collaboration with others. "The genius of Marvin Gaye is the genius of those of us who were able to collaborate with him and help him to achieve his goals," says Art Stewart, a superb engineer who worked with Gaye on some of his finest recordings.

Gaye's collaborations took many forms. He reworked words to a song begun by a fellow lyricist. He completed vocal gestures hinted at by another singer. He tapped into the energy and extended the vibration of another musician. He mapped musical secrets locked in his own soul through the charts of a composer, since he could neither read nor write music. He pried loose deeper dimensions of his sensuality in partnership with sensitive producers. Or he lay prostrate on a couch singing in the studio as an engineer captured an artist exploring his multiple voices. In all of these ways and more, Marvin's art thrived on communal cooperation.

"You can't touch what Marvin did," says Harry Weinger, a Universal/Motown VP whose prodigious scholarship in the company's vaults has produced deluxe editions of three of Gaye's classic albums: *What's Going On, Let's Get It On,* and *I Want You.* "But I think I understand why he found it so inviting to work with other people. I love to write, but it's a struggle. If you give me something somebody has already written, I love to edit it; I can work that thing up and make it go. With Marvin, I think his mind was at times distracted, since he was full of so much that he couldn't quite focus. When Leon Ware, for instance, brought him a melody and charts and an idea [for *I Want You*], it helped him to focus and say, 'I can work with that.'"

Marvin's methods of creation appear to echo Berry Gordy's efforts to harness the musical genius of urban black America. Gordy sought to transform the blueprint of Henry Ford's automobile empire into an ebony musical kingdom. Motown Records Corporation adapted the assembly line as a metaphor for producing hit records. Gordy fixed on elements that made cars and musical careers sleek and appealing: regularity and efficiency of production; mechanical and technical brilliance wed to aesthetic value; the elevation of a system that, with few exceptions, credits the product, not its creators; and an obsessive attention to quality control. In the flawed genius of both Ford and Gordy, the quality of *their* control was paramount.[11]

But Gaye's outsized talent and ferocious hunger for independence routinely cut against Gordy's formula, especially in his mature artistry. Marvin's career can be divided in many ways—solo efforts versus duets with female singers; the sides he recorded with the legendary team of Holland-Dozier-Holland in contrast to his work for gifted songwriter-producer Norman Whitfield; or his sixties music versus his seventies-era songs. But the simplest way to chart his artistic freedom is to consider the event that separated both territory and time in Gaye's musical universe: the 1971 release of *What's Going On*, arguably the greatest pop album ever recorded. Before that album, Gaye bitterly fought to abide by his rules. After its release, even though he still raged against the machine, his eccentric path was oiled by the recognition that, at least for a spell, the Zeitgeist rested on his book of musical prophecy. He was Hegel with a downbeat. (Of course, it can't be denied that the seismic shift in Gaye's perception in the culture with that album may at times obscure the compelling work he did before and after his signal achievement.) In the guise of towering auteur, Marvin Gaye worked only when he was inspired, spoke mostly when he had something to say, introduced race and politics into the music of a company hell-bent on crossing over to white America, and gave acknowledgement to other artists in a world ruled by creative anonymity, save for its biggest stars.

"I sometimes resent artists getting all the credit, because although they may have phenomenal voices, they didn't write those phenomenal songs," says Johnny Bristol, a gifted singer-songwriter-producer who worked with Marvin Gaye and Tammi Terrell on the duo's first two hits. "Nor did they produce them. If they could have, they would not have needed us. So it's very sad that the people who are behind the scenes doing all the hard work, and staying up late at night and weekends to have the product ready for the artists when they come back off their money-making tour [don't get credit]. All [the artist] had to do was walk in and say, 'Here's the paper and I'll sing the song.' The producer's already written the song, produced it, got with the arranger, stayed up nights trying to finish it and get it ready. And yet they bend over and take more bows than any one person should bend over that far to do. You deserve credit for what you've done, but don't ignore the people who helped make it possible for you to be exposed in that light." Ironically, Gaye subverted the rules while actually fulfilling the spirit of collective creativity on which Motown's musical philosophy rested. In a way, he enlivened Motown's ideals by resisting its practices.

Before Marvin found his groove in collaborative creativity, he experienced the ups and downs of any young singer searching for his true voice and style. He found plenty of company in the artists who made up Gordy's "Sound of Young America," as the founder took to calling the rhythms spilling out of Motown. Marvin Gaye and his compatriots were grateful to have a place to work and fashion their musical destinies. Often their eagerness and inexperience caused Motown's young artists to ignore their best interests. Many artists even toured without first ironing out the terms of their compensation. "We used to get on the bus and we hadn't *seen* a contract," says Gladys Horton, a lead singer for the Marvelettes. "We didn't know how much money we were making. That would never happen in this day and time. Berry had a bunch of teenagers. You're very powerful in your teenage years; you *want* something. He was able to capitalize on that."

What many of the youth wanted was a chance to become stars. Some of them got to shine at Hitsville, U.S.A., the two-story house at 2648 West Grand Boulevard in Detroit that Gordy converted into Motown's first headquarters and studio. But opportunity was costly. "When I met Raynoma (Gordy's wife) and Berry, they weren't on West Grand Boulevard yet," says Louvain Demps, a member of the Andantes, the backup singing group for Motown that appeared on over 20,000 recordings. "They were in a duplex on Dexter Avenue. That's where they started out, because they didn't have a studio or anything. I met them, and became one of the Rayber Voices—the name came from the combination of Raynoma and Berry—when they said you could pay them a hundred dollars and they'd record your music. Always scheming!"

As a 19-year-old aspiring singer, Demps took them up on their offer. She sang backing vocals with the Rayber Voices on the company's first release, Marv Johnson's "Come to Me," issued on Motown's Tamla label in 1959. During this time, the company got new digs, first renting, and then buying the eight room house. "I went with Ray before they purchased the property and were still looking at it. Later, when they purchased it, Gordy went to work over there fixing it up as his studio." If Berry Gordy was the midwife of black musical aspiration, then Motown was his hospital. Hitsville was the delivery room. That may sound hokey, but Hitsville was the birthplace for watershed moments in the cultural imagination: the simple eloquence of Smokey Robinson's lyrics, which led Bob Dylan to dub him "America's greatest living poet"; the transcendental musings of Stevie Wonder, who was Emerson in dark shades; the Temptations' elegant masculine vulnerability; the lyrical feminine yearning of the Supremes; and Gaye's deft explorations of social and sexual identity.

At the beginning of his Motown career, Marvin was neither interested in embracing the raucous sentiments of rock and roll nor sweetening the strains of soul music. Instead, he yearned to swim in the streams of popular music that buoyed the art of America's greatest balladeers.[12] "He wanted to be the next Nat King Cole and Frank Sinatra," says Claudette Robinson, the still-gorgeous former member of the Miracles. "He had such a smooth, silky type of voice." Her praise resounds because Robinson was married for a quarter century to Miracles lead singer Smokey Robinson. His cascading falsetto is one of the most recognizable vocal signatures in pop music.

Janie Bradford, who was Hitsville's first receptionist, and who penned "Money (That's What I Want)" with Berry Gordy, agrees with Robinson. "I loved him doing that style, because as you notice, even with R & B he wasn't all over the stage," Bradford says. "He was just this quiet singer." Warren "Pete" Moore, another member of the Miracles, remembers the first time he and renowned vocalist Chuck Jackson heard Gaye's ethereal tones. "One day, me and Chuck went by Hitsville," Moore recalls. "We went into the office, and the studio door was open, and we heard this voice—I hadn't met Marvin at this point—and he was singing some dreamy stuff, because at that time Marvin wanted to be the next Nat King Cole. We walked into the control room, and Chuck, who is *good*, asked, 'Who is this guy?' Chuck made a statement that I'll never forget. He said, 'Man, this guy has got the prettiest voice I have ever heard in my life.'"

Despite the good impression Gaye made on Moore and Jackson, his periodic recording visits to the standards catalogue failed to click with a broader public. His first Motown album, 1961's *The Soulful Moods of Marvin Gaye*, featured classic tunes like "(I'm Afraid) the Masquerade Is Over," "My Funny Valentine," and "How High the Moon," and legendary song-writers like Irving Berlin, Cole Porter, and Rodgers & Hart. It was largely ignored. Decades later, the album was panned because Gaye's delivery "is so smooth it's virtually soulless," and although most "of the album is standards," he "doesn't do them justice."[13] Another critic was kinder, arguing that while "it is hardly the innovative" work contained in *What's Going On* or *Let's Get It On*, "for the most part these are fine performances considering the versatile range of his voice and depth of feeling he brought to most of his performances."[14]

In the coming years, Gaye would release A *Tribute to the Great Nat King Cole* (1965), a lovely testimonial to an enduring musical influence that at the time of its release was barely noticed. A year before, in 1964, he made *When I'm Alone I Cry*, which one critic dismissed as "only of interest to collectors" since on it Marvin proved "that he was a great soul singer, but a mediocre jazz vocalist."[15] Such a conclusion is unnecessarily harsh, especially in light of Gaye's fine work on *Vulnerable*, fin-ished in 1978, but released posthumously in 1997. On this work, Marvin embraces seven ballads surrounded by dense string and brass orchestral arrangements of pianist-composer Bobby Scott. Gaye had taken a crack at this material before, in 1967, when he and Scott concluded that the singer wasn't yet vocally mature enough to sublimely interpret songs like "The Shadow of Your Smile," "This Will Make You Laugh," and "Why Did I Choose You." Marvin revisited the material in 1978 when he was more confident. Marvin's command of vocal overdubbing, and his lovely shifts between his celestial falsetto, aching tenor and his gripping lower-register, gave his renditions depth and complexity.[16] Marvin proved that he could use multiple vocals to enhance his R & B tunes and to bring fresh urgency to the standards. As one critic wrote, *Vulnerable* showed that "Gaye could turn even the most hackneyed lounge-act tunes into forthright, spellbinding testimony."[17] His enlarged technique works poignantly on "She Needs Me." After an overture of sweeping violins and sparkling harp tones garnished by wisps of fluttering flute, Marvin cries, in his natural tenor, "I love you." One of his own background voices gently floats an "ooh" beneath his phrase. Later, Marvin effortlessly glides to the top of his sweetly wailing falsetto, declaring that his lover, appearances aside, needs him. His confidence is boosted by doo-wop blended harmonies—all supplied by Gaye. They spin the song into melodic fury, and even deeper into the mysteries of mutual attraction it proclaims. Unfortunately, in 1985, CBS Records released some of Gaye's earlier, discarded, 1967 versions of the material on *Romantically Yours*.[18]

It wasn't just on his studio efforts that the public failed to warm to Marvin's ballad crooning; it crossed over to live performance. "We were in San Francisco right after Tammi Terell [who was Marvin's most successful and beloved duet partner] fell ill, and lovely Brenda Holloway was onstage with him, doing her part," remembered legendary Motown artist Martha Reeves. "And between numbers, before she joined him, Marvin was trying to do a version of 'Days of Wine and Roses.' So you heard one guy holler out, 'I don't wanna hear that! I wanna hear 'Stubborn Kind of Fellow'! You better sing 'Hitch Hike.' And the wine bottles flew up on the stage. I mean, they were really adamant about not wanting Marvin to sing ballads. They wanted to hear him do his groove thing. So he kind of turned his mind for a while back to the R & B thing, and laid the desire to sing ballads aside."[19]

Ironically, it was Marvin's treatment of standard tunes that first caught the ears of Chuck Jackson and Pete Moore. When they happened on Gaye in Hitsville's "Snakepit"—so named because of the studio's lower-level location, and for the intense competition among writers, arrangers, and artists—they heard him recording songs for *When I'm Alone I Cry*. Moore disagrees with critics who feel that Marvin lacked the skill to sing standards. "It's a great work," he says, referring to Gaye's first effort. "I don't know how many dudes even *heard* this album." Harry Weinger thinks that while Gaye had a beautiful enough voice to record such music, in the sixties he lacked the experience to bring the tunes to life. "The key thing about *Vulnerable* is, had Marvin matured and got older and lived a little longer, and had different experiences, [he would have been more successful]," Weinger says. "He went back and refined the vocals over and over again. So when he saw himself that a sixties person could not really understand these songs, he had to go back and redo them. In the beginning, it's just imitation, and he's pleasant enough, and he has a wonderful voice. He can do 'Witchcraft' and 'One More For The Road.' But you're playing the persona; you're not living the material. Not in the sixties. I think if Marvin were around now he'd probably make a killer standards record. Can you imagine? Imagine Marvin at 60 [doing] 'Bewitched, Bothered and Bewildered,' and 'At Last'!"

Janie Bradford is more philosophical about why Gaye failed to strike fire on his version of these songs. The white musical establishment plays a big role. "Think about the times," Bradford tells me. "Okay, they let Nat King Cole in, and we couldn't keep him on TV because we did not have the money back then. They let him in, but they wouldn't back him. So they could claim, 'You can't say we didn't give you a show.' So Marvin didn't reach any status singing that kind of music. It was not his voice or his style or his personality. The timing was bad. And since Marvin Gaye is a black boy, in their minds, he's got to sing R & B and rock and roll, and this kind of music. Their feeling was, 'There was only one Nat King Cole. How can there be another?'" Marvin was trapped by insidious racial politics whose rule was clear: One Negro at a time. Gaye's stubbornness and artistic desire kept him hungry to master the standards. Nevertheless, he continued to release hit R & B singles and albums that crowned him Motown's Prince.[20]

If collaboration was the order of his later career, it marked his earlier efforts, too, even if they were shaped more by company dictate than creative drive. Before *What's Going On*, Marvin was assigned producers, songwriters, and singing partners. Still, whether by slow downs or periodically absenting himself from production, Marvin managed to squeeze a bit of control from Motown's high-powered machinery. Marvin's legendary stubbornness would prove as great a headache to the company as its refusal to grant artistic freedom would be to its artists. Marvin ignored most pressures to bow at Motown's procedural altar just because he was Berry Gordy's brother-in-law. His near kinship simply spurred him to greater demands for artistic breathing room. "Marvin played the drums, he played the keyboard, he played a MELODICA, he played any synthesized instrument that was invented at the time, and made a lot of tracks on his own," says Martha Reeves. "There're one or two songs that we recorded behind him where he actually played the footboard of the Hammond B3 organ. And he had his own groove. He would stay in the studio for hours to get the groove that he was hoping for, and he enticed the musicians to come go with him in some of the things he was doing. He had to face a lot of opposition from Berry Gordy, who had never really let any artist have their way and do their own thing. But Marvin insisted. And I don't think it was because [Berry] was his brother-in-law. I think it was because he was a profound artist who wanted and knew what he could do. He wanted to do things his way." If he couldn't sing like Sinatra for a living, at least he could emulate the artist in carving his own niche in the musical stratosphere.

Gaye's genius broke down many barriers, not only in the broader culture, but at his musical address. Among Motown artists, Marvin Gaye might be considered their Curt Flood—the black baseball player whose pioneering efforts to choose the team he wanted to play for resulted in free agency in the big leagues.[21] Marvin's insistence on listening to his own voice and clearing his own path earned him a level of artistic liberty that benefited others. No artist stood to gain more from Gaye's efforts than Motown prodigy Stevie Wonder. It was because of

Gaye's trailblazing exploits, and Stevie's talents, that Wonder signed a lucrative contract and won artistic freedom when he turned 21. "I think Stevie Wonder and Marvin Gaye were the most talented artists at Motown Records," Martha Reeves says, "because they could produce themselves, and they knew how to get along with the Funk Brothers (Motown's in-house backing band of stellar musicians). And they knew how to get them to play what they wanted. But Marvin's creative genius shows in a lot of the notes that he had singers to sing, and some of the string parts that he invented himself and composed. These are indications that he had a higher level of artistry and thinking than most."

Still, there is little doubt that Marvin's gold records during his first heyday at Motown resulted from his striking gold in the artists, songwriters, arrangers and producers with whom he collaborated. He started as a studio session drummer, but won the opportunity to show his wares because of his undeniable talent, good looks, Gordy family connections, and amiable personality. "When I was a secretary, I had to call drummers on the list," recalls Martha Reeves of her duties of supplying studio musicians for recording dates. "When Benny Benjamin wasn't available, I would call this man named Marvin, who had been traveling with Smokey Robinson as his backup drummer. And he would come in, and he'd wear this straw hat on his eyes. He had this pipe in his mouth most of the time, and he wore sunglasses, so you couldn't really see his face. He didn't say much of anything but, 'Hey, baby,' or 'Hi, baby.' He always referred to you in a sweetheart name, and never called you by your name. And he'd come in and do the sessions and quietly go home. He was always on call." Gaye's legendary lack of promptness began long before he found worldwide acclaim. "If the session was at one o'clock, you'd have to tell him it was 11:30, and he *might* make it by 2 o'clock," Reeves says with a chuckle. "He was a guy who was habitually late in showing up, but when he showed up, he brought all his goodness with him."

Gaye's failure to become a black Sinatra only enhanced his standing at Motown. His transition from standards balladeer to gritty soul singer was jump-started by his teaming with Martha and the Vandellas, who sang backup on his fourth Motown single, 1962's "Stubborn Kind of Fellow." Gaye would later return the favor for the group when he played drums and supplied the all-important title on their career-defining hit, 1964's "Dancing in the Streets." "When he first started out, [his music] was nice and mellow," Louvain Demps recalls of Marvin's work. "It was not really what you would call a money maker, because it really wasn't what Berry would call his thing. Berry's favorite saying was, 'Keep everything in the pocket.' He wanted that harder kind of sound. I think Martha Reeves and the Vandellas helped him in that area, because they had a different kind of sound. If you listen to their records, their sound was punchy and sharp, and the Andantes' was more sweet and flowing." The Andantes' sweet sound would bless Marvin's 1964 single, "How Sweet It Is (To Be Loved By You)," but for now, a more propulsive energy was sought.

"I did sing backup for him, non-payable," says Martha Reeves, who in 1989 successfully sued Motown for back royalties. "We loved him so, and we were proud to sing with Marvin on 'Stubborn Kind of Fellow' and on 'Pride and Joy' (released as a single in 1963). A lot of girls competed with us after that. I think the Supremes did some backup for him, and the

Andantes sort of took over, but we were the first girls to give Marvin a hit." Reeves acknowledges that it was their sharper sound that fueled Gaye's stirring and gritty performance on "Stubborn Kind of Fellow." The proof is in the song's first line. After a brief but pungent background intro of gospel-tight harmonies from Martha and the Vandellas, Gaye cries at the top of his tenor range, "say yeah, yeah, yeah." Then, begging for repetition, he coarsely pleads, "one more time." A new Marvin Gaye was born.

"'Stubborn Kind of Fellow' was an immediate hit," Reeves acknowledged. "And we stood there on that microphone, standing in back of him, because there were only three tracks at that time—the musicians were on one track, the mixing was done on one track and the singing was on one track—and coaxed him to sing in that strong, powerful voice that he delivered on 'Stubborn Kind of Fellow,' and that he continued on 'Hitch Hike' (released later in 1962 as the follow-up single to "Stubborn") and 'Pride and Joy,' establishing his style as the resident blues singer. He wanted at first to be a balladeer. And we sort of knew that, so we stood behind him and egged him on and gave him a little bit of our soul and spirit. I grew up singing in my grandfather's church, and when we started singing behind Marvin it was like gospel. And all he had to do was remember what he learned in his father's church. Just get a couple of 'Oh, Lord's' in there, and come on with the feeling that was supposed to be on the songs. That made them popular, and made them sell."

The success of "Stubborn Kind of Fellow," (written by Marvin, Mickey Stevenson, Motown's A&R head, and George Gordy, Berry's brother), "Hitch Hike," (penned by Marvin,

Stevenson, and Clarence Paul), and "Pride and Joy," which he wrote with Stevenson and Norman Whitfield, inaugurated a period of commercial acclaim for Marvin. His songs scaled the pop rankings and stormed the R & B charts. Although "Stubborn" was about a man determined to love a woman who was unmoved by his charms—supported by an entrancing mid-tempo shuffle and a floating flute solo—it might as well have been a song boasting Gaye's resistance to a marketplace that scuttled true artistry.[22] "Hitch Hike" was a throb of high energy rhythms that characterized the dance of the same name. The tune permitted Gaye and his collaborators to cash in on the trend of making songs tied to dances like the Hully Gully, the Fly, the Pony, the Limbo, the Cha-Cha, the Sway, the Fish, the Frug, the Shake, the Locomotion, and the Mashed Potato.[23] "Pride and Joy" was an up-tempo jaunt. Marvin plumbed his bass voice behind a grinding gospel groove and walking bass line to proclaim pride in his lover. It was meant to soothe and placate his wife Anna Gordy Gaye. Her jealousy, driven in part by their big age difference, lay behind some very public arguments. "Pride and Joy" was Marvin's reassurance to his wife that he loved her despite their occasional clashes.

In the midst of Marvin's success with Stevenson, which made him Motown's most accomplished act behind the Miracles, he was passed along to Holland-Dozier-Holland. This trio of singers-songwriters-producers consisted of brothers Brian and Eddie Holland, and Lamont Dozier, who went on to make some notable records of his own in the seventies. Marvin felt that he was more victim than beneficiary of Gordy's production philosophy.[24] He openly fought with Berry, chafing at being made a cog in Motown's hit machinery.[25] Despite his differences with Gordy, Marvin settled down to working with Holland-Dozier-Holland, and developed a genuinely collaborative relationship with the team as he grew to appreciate their talents. Marvin's first song with the trio was 1963's "Can I Get a Witness," a tune steeped in church backbeats and bathed in gospel piano riffs. On "Witness," the first Marvin Gaye song I remember hearing as a five-year-old, Marvin alternated between sweet and gritty vocals. He decried an undependable lover while begging for affirmation in the song's title phrase. "Can I get a witness?" is often tossed out by black preachers hunting for verbal feedback from their congregations. After "Witness" hit the 15th spot on the R & B charts, and number 22 on the pop charts, Marvin enjoyed a banner year in 1964 with a string of Holland-Dozier-Holland hits, including "You're a Wonderful One," "How Sweet It Is (To Be Loved By You)," and "Baby Don't You Do It." And then, just as quickly as they'd come to produce Gaye, Holland-Dozier-Holland moved on to work with the Four Tops and the Supremes, writing ten number one hits for Motown's most feted girl group.

Marvin's collaboration with Holland-Dozier-Holland gave him valuable knowledge about his vocal gifts. If Mickey Stevenson and Martha and the Vandellas put him in touch with his gospel roots, then Holland-Dozier-Holland forced him to stretch vocally by reaching for notes at the top register of his natural singing voice. They cast the songs in higher keys to get the desired performance from Gaye, a lesson he put to brilliant use on later classics like *Let's Get It On*. In 1965, Marvin gained another collaborator he had long admired for his artistic genius and business savvy: Smokey Robinson. Robinson was not only the sweet voiced leader of Motown's biggest act at the time, but he was also a vice president and significant force in the company's A&R department. He and Marvin were fast friends.[26] "When we moved into our first house, which I think was about 1962, he lived around the corner from our home with Anna," Claudette Robinson explains. "And he would often come by the house and just sit around the dining room table and talk. He was a confidant in many ways." Marvin also bonded with the Miracles on the road during tours in the early sixties after he played drums on their 1961 hit "Shop Around." "Marvin was kind of bopping around, helping out artists, being a hell of a drummer and piano player as well," notes Miracles member Pete Moore. "So Smokey and I said, 'This guy is good.' So we took Marvin on the road in 1961 for about three or four months. And then one day he told us he didn't want to go out on the road anymore, and that he wanted to pursue his career as a singer."

By the time Robinson began working with Gaye in 1965, they were familiar with each other's musical tastes and talents. Berry Gordy hoped that Marvin's work with Robinson might finally land him at the top of the charts. "Berry went to candidly talking one day at a production meeting," Moore says. "He wanted Smokey to do some songs with Marvin to increase his popularity. All those songs, 'Stubborn Kind of Fellow,' 'Hitch Hike,' 'Can I Get A Witness,' were big songs, but they didn't really get Marvin over as a superstar. Smokey called me one day and said, 'Hey man, I'm working with Marvin,' and so we worked together. In those days, we worked at Smokey's house a lot. He had an upstairs room with a piano. Our cowriter at the time was a guy named Marvin Tarplin, who was the Miracles guitar player. The three of us wrote some pretty impressive songs during the course of our songwriting career as collaborators. And Marvin was there that night, and we told him to come up with a good sound. Everything started with Marvin, who would come up a with real hip, slick lick or something, and then he would run that past me and Smokey. Then we would work it out, and come up with the melody. Then Marvin Tarplin came up with a lick, and we said, 'Man, this is good.' So we worked it out, and came up with a song called 'I'll Be Doggone.'"

"I'll Be Doggone" turned the trick and gave Marvin his first number one R & B hit. The song was a pop hit as well. Next up in 1965 was "Ain't That Peculiar," as Robinson, with help from Moore, Tarplin, and Miracles member Bobby Rogers, continued to transform colloquialisms into vernacular poetry. Although Rogers has said that the phrase came from Robinson when he heard a guitar riff from Tarplin while the Miracles were on tour in England, he gave me further insight into the song's origins.[27] "A few of the songs we wrote with Smokey were about Marvin and Anna," Rogers told me. "One of them was 'Ain't That Peculiar' which we wrote about them." When I asked him if Marvin knew, he told me, "Only we knew that. Now I'm telling you." Then he sung the tune's opening lines for illustration. "'Honey, you do me wrong, but still I'm crazy 'bout you/Stay away too long and I can't do without you.'" When I asked Rogers if he and his co-writers saw Marvin's heartache in his marriage to Anna, he simply said, "I don't think he was thinking that, but we saw that." Smokey and his cohort wrote and produced two more songs for Marvin, "One More Heartache" and "Take This Heart of Mine," both released in 1966. Neither tune duplicated the chart success of the earlier singles. Robinson's work with Gaye encouraged Marvin at a critical time in his career when he was unsure of his songwriting talent. Smokey's lyrical prowess inspired Marvin, even as he was daunted by his peer's literary talent—and that of Holland-Dozier-Holland and Norman Whitfield.[28]

Marvin renewed his desire to sing more popular fare when he released an album of show tunes in 1964, *Hello Broadway*, a year before his tribute album to Nat King Cole. But neither of these efforts proved as important to his career as a decision Berry Gordy made in 1964: to exploit Marvin's image as a sex symbol by pairing him with the company's elite female artists. Mary Wells, who had a big hit in 1964 with the Smokey Robinson song, "My Guy" was Marvin's first partner. Their union yielded the 1964 single "Once Upon A Time," a soft, airy, Latin-tinged ballad that made a solid showing on both the pop and R & B charts. The single's B-side, "What's the Matter With You Baby," is a jump-beat grinder that evokes passionate performances from both stars: Wells accuses her lover of doing her wrong as Gaye begs for a second chance. Their album, *Together*, produced by Mickey Stevenson, did well enough to anticipate future efforts. But that was not to be. Wells departed Motown for 20th Century Fox and a lucrative contract just as her biggest hit, "My Guy," was rising to the top of the charts. Marvin was then teamed with Kim Weston, a gifted twenty-four-year-old vocalist and the wife of Mickey Stevenson. That union, too, was fated to fizzle before they realized their potential as a duo. Kim possessed a sweet, sultry voice, one that matched nicely with Marvin's gentle tones and playful growls. But Motown failed to use her talents properly.

"I met Marvin right after I signed with Motown," Weston tells me, "when he came off the first Motown Revue. I had a demo session with a young man who happened to be the cousin of Eddie and Brian Holland. That's how I got to Motown. And I was waiting for them to do something. The tour came back in while I was waiting, and that's when Marvin and I first met. He and I had a special rapport, because Marvin was raised in the church, very much like my upbringing in the Pentecostal Church. We could talk about how we were raised not being able to do anything; *everything* was wrong. And we had a similar feeling about how people are supposed to live their lives: You treat people like you want to be treated. He was very shy, and he became like a brother to me." Their warm feelings and youthful innocence translated well on wax, producing the album, *Takes Two*, which came out in August of 1966. But Motown didn't release a single off the album until Weston was out of the door. Her husband, Motown VP Mickey Stevenson, decided to jump ship when he realized he wouldn't receive stock options, and when he concluded that his wife's career would never be fairly promoted. When Motown released "It Takes Two" as a single to please Weston, it proved to be too little too late. The song shot to number four on the R & B charts and to number fourteen on the pop charts. "We had done the album almost two years prior to its release," Weston explains. "I think I'm the only artist at Motown that would have a hit and it would take another six to nine months before I could get a release. So that was why I was leaving."

Weston's untimely departure paved the way for a historic pairing that, it is safe to say, changed the face of black popular music. The union of Marvin Gaye and Tammi Terrell not only produced high art of timeless beauty, but it redefined both the image and the ideal of the dual-sex pop duo. Moreover,

Marvin's matinee idol looks were perfectly matched by Tammi's stunning café au lait beauty. Terrell was just twenty when she joined forces with Gaye, but she was already vastly experienced. The Philadelphia native, named Thomasina Montgomery when she was born in 1945, was drawn to her vocation early in life. "Tammi saw some entertainers that she liked at the Uptown Theater, and we snuck in the backstage," her younger sister Ludie Montgomery remembers. "That's how it all started. She was about eight, and she knew exactly what she wanted to be as a little kid, and I think that's what made all the difference in the world. She absolutely, positively knew that early. She was going to be a star. She didn't say a singer; she said a star. And she started to pursue those things and my parents supported her." Tammi's father, Thomas Montgomery, a barber who also dabbled in local Philadelphia politics as a ward leader, was the brother of noted lightweight boxer Bob Montgomery. Her mother, Jennie Montgomery, was an actress who took Tammi to local talent shows in Philadelphia and New Jersey. "Tammi and I studied ballet, interpretive dance, jazz and tap," Ludie says. "We also took piano, and Tammi excelled, a prodigy really. She was like a little old lady." By the time she was 13, Tammi's prodigious talent made her the opening club act, as Tammy Montgomery, for artists like Gary "U.S." Bonds and Pattie LaBelle & the Blue Belles. She also sang with Steve Gibson and the Redcaps.

Tammi was discovered by producer Luther Dixon when she was 15, and signed to Scepter Records. After a few singles, including the Shirelles-backed "If You See Bill," she signed with James Brown's Try Me label, which issued her single "I Cried" in 1963. Tammi toured with Brown's Famous Flames

Revue and had a love affair with the singer as well. Her single, "If I Would Marry You," appeared on the Checker label in 1964, the year she was a pre-med student at the University of Pennsylvania. In 1965, Tammi toured with Jerry Butler for six months, including a stop at Detroit's Twenty Grand Club, where Berry Gordy spotted her and brought her to Motown. Gordy teamed Tammi with Harvey Fuqua and Johnny Bristol, who produced the singles "I Can't Believe You Love Me," "Come On and See Me," a remake of the Isleys Brothers tune "This Old Heart of Mine (Is Weak For You)," and "Hold Me Oh My Darling." (Many of Tammi's solo performances would be reshaped into duets with Marvin when he overdubbed his vocals months, and at times, years later). When those cuts failed to generate heat, at Fuqua's suggestion, Tammi was paired with Marvin in 1967.[29] By this time, Holland-Dozier-Holland had gone on strike out of frustration and anger at being unfairly compensated for the nearly 50 hits they had produced for the company in the span of four years. In fact, their compositions had come to define "the Motown sound." Into the musical gap stepped Nickolas Ashford and Valerie Simpson, a dynamic songwriting duo who were formerly associated with Scepter Records. They had already written Ray Charles's 1966 hit, "Let's Go Get Stoned." Now they were Motown staff songwriters signed to Jobete, Gordy's publishing firm named after his three children, Hazel Joy, Berry and Terry. Ashford and Simpson aimed to make a mark with gorgeous love ballads whose sensuous yearning was matched by hypnotic hooks and soaring melodies. They didn't have Marvin and Tammi in mind when they penned two of their first songs for Jobete, "Ain't No Mountain High Enough" and "Your Precious Love," but they felt, as did producers Bristol and Fuqua, that the duo could bring the lyrics to life with their vital energy and superb vocal gifts.

"I think it was a perfect match," admits Johnny Bristol. "You had Marvin's sound of soulfulness and Tammi's emotional, tender light voice. To me, they blended better than any of the duet partners Marvin sang with. I'm not saying that they all weren't good, but just listening to the blend of the intonation of their voices, I preferred them. There was an obvious difference between them and his other partners. Kim Weston had a more powerful voice than Tammi, so she could do 'It Takes Two.' But Tammi had the lightness of the romance to do 'Ain't No Mountain High Enough' and 'Your Precious Love.'" Harry Weinger attributes the difference in chemistry to more mundane matters, such as the kind of relationship Marvin had with Kim Weston outside of the recording booth. "Kim Weston said, 'When Marvin and I recorded together we were friends. We did shows together, our families knew each other. It was comfortable. When I heard Marvin and Tammi, I heard what we could have done.' When you listen to Marvin and Kim's stuff, it's friendly: 'I Want You 'Round,' 'It Takes Two.' It's very arm in arm, very friendly. With Marvin and Tammi, it's more that you're rubbing a little bit. It's more of when you look somebody in the eye and then you look at where the ear and the jaw connect, and you have a special spot. That's more of what it's about." Weston also links the different chemistries to how Marvin functioned in the lives of each of his first three partners. "When Marvin worked with Mary Wells, she was a very sweet, but rather naïve person, and so his thing was basically helping her artistically more than anything," Weston says.

"With Tammi, she had gone through an awful lot in her young career. She was fragile mentally. Marvin was trying to protect her. Our situation was not a situation where he had to help me so much, but I admired his artistic ability."

Marvin and Tammi's success was driven by several factors, including their captivating physical beauty, and hence, the erotic tension suggested by the very idea of their pairing, and the vocal chemistry produced by the glove-to-hand fit of their sweet and arching voices.[30] But their appeal was also fueled by Marvin's need to match the hunger and vigor that Tammi brought to their recording sessions as the vocal underdog, and as the partner who brought the lesser known aesthetic quality. Marvin was undoubtedly the veteran, but the younger Tammi, besides an impressive resume of vocal accomplishments, possessed a feisty, irreverent attitude that belied her sweet, seductive persona. "We were both from Philly," says Weldon McDougal, a Philadelphia-based Motown publicist and promotions man in the sixties. "But once I was in Detroit, and she came to me and said, 'I'm going to do this duet with Marvin. I'm gonna make this motherfucker sing! I'm tired of people thinking that I can't sing.' And about a month later, Marvin came in, and when I asked him how he was doing, he said, 'Man, that damned Tammi Terrell! I got to do my part over because of her.' And I'm saying to myself, 'Damned, she really tore him up!'"

Tammi's street-smart roots, although obscured on record, often pushed through her personal interactions with Marvin, adding grit to their vocal magic on stage and wax. "She would tease the hell out of him, and he couldn't stand it," says Elaine Jesmer, a Los Angeles publicist who worked with Gaye and later

penned *Number One with a Bullet*, a largely unflattering fictional portrait of Motown's major figures.[31] "She would pick on him by saying, 'I can sing higher than you,' and 'I can sing better than you,' and 'By the way, you better show up next time in our recording session.' She loved to do this. I think it was just to needle him. I knew she knew he was good. She just made him work a little harder, and he had not had that happen in a long time."

Harry Weinger believes that Marvin and Tammi's appeal grew from their role-playing on record, their friendly sense of competition, and from their ability to sing a portrait of two people in love, even when they weren't in the same recording studio. "There's a telepathy and sweetness there," Weinger says. "They knew they were playing a role, but there's a love there, even on the songs where they're not together—like 'Ain't No Mountain High Enough,' which Tammi cut as a solo track, and Marvin added his vocal later. It's a testament to his craft, his skill, that he could make it sound like they're standing right next to each other. If they did push each other to do better, it happened when Marvin had to overdub Tammi. It's almost like he had to be as pretty as her, as good looking as her. His voice had to sound as fine as she looked. He had to step up."

Marvin had to raise his level of performance when they stood next to each other in the recording studio, even though they had never met each other (and Gaye had never heard her voice) before their first duet. They found such an intimate vocal groove that they spurned separate sources of amplification. "It's interesting that the songs they did record together at the same time, they sang on one microphone," Weinger says. Other aspects of their recording pattern sheds light on how most Motown artists of the sixties interpreted lyrics and converted music into records.

For instance, Marvin and Tammi gave stirring vocal performances on record with little rehearsal. "That was pretty much true with all the artists in the studio," explains Johnny Bristol. "They hardly ever got a chance to hear the product before we got to the studio. Most of the music was recorded while they were out of town. We would just call them up, maybe, and get a key on the telephone. Or it may be someone we're so familiar with that we have a general idea of where the key should be. So we could go ahead and cut the tracks, and then, when they came back in town, we had them booked in the studio and they would come here and learn the product, and record it, in that same three hour session." Even within a system where such vocal excellence was routine, Marvin and Tammi proved to be exceptional. "It takes people who can catch on quickly," Bristol says. "There were those for whom it took a little more time. In a three hour session, you might not get but one song. But with Marvin and Tammi, we'd get three or four sometimes. With Marvin, everything he sang was good; there was no such animal as a bad take, so I had to use a new track every time I let him sing, because I didn't want to lose what he did previously. Tammi was very good as well. They just seemed to click. They liked each other as people."

The public liked Marvin and Tammi as well; they embraced their music with great enthusiasm. "Ain't No Mountain High Enough" debuted in April 1967, climbing to number three on the R & B charts while cracking the top twenty on the pop charts. From the tune's kick-start drum licks and nimble bass line, and Marvin's plaintive opening statement, "Listen, baby, ain't no mountain high, ain't no valley low, ain't no river wide enough, baby," followed by Tammi's serenely reassuring offer, "If you need me, call me, no matter where you are, no matter how far," the song builds on infectious light-gospel grooves, full of tambourine slaps and discrete but spirited backing vocals, as both singers declare that no natural or metaphysical barrier will prevent their love from flourishing. For the next two years, Marvin and Tammi would consistently hit the charts with songs written by Ashford and Simpson, who also took over producing the duo when "Ain't No Mountain High Enough" and "Your Precious Love" hit big. The latter tune was released in August 1967 and charted in the R & B top ten and rose to number five on the pop charts.

These songs, as well as the duets the pair would write for Marvin and Tammi over the next year, are so firmly entrenched in the nation's collective memory that it is hard to imagine black American romance being as articulately expressed if they didn't exist. Nickolas and Valerie, who would later marry and perform as a duo, but were then only writing and composing partners, tapped the gospel roots that nourished them as members of Harlem's legendary White Rock Baptist church choir. Their elegant, sophisticated arrangements and their literate, inspiring lyrics—which fused the Christian love ethic with an uplifting philosophy of relationships powered by the erotic charge of mutual respect—were the perfect vehicle to disseminate Marvin and Tammi's urbane sensuality. These songs also provided an edifying glimpse into the black sexual imagination at a time when the civil rights movement was still waging war for black social and political equality. In their subtle fashion, these songs protested malevolent stereotypes of black domestic unions while waving the flag of romantic universality. While they implicitly made the point that black folk are like all others, they made the equally powerful point that all others can learn and benefit from black love. That's why the songs were both R & B and pop hits; they crossed over to the white mainstream by slipping through the streams of bigotry that poisoned interracial understanding.

Ashford and Simpson's first two hits on Marvin and Tammi—plus the deliciously vibrant November 1967 single "If I Could Build My Whole World Around You," written and produced by Bristol and Fuqua, which was a top-ten R & B and pop hit—were included on the album *United*, which snagged the number seven spot on the R & B charts. 1968 was a banner year for Marvin and Tammi's collaboration with Ashford and Simpson, as they unleashed a cache of songs that captured the R & B and pop charts. In March they scored big with "Ain't Nothing Like The Real Thing"; in July, it was "You're All I Need to Get By," and in September, it was "Keep On Lovin' Me Honey." They also released their second album, *You're All I Need*. Their success extended into 1969 with singles like "Good Lovin' Ain't Easy to Come By" and "What You Gave Me," and with their third album, *Easy*.

But tragedy shadowed the duo's success almost from the start. In July 1967, "Ain't No Mountain High Enough" entered the pop top 20, and later earned a Grammy nomination for best R & B group performance. That October, Marvin and Tammi made an appearance at a Homecoming concert at Hampden-Sydney College, located in Virginia, 60 miles southwest of Richmond. The all-male liberal arts school boasts William Henry Harrison, the ninth president of the United States, among its alumni. Hampden-Sydney's student newspaper, *The Tiger*, featured an October 13, 1967 cover story that described the two nights of Homecoming festivities sponsored by the school's German Club. On Friday night, the Drifters, the Tropics and the Robinson Brothers were scheduled to perform, and on Saturday night, Marvin Gaye and Tammi Terrell, and Bill Deal & The Rondells were slated to appear. In the article, German Club president Bill Carter called Gaye "the smoothest of the pop-showmen." Carter also said that Tammi Terrell "combines with Marvin Gaye to form the most professional and enjoyable male-female act in the business." Carter concluded, "Marvin and Tammi are the male-female of Sam and Dave—perfect together."[32] It is noteworthy to recall that the school was not yet integrated; the presence of black entertainers underscores the crucial role they played in knocking down racial barriers.

An even more momentous event was waiting in the wings of the school's Homecoming on Saturday night. Marvin and Tammi's band arrived three hours early, and played poker with the German Club's vice-president Bill Selden, Jr.. Gammon Gymnasium, where the concert was held, was extremely hot, but that didn't keep a few thousand people from crowding around the stage as Marvin performed several of his solo hits. Tammi was ill from the time they both arrived at the college, and rested with the lights off in the makeshift dressing room made up of two coaches' offices. Tammi said that she simply had a headache and that she'd be fine. When it came time for her to join Marvin on stage, Tammi only made it through two songs, and in a cruel irony, she began "Ain't No Mountain High Enough," but collapsed on stage, dropping to her knees before

Marvin caught her, and with the aid of a band member, helped her off stage. Marvin finished the concert alone, which would be his lot from then on, as it turned out to be Tammi's last live performance. She was diagnosed with a brain tumor that slowed, and finally, incapacitated her for two years, making it difficult to record and impossible to perform.

"It was horrible, devastating," says her sister Ludie Montgomery. "I was her companion for two years because my mother wasn't well. I had to console and comfort her, and be there for her, while she was in the hospital, at home, through the whole ordeal. At one point she was fine. Then she was paralyzed, lost weight, blew up. She went from one extreme to another. They couldn't take the tumor out. But she always believed that she was going to get better, and be able to continue her career. She didn't think she was going to die until the end. She was accepting of it. We would talk about it all the time; we were consumed. There were a lot of people around during the beginning of her illness, but after she was sick for a while, they sort of dwindled away, except for immediate family. That's what made it so sad. Marvin came; he was one of the few. He would call all the time."

Tammi's condition was rumored to have been the result of beatings she took over her young but fractured life. "I think you hit people in the head enough, they get brain cancer eventually," says Elaine Jesmer, a close friend of Tammi's. "And I knew two of them were musicians." "That's just rumor," Ludie says about the belief that such beatings caused her sister's death. "I'll elaborate on that in my book I'm writing on Tammi." Beyond dispute is the fact that the duo's success drove Tammi to begin work on their second album, *You're All I Need*, as her health deteriorated. She cut a few new songs, while Marvin over-dubbed vocals on six of Tammi's older solo recordings, including "Come On and See Me." As her songs were soaring to success, including the immortally rendered, "Ain't Nothing Like The Real Thing," Tammi's health was plummeting. She lost sight and several motor functions as she underwent eight surgeries. For their last album, *Easy*, Marvin continued to over-dub Tammi's early tracks. When she could no longer sing, Valerie Simpson valiantly stepped in to complete the task, making sure that Tammi continued to receive royalties during her illness, a plan thought up by Berry Gordy. It is Simpson's voice, and not Tammi's, that is heard on several of the songs from *Easy*, including "Good Lovin' Ain't Easy to Come By," "What You Gave Me," and "The Onion Song." Simpson was a natural choice to fill in for Tammi: her sweet and soulful voice was very close to Tammi's; she produced Marvin and Tammi on two albums and on more than two dozen songs; and she sang Tammi's part on the demo tapes she made of the songs she and Nickolas penned for the duo.

Marvin managed to stay incredibly busy during Tammi's illness. He released four albums in 1969 alone, among them *Easy*, *Marvin Gaye and His Girls* (a compilation of 12 previously released duets with Mary Wells, Kim Weston and Tammi Terrell), and *MPG*, which contained "Too Busy Thinking About My Baby," a big hit for Gaye on both the R & B and pop charts. Unlike the rest of the album—a brooding exercise in angst and a vicarious probing of the dark emotions that stormed Marvin as his marriage failed, captured in the finely cross-hatched black-and-grey cover photo where Gaye fairly glowers, or, as Harry Weinger says, looks as if "he's going to fucking kill you"—"Too Busy" is an upbeat romp through innocent love and unspoiled affection. Marvin also created more elbow room within Motown's claustrophobic artistic quarters by seizing the production reins for the Originals, a quartet of unheralded Motown backup vocalists who had been patiently waiting their turn to shine. "He just came through one day and heard us, and decided to do something on us," remembers Originals second tenor Hank Dixon. "It seemed like nobody else was going to do anything. Marvin was a little of a rebel. He had his own ideas of the way things should be. He wasn't a follower at all; he was a changer. At that time, [Motown] wasn't listening too much to change, so he got in a lot of trouble. He was a man before his time, really." With Anna, Marvin wrote "Baby I'm For Real," a love song whose structure and sound borrowed from Gaye's doo-wop past and foreshadowed his future direction: expertly arranged background voices tingling with air-tight harmonies in a mellow groove. The company held onto the song for nearly a year. "It was different, a ballad," says Originals bass Freddie Gorman, who co-wrote "Please Mr. Postman" for the Marvelettes. "During that time you had a lot of psychedelic kind of music. So it was released on an album, and then from the album, the disc jockeys began to play it." The song's popularity on radio forced Motown to release it as a single in 1969. "Baby I'm For Real" scampered to the top of the R & B charts and sold more than a million copies. The song's success announced Marvin's prowess as a writer, arranger and producer, and proved, at least in his mind, that Motown no longer needed to smother him in its assembly-line clutches.[33]

In truth, Marvin's greater artistic freedom had already been set in motion by his successful 1967 pairing with producer

Norman Whitfield. The producer had worked with Marvin five years earlier on "Wherever I Lay My Hat (That's My Home)" and "Pride and Joy," both of which appeared on Gaye's second album, *That Stubborn Kinda Fella*. In February of 1967, a month after Marvin first tinkered with the seven ballads he had commissioned from Bobby Scott, he began work on a song he completed in April. The cut wouldn't be released as a single until October of 1968. Ironically, that song, "I Heard It Through The Grapevine," was the biggest hit in Marvin's career and Motown's history, selling over four million copies and reaching number one on the pop charts. The song was also a critical smash, ranking at one time as the greatest single in rock history.[34] "Grapevine" reeks of paranoia and seethes with suspicion: A man is wounded by the rumor that his lover will soon leave him for a former flame. The rumor nearly chokes the injured lover's sanity—and penetrates his male pride. The music ratchets up the sinister atmosphere: muted staccato piano chords, insistent cymbal taps, a nervous rattlesnake tambourine, faux-Indian tom-tom beats, blaring trumpets, and beneath it all, an ominous bass-line figure. Marvin's delivery of the third line in the opening verse underscores the song's seamless fusion of anxiety and ardor. His indecently vulnerable falsetto squalls his knowledge that his beloved will "make me blue" with "some other *guy-y-y-y* you knew before." By the time he confesses that "I'm just about to *lo-oh-ose* my mind," you have no earthly reason to doubt that it's true.

For late baby boomers like me, "Grapevine" conjures youthful glimpses into the mystery of adulthood. For the artistically inclined, it's an aural portrait of earlier epochs. "My father worked for Ford, so we always had a new Ford wagon," Harry

Weinger tells me. "And the kids were all in the back seats, and I remember leaning...because the speaker was back there. So I'm eleven years old, and I remember the first time I heard 'Grapevine.' It's like 'Purple Haze' [was] for some people. I'll never forget that feeling, my head against the window, drifting into that world, with that song. And I could hear that song over and over and over again. So years later, I was seeing someone who was a painter, and we were playing the record, and she says to me, 'It's a painting; I can see it. First of all, it's the voodoo drums, the talking drums. And then the rattlesnakes, the jungle. And then when the horns come in? It's the elephants announcing their arrival. So the whole thing is an ancient call.'"

In purely artistic terms, Marvin's performance on "Grapevine" is striking. But in light of the barriers that might have kept him from a career defining moment, his accomplishment is remarkable. When Marvin recorded the Barrett Strong-Norman Whitfield tune, Berry Gordy had it shelved for a year-and-a-half. He thought that the image it projected didn't fit Gaye's lover-man persona. Marvin wasn't even the first Motown act to record the song: first the Miracles, then the Isley Brothers, trafficked in the rumor mill before Marvin gave it a try.[35] A fourth version of the song, recorded by Gladys Knight and the Pips *after* Marvin's take, was released a year *before* Gaye's interpretation made it to the airwaves. What's more, Gladys Knight and the Pips made a thrilling, up-tempo version of the song—full of churning gospel rhythms and urban bravado that was more defiant than defeated. If Gladys Knight and the Pips' treatment brings to mind the film *My Best Friend's Wedding*, Marvin's evokes *Fatal Attraction*. Their dramatic differences aside, Gladys Knight and the Pips had just had a big hit with the song, selling 1.7 million copies and racing to the second spot on the pop charts. Marvin's version barely made it on his 1968 album, *In The Groove*. Billie Jean Brown, head of Motown's Quality Control department, was scrounging around to find enough material to complete his album. Even after the tune was slid onto the album, it was only when Chicago disc jockey Rodney Jones played the song on his WVON radio show that a public outcry for the record forced Motown to make history by making it a single.

"Grapevine" marked a turning point in Gaye's career. Although Motown issued a few more singles and albums from Gaye before his epochal 1971 single, "What's Going On," "Grapevine" almost single-handedly gave Marvin the leverage he needed to have more say-so in how he was recorded and produced. Marvin admitted that he hadn't been greatly enthusiastic about the song, and only recorded it to please Whitfield and Strong.[36] A few years later, Gaye discussed the circumstances of the recording with *Rolling Stone* and said that a higher power directed his decision. "'Grapevine' was a divine thing," Marvin said. "*I* didn't choose it. I was being a good artist at the time. They tell you, 'Marvin, you gotta come in and do this tune, because this song is a good song for you and it was written by so and so, so come right in there and be a good guy and cut it, OK?' And that always bugged me. Generally, I say go take your song and stuff it. But this particular time I said oh, hell, I'll be a good artist. But it was the Lord who was working and He knew I should have gotten to do it, so I did. And that's why it became a big hit."[37] "Grapevine" was also the musical earnest that reaped huge artistic—and financial—dividends for Marvin and Motown with *What's Going On*.

In the midst of his musical triumphs, Marvin faced the sad refrains of suffering that silenced his most popular duet partner. The harsh irony of Tammi's situation was not lost on Marvin, who reflected on the sharp contradiction between their image as a wholesome, healthy young duo radiating emotional and sexual confidence, even as each suffered private agony: for Tammi, her failing health, and for Marvin, tough times at home with Anna, with more fighting and feuding than ever before. When Tammi died on March 16, 1970, at the age of 24, a bright and beautiful star had been extinguished, not only in the recording firmament, but also in the dark bosom of Marvin's psychic composure. Although the cliché begs to be resisted, it summons a truth hard to overlook: Marvin Gaye would never be the same. His haphazard pattern and mortal fear of performing live grew almost unmanageable, sending him into self-imposed exile. With the exception of two isolated concerts, he wouldn't perform live for nearly five years after Tammi's death. "I think Tammi's death triggered something in my boy," Marvin Gaye's father told a *Rolling Stone* reporter in 1974. "He troubled up and I would call and ask him, 'Marvin, why aren't you working?' He would say that he was tired of his music, but his excuses didn't satisfy me. It just didn't sound like him. I have to attribute the fact that he wasn't working to the girl's death. It took something from my boy."[38] Marvin's sense of vocation was transformed as well; he withdrew into existential rumination and musical brooding. With the exception of a few recordings, he didn't reemerge until he had been remade in the shape of his restored, perhaps redeemed, artistic vision.

CHAPTER TWO

"If This World Were Mine"
The Politics of Soul Music

As a new decade dawned in Detroit—Motown's birthplace and the home of its most glorious creations before relocating its offices to Los Angeles in 1972—blacks emerged from the city's shadow of a bloody 1967 riot with the hope of finally achieving true equality.[1] Motown inspired African Americans to believe that hard work and true talent can be rewarded. Because it gave voice to black genius, Motown couldn't avoid being seen in racial terms. Berry Gordy was an icon of black entrepreneurial power, especially since "[n]o one could have predicted that an unskilled car-factory worker one generation removed from the cotton fields would be one of the most successful black businessmen in American history."[2] Motown was an extraordinarily successful *black* business that harvested the gifts of black artists denied opportunity in the white world.[3] The black freedom struggle in the sixties greatly accelerated the national embrace of Motown. As critic Suzanne Smith noted, "the civil rights movement created the environment in which broader cultural integration—as typified by Motown's wide appeal—could occur."[4] Still, Motown was cautious about identifying too strongly with the black revolution. Although it readily depended on its black base for support, Motown eagerly desired to produce a sound that could cross over to white audiences. The styles, themes, sounds, and behavior of its artists were carefully tailored to project an unthreatening image of black identity.[5] The gulf between whites and blacks was effortlessly bridged by the rhythms pouring from Hitsville, creating a treasured sanctuary in the geography of racial harmony at 2648 West Grand Boulevard.

That didn't mean that Motown ignored the rising tide of black pride and racial consciousness. In 1963, Motown recorded Martin Luther King, Jr.'s June 23 speech before 125,000 demonstrators in a historic civil rights march in Detroit, and released it on August 28, the day King gave his legendary "I Have a Dream" address at the march on Washington.[6] The album, entitled *The Great March to Freedom*, was the company's first spoken-word recording, paving the way for Motown's spoken-word label, Black Forum, which would provide "a medium for the presentation of ideas and voices of the worldwide struggle of Black people to create a new era…[and as] a permanent record of the sound of the struggle and the sound of a new era."[7]

Black Forum's first productions included *Free Huey!*, a speech by activist Stokely Carmichael in support of the imprisoned Black Panther leader Huey Newton, and Martin Luther King, Jr.'s speech, *Why I Oppose the War in Vietnam*, which later won a 1970 Grammy Award. In 1970, Black Forum released *Poets of the Revolution*, featuring the poetry of Langston Hughes and Margaret Danner. Later it released *It's Nation Time* by poet-activist Amiri Baraka; *Elaine Brown: Until We're Free*, a collection of songs by the Black Panther leader; *Black Spirits*, which featured the work of figures like Baraka, Clarence Major, the Original Last Poets, and David Henderson; *Guess Who's Coming Home: Black Fighting Men Recorded Live in Vietnam*, a recording based on the research of the late Wallace Terry in Southeast Asia among black soldiers; and *The Congressional Black Caucus*, a recording of keynote speeches, including those of Ossie Davis and Bill Cosby, presented at the caucus's first annual banquet.[8] After the assassination of Martin Luther King, Jr., in 1968, Berry Gordy dispatched Stevie Wonder, Gladys Knight and the Pips, the Supremes, and the Temptations, to perform at a benefit concert in Atlanta for the Poor People's March, the campaign on which the leader was working when he was murdered.[9]

Despite these significant interventions, the Black Forum label was comparatively obscure, and aside from King's efforts, its offerings weren't nearly as aggressively promoted as Motown's musical fare. Motown vigilantly separated its support for venting black struggle and its keen desire to captivate and capitalize on white America through pop music. The rigid segregation of politics and music kept Motown's enormous popularity intact. But the rise of a new black political consciousness, the flames of urban riots and rebellions, the war in Vietnam, the expansion of American protest music, the relentless appropriation of black music by white artists, the evolution of student activism, and the resurgence of progressive politics began to shape the music of some of black America's bravest artists. Many black jazz artists had already been politicized in the fifties and sixties, and the recordings of Sun Ra, John Coltrane, and members of the Association for the Advancement of Creative Musicians (AACM) showed how the line between music and social conscience could be artfully blurred.[10] The work of Nina Simone ("Mississippi Goddamn"), Les McCann and Eddie Harris ("Compared to What"), Julian "Cannonball" Adderley ("The Price You Got to Pay to Be Free") and Eugene McDaniel (*Headless Heroes of the Apocalypse*) proved that the black aesthetic and the black politic could be one.[11] Curtis Mayfield defined the gospel-drenched Chicago sound with music of haunting eloquence and lyrics that touched the soul of black struggle. His work with the Impressions produced not only elegant romantic ballads, but edifying songs of racial pride. In the mid-sixties, Mayfied wrote socially uplifting tunes such as "Keep on Pushing," and "People Get Ready." While not explicitly political anthems, these songs nevertheless brought inspiration to the civil rights movement. In 1968, Mayfield more straightforwardly embraced black pride on his stirring "We're a Winner," followed in the next couple of years by such message songs as "This Is My Country" and "Choice of Colors." In 1969, Sly and the Family Stone's album *Stand!* ventured into socially conscious territory with songs like "Don't Call Me Nigger, Whitey" and "Everyday People." In the early seventies, they added the masterly and stylishly bleak manifesto *There's a Riot Goin' On*.

Motown slowly came around. Stevie Wonder was the first Motown artist to nod to politics on a single when in 1966 he released a well received version of Bob Dylan's "Blowin' in the Wind." He followed it later that year with the similarly themed "A Place in the Sun" on his album *Down to Earth*, which was the first Motown album cover to depict a ghetto landscape.[12]

Despite these recordings, the songs failed to ignite a trend of socially conscious music at Motown. In 1968, the tide turned with the release of the Supremes' "Love Child," a song that probes the plight of unwed teen mothers. "Love Child" leaped to the number one position on the pop charts and became the biggest hit of the Supremes' career. With the commercial appeal of socially relevant soul music established, Motown waded a bit further into these waters under the innovative guidance of Norman Whitfield, who was, according to one critic, an architect of the "ghetto sound" that speaks directly "to the concerns of inner-city blacks."[13] Along with Sly Stone, Whitfield seized on the wah-wah pedal—which distorts the guitar's sound—as the emblematic tool in the expanding technological repertoire of electrified black music. Stone and Whitfield helped to extend funk modernism—multiple rhythmic patterns that blend frenetic bass-lines and turbulent drumbeats in jolts of regulated frenzy. Besides the aesthetic dimensions of funk modernism, which draws on a collage of jazz and blues sounds, its metaphysical heart beats in lyrics that explore black existence. A key form of funk modernism, lyrically speaking, is urban realism; artists probe the complex social and moral properties of black urban identity and the political issues that shape black life. Whitfield, and his writing partner Barrett Strong, did this brilliantly on several "message" tunes for the Temptations in the late sixties, including "Cloud Nine," "Ball of Confusion (That's What the World Is Today)," and "Message from a Black Man." Another song the duo wrote for the Temptations, but which was seen as too controversial for the group to release as a single, was "War," a throbbing anthem whose refrain asked and answered the question: "War—Huh! What is it good for?

Absolutely nothin'!" Instead, Motown's Edwin Starr released the song and rode a wave of angry fuzz guitars to fame and the top of the pop charts in 1970.

Marvin Gaye borrowed from and brilliantly re-imagined the political and musical landscape when he spoke again in 1971 after his nearly year-and-a-half pause between albums. Gaye had released 40 singles and 21 albums between 1962 and 1970. In some years, he released as many as six singles and four albums. Admittedly, a year-and-a-half seems a short time not to have an album in today's music market, where artists routinely go a year or longer without recording anything new. At the time, however, it was a huge gap in a recording artist's itinerary, especially a prolific singer like Gaye whose art helped to fuel Motown's musical engine. But the pressure to smoothly fit into Motown's assembly line approach to art riled Gaye. With the blockbuster commercial triumph of "Grapevine," and to a lesser degree, his production success with the Originals, Marvin stalled the company's demands to conform to its pace and style of making music.

Marvin's retreat from the studio was not only driven by Motown's actions and the plagues on his personal life—Tammi's death and alienation from Anna—but by the social crisis of black America and the trauma of war. Marvin dug more deeply into black culture and history and read the books of thinkers and activists like Malcolm X and Dick Gregory. He sought to reclaim a vital connection to poor and working class black folk, like those who populated the East Capitol projects of his Washington, D.C. youth. He also shirked his clean-cut sex symbol image by growing a beard and slipping out of his trademark suits into sweats and sneakers.[14] Marvin's new style of dress brought him closer to the informally clothed youth who took to the streets to protest social injustice. His brother Frankie had been drafted in 1967 into military service in the war in Vietnam where he was involved in vicious firefights. Marvin wrote to Frankie of his growing disenchantment with military actions in urban riots and with police brutality against student demonstrators at Kent State.[15] When Frankie returned home to Washington, D.C. in the spring of 1970, Marvin left Detroit to greet him—and to relentlessly question him about his experiences in Vietnam. Marvin would put the information to poignant use on his next album.

Another reunion would prove even more critical to lighting Marvin's artistic fires—and would confirm that Gaye did his best work in collaboration with others, especially since the reins of his musical association were now largely in his hands. Shortly after his return to Detroit from Tammi Terrell's funeral in Philadelphia in late March 1970, Marvin ran into Al Cleveland, a staff writer for Motown. Cleveland gave Marvin a song he'd co-written with Four Tops member Obie Benson that he thought might be good for the Originals, who were enjoying another rush of success with their second hit single "The Bells."[16] "I had a duplex here [in Detroit], and Al Cleveland was my neighbor upstairs," Benson recalls in explaining how they came to write the song together. Benson says the song grew from personal experience in California. "I was in San Francisco, up in Haight-Asbury, and I saw these [young] people speaking in the park. And then I saw the police come in and start running them over, and beating on them. And I thought, 'what's going on?' See, it's really a love song. These people had so much love, and the police were just beating them because they were hippies. Then we were sending people over to war, and they didn't want to go. And there were mothers who had that experience in their lifetime of sending their offspring off to fight. So that question had to be answered." Benson came up with the tune, and then with Cleveland's gifts—"Al was a poet"—they refined the lyrics.

Benson and Cleveland met with Marvin at his Detroit home. "I was playing the guitar and Marvin played the piano, and he put it in another bag, you know? He said, 'Man, I'm going to do this for the Originals.' But his wife, Anna, came in, and when she heard him singing the song, she said, 'I don't care who you produce, but you ought to do this song yourself.' And that's when me and Al said, 'Hey man, we'll give you a third [writing credit] if you'll sing it! If you don't sing the song, *we're* going to play it.'" Benson was trying to appeal to Marvin's famously competitive nature to goad him into performing their song. "I did that because his ego was really big," Benson admits. "And what it really was is that he was impressed because I always thought he was a great singer." Besides, Benson's group, the Four Tops, had already been denied permission by the company to record the song. "I couldn't get the tune onto our album. I took it to Marvin to show Motown that it was a great song, no matter who sung it. And when he got through singing it, I knew it was a great song. Nobody else could ever sing it like Marvin." Of course, the fact that Motown had rejected the tune for the Four Tops made Marvin anxious to embrace it. "That made Marvin want to do it even more. Motown thought the song was a protest song, whoever did it. But when Marvin put that melody in, he did the different jazz-type and modern changes, and got real creative. In other words, it was three cats that had three different talents, but it was one great fucking song!"

But they weren't through. A fourth person contributed to the mix. "Marvin went to Dave Van DePitte, who was a jazz musician and arranger, and he took the whole production and he wrote the music under what was happening." Van DePitte had worked with Marvin when he produced the Originals. It was his charts that helped Marvin flesh out his musical vision at Motown for much of the seventies. In a 1972 *Rolling Stone* interview, Marvin explained Van DePitte's role in his artistic creativity. "*What's Going On* was my first production ever. I conceived every bit of the music. I hate to *brag* and everything like this, but I had no musical knowledge, I can't write music, can't read music. But I was able to transmit my thoughts to another person, and David Van DePitte, through the graces of God, had enough talent to be able to receive it and put it on paper for me." Marvin says he thought at one time that he might go to school to learn music so that, like great composers, he could translate his own musical ideas—and because he wanted the glory for himself. "As I listen to composers like Gershwin…I mean I'm awed by him, that he wrote all his music himself. You know, I can go around all day and say, 'Hey, dammit, I composed that album,' and Dave can come back and say, 'No you didn't, I wrote it,' and I'm going to take it to a judge and say, 'Well, I *thought* it,' and he'll say, 'Wait a minute, well, who wrote this music?' Dave Van DePitte. Well, you get it; it's yours. But I'm gonna learn how to write music, so I can do it. Why? Because I want all the credit.'"[17]

Marvin did possess the keen gift to hear music in his soul and to make every effort to translate it through powerful lyrics and the creative use of the instruments at hand—whether a piano, a drum set, or his voice. "You'd just be sitting there talking, and you could relate anything to him, and when you looked up, he's singing about it," says Benson. Art Stewart, the engineer, agrees. "He could say things in such a way that [even if] you probably didn't think like that, when you heard him sing, you said, 'Yeah, that's exactly what I would have said.' And then to sing it in such a style that you could understand it and feel the warmth, the pain, the love, the compassion that this guy could feel. And Marvin could really interpret songs; that was his genius. He could approach it in so many different ways, in terms of melody, in terms of lyrical structure, just in terms of taking a song and singing a line with one emphasis, and then turning around the next second and changing the emphasis on a word or on a note. It would take it to another level."

I got a taste of this when I compared the originally released version of Marvin Gaye's song, "Let's Get It On," to the "demo" version contained in the deluxe edition double-compact disk that was recently issued. On the original version of the song, Gaye is forthright about his erotic passion for his lover, and declares with a punchy staccato line, "I've been *really* try-y-y-y-in' baby, *tryin'* to hold *back* these feelins' for so-o-o-o long." You can feel his ardor torching the syllables that are gruffly elongated to communicate his desire. On the "demo" version, Gaye takes a bluesier approach, on both the music and in his delivery. Instead of belting his first phrase, Marvin sneaks up to his subject, albeit quickly, avowing that "I've been *try-y-y-in'*, tryin' for so long, baybay-uh, *tryin'* to *hold* back this *feelin'* for so long." By subtracting the word "really" from the demo version, Marvin lays even greater emphasis on the first "tryin'," rolling it in gospel melisma. And by placing "baybayuh" after "for so long" in his "demo" version—it's after the first "tryin'" in the original version—he draws it out and rests the full weight of his affection on the term, giving it a vernacular meaning in his pronunciation. And by repeating "for so long" twice in the "demo" version, Gaye stresses the pent up emotions that long for expression. The first version is more assertive, the second more plaintive. Gaye achieved these contrasting meanings by modulating his wailing, and by striking, rearranging and stressing different words in the same line.

Marvin put this gift to good use in the five days in June and July of 1970 that it took him to record the single "What's Going On." It may also help explain how he got writing credit on the tune, and on every song that filled out his monumental album. Marvin rarely sang what he was originally presented by a songwriter. He often edited, fiddling with lines, giving new shades of meaning. And he repeatedly pursued the lyric down multiple avenues of interpretation. "Working with him, I would always think that when he sang a line, or sang a phrase, I was quite satisfied with it," Art Stewart said. "But he very rarely was. So we did a lot of takes, as they're called, and we'd use a lot of different tracks. He rarely would just sing a line and say, 'Okay, let's go on to the next thing,' because he just wanted to approach it from every angle to make sure he was putting on tape what he really felt in his heart." The talented songwriter-producer Ivy Jo Hunter, who worked with Marvin on several occasions and with whom he cowrote "Dancing in the Street," says that Gaye possessed a rare level of musical literacy. "He knew music well enough to read interpretation into a piece of music, to know that there was more than one way that this piece could be done.

Most artists don't have that ability. They hear what you give them. They know the riffs that are standard to their style, and they've got to make an adaptation within those boundaries." Marvin undoubtedly felt in his element as he set out to interpret Benson and Celeveland's song, and thus, to make it all his own. He had help from the Funk Brothers, who have only recently got their artistic acclaim—with a full-length 2002 documentary on their work, *Standing in the Shadows of Motown*, and a lifetime achievement Grammy Award in 2004. They boasted musicians as comfortable with jazz as they were with rhythm and blues.

For the first session in the Snakepit on June 1, 1970, the weed smoke was thick when Marvin the producer and artist took to the piano. The Funk Brothers and other guest musicians enveloped him in a mellow jazz groove that was both percussive and percolating. On "What's Going On," James Jamerson's famously peripatetic bass, coupled with a conga thump, form the opening downbeat that introduces the well-known saxophone chords, piercing yet solemn, that float through a wall of sound. "Mother, mother, there's too many of you crying," Marvin gently announces, his love for his own mother, and for the mothers of the world facing loss, readily apparent. "Brother, brother, brother, there's far too many of you dying," he concludes the couplet. Gaye caresses the lyrics with a poignancy that was perhaps informed by his brother's brutal passage through the jungles of Southeast Asia, as well as his and Benson's observations of problems closer to home. Marvin goes on to lament the hostilities on foreign soil—"war is not the answer," he urgently intones—and to decry the mistreatment of demonstrators for social justice. "Don't punish me, with brutality," he rhythmically pleads. Instead, he asks to be taken seriously, to be listened to, to be understood. "Talk to me, so you can see, oh, what's goin' on," Marvin declares, building upon the song's first forceful verse. The song's aesthetic tension is released into Marvin's haunting falsetto, which arcs above a luxurious landscape of scatting background voices, most of them his own. (Mel Farr and Lem Barney, football stars for the Detroit Lions and Marvin's friends, supply the single's background party voices—the same vocals that famously greet the listener on the song's album version before a single note is heard). Marvin's voice is silky, sensuous and serious all at once; his lyrics serene but socially aware. The backing orchestra assembled to accompany the Funk Brothers is elegant and understated. The juxtaposition of strings and percussion, and the sophisticated slide of trombone riffs beneath gently slicing saxophone spurts, sweetly complement Gaye's moral mission to inform and inspire.

"What's Going On" was a remarkable, radical departure for Marvin and Motown. This was high concept, high-minded popular music; it was smooth and effortlessly classic. He had transformed the Snakepit into a sanctuary of progressive jazz-influenced black music. The song, and the album that followed, evoked Gaye's great studio gifts. "He was the ultimate recording artist," said Ivy Jo Hunter. "He had such emotion, and he gave such recordable performances. A lot of people can sing, but they're not recordable. You can't get that nuance; it's not transmissible. You can't communicate the real thing that they have in that medium. You go to see those people live [and] they're fantastic artists—alive and vibrant. You take them in that studio and they're either too loud for the mic or they can't be still and stay in one place. Recording is an art form; you're either aware of what you're doing or you're pliable enough to let a producer manipulate you into what he wants. Marvin was the kind of artist that you didn't have to manipulate. You had to give him rein. You had to argue with him from time to time to save your production, because he'd take it somewhere else. But he had concept, which many artists don't have."

Marvin's conceptual acuity was evident on "What's Going On"—from the ingenious contrast of the harsh subjects he broached and the soulful music through which he chose to address them, and the integration of symphonic sweeps and jazz licks into his melodic vocabulary. "Marvin had changes in his music like jazz," Benson pointed out. "It wasn't just two bars and four bars. Marvin's stuff had different colors in it, harmonically." Ivy Jo Hunter elaborates on this strength in Marvin's music. "The chord structure of his music, if you notice, is very extended," Hunter says. "It is not the triads; it's the sevenths, ninths, thirteenths. We don't usually expand the chords that far in rock and roll or R & B. These chords gave his music another quality, not just your ordinary sound. That's why when you hear 'What's Going On' you think, 'Marvin!' Coming from the Moonglows, he had extensive experience with harmony. They tell you about his drum playing, but you never hear about his piano playing, which was very good." (If one listens to his live concert in D.C.'s Kennedy Center in 1972, contained on the deluxe edition of *What's Going On*, one gets a sense on the opening track—a jazzy recapitulation of his sixties hits—for Gaye's piano playing, full of blues lines and jazz chords bathed in gospel passion that, in tandem with his smoldering, smoky, wailing vocals, is a stirring diapason of the seventies black urban cosmopolitan sound)."If you listen to things like *Trouble Man*, that is jazz! When left to his own devices, that's what he did. But now Motown, they wanted an instant market, and since he took off yelling and screaming, they kept him yelling and screaming. They didn't have a lot of imagination. Whatever was selling they sold. That was not just them; that was the industry. You needed to develop a formula and readapt it as many times as possible. They called it the 'Motown sound,' but it was really redundancy."

Marvin was trapped by Motown's hunger for redundancy. Berry Gordy disliked "What's Going On," reputedly saying it was the worst record he'd ever heard.[18] "I remember being in the Bahamas trying to relax and take a vacation," Gordy later said in a television interview. "[Marvin] called and said, 'Lookit, I've got to release this album. I've got these songs, it's great.' When he told me they were protest songs, I said, 'Marvin, why do you want to ruin your career? Why do you want to put out a song about the Vietnam War, police brutality and all of these things? You've got all these great love songs. You're the hottest artist, the sex symbol of the sixties and seventies…'"[19] Obie Benson cites another reason for Gordy's resistance. "Berry had this big company with all these acts and he didn't want controversy." Despite the message music that Stevie Wonder, the Supremes, and the Temptations had cautiously floated in the musical mainstream, Motown wasn't prepared to suffer the potential backlash over Marvin's social criticism—even if it was draped in love and sung with sweet passion.[20] The music was a problem as well: too jazzy, too unorthodox for a black pop market, and dangerously shredding the three-minute attention span that most R & B and rock and roll records played to. Motown flatly refused to release "What's Going On." (Of course, the company had done this before, with "Grapevine" and on "Baby I'm For Real," the song he produced for the Originals, both of which turned out to be hits.)

Marvin was equally adamant: he wouldn't record another note until the company put out his single. Harry Weinger is less ceremonious in capturing Gaye's attitude. "He does the song in the summer of '70," Weinger reminisces. "He knows he's got something, and Berry Gordy is saying no. He says, 'Well fuck y'all. I'm not recording.'" Motown and Marvin would stalemate nearly half a year. When Berry Gordy insisted the company needed product from Gaye, he discovered all they had was "What's Going On," to which Gordy replied, "Ah, that Dizzy Gillespie stuff in the middle, that scatting, it's old."[21] Desperate to get Gaye's voice in the marketplace, Motown Executive VP Barney Ales talked to Quality Control head Billie Jean Brown, and they agreed to put the record out—without Gordy's knowledge.[22] On the day the single was released, in January 1971, Ales flew to Los Angeles, where Gordy had virtually taken up residence, to explain the decision to his irate boss. But by the time Ales landed in Los Angeles, Motown had reorders for 100,000 records. When Gordy found out that Gaye had sold more than 100,000 singles in one day his mind changed instantly. The song eventually climbed to number two on the pop charts and claimed the top spot on the R & B list. Now Motown needed an album to support the single. Weinger continues: "Berry Gordy says, 'Okay, I may not like it, but I need a million more like it.' And Marvin says, 'Oh, no problem.' Well, he hasn't written a thing.'"

Gaye had barely sketched out a few other songs for the

album. The music existed mostly in his imagination, waiting to be mapped, transcribed and articulated in David Van Depitte's expert—if exasperatingly generated—charts. Marvin had become notoriously difficult to get to the studio, and now that Motown was desperate for more of the music that it had spurned, he was in no mood to comply with their wishes, at least not right away. On one of his visits to Detroit, Gordy came to his house and met with Gaye face to face. He knew that Marvin had agreed to appear in a film that would begin shooting in Los Angeles in early April. Gordy struck a deal with Marvin: he could make *his* album, just the way he wanted, producing himself, if he could finish it by the time he was to begin filming. Gordy made the offer to Marvin at the beginning of March. He would have a month to complete the project. But by the time Marvin got in the groove, it was already mid-March, leaving him less than 15 days to fashion his masterpiece. In fact, Gaye recorded *What's Going On*—widely considered the greatest album in black popular music, and arguably, in all of American pop music—at the end of March in a whirlwind ten days!

In a week-and-a-half period, Marvin heavily relied on a host of collaborators. First, he depended on other writers to help him eloquently articulate his ideas. He enlisted the Andantes to supply sweet background support. He sorely needed David Van DePitte to chart his inchoate but inspiring musical vision. And he recruited the Funk Brothers and members of the Detroit Symphony to bring that vision to life with their excellent musicianship. That the album was completed is a miracle of converging circumstances and realities—in the land of social and political affairs that was the album's rhetorical backdrop; in the world of Motown, which put aside business as usual to help in the creation of art of the highest order; and in Gaye's own musical universe, where the stars of fate burned brightly in his heart and lit his path to noble transactions with his Muse. In the frenzied but portentous space in which he labored, Marvin embraced the challenge to turn inspiration to art with a rigorous concentration that taxed and transformed his co-creators.

With James Nyx he hammered out "What's Happening Brother," a mellow but haunting morality tale about the ruin of war narrated by a returning soldier—a story clearly rooted in Frankie Gaye's experiences. By portraying the difficulties faced by the soldier once he comes home—"Can't find no work, can't find no job my friend/Money is tighter than it's ever been"— Gaye and Nyx are able to link foreign hostility ("War is hell, when will it end") to domestic suffering. Despite the cries of politicians, it truly appeared to be guns *or* butter. When they focus on what their subject wants to catch up on—dance spots, the baseball team's pennant chances, social trends—Gaye and Nyx underscore an awful effect of war: it disrupts life and robs one of the pleasures and distractions that others take for granted. All the while, Gaye's honey tenor is surrounded by a glorious cushion of the Andantes' angelic "ahs" and "oohs" as heavily percussive rhythms are stroked by a tingling bass. On "Flyin' High (In The Friendly Sky)," cowritten with Anna and Elgie Stover, Marvin, intentionally or not, is both confessional and prophetic as he addresses drug addiction in a falsetto that rings through a pared back landscape of roving bass, soft cymbals and gentle snare drums. "And I go to the place where the good feelin' awaits me/Self-destruction's in my hand," Marvin achingly admits. He relies upon his own voice in the background to echo and answer his plaintive confession that his actions are "so stupid-minded." Gaye's trailing voice faintly, parenthetically intones "can't help it, I can't help it"—symbolizing a point-counterpoint of ego division that calls on the healthy force in his conscience to bear witness against its sick, ensnared double.

"Flyin' High" gives way to Gaye's jazzy, conga-laden lament over the plight of children—their neglect, their dismissal, their suffering. "Save the Children" begins with a question that anticipated the resurgence years later of a branch of ethics concerned for the other, as he softly asks, "I just want to ask a question, Who really cares?" In Gaye's song—cowritten with Benson and Cleveland—the object of care is singular: a despairing world whose fate is tied to our treatment of children. Hence, we must "Save the babies, save the babies/If you wanna love, you got to save the babies." On "God Is Love" and "Wholly Holy" Marvin probes his religious passions. In the first, brief song, written with Anna, Stoger, and Nyx, Marvin claims that Jesus "loves us whether or not we know it/And He'll forgive all our sins," over a sprightly arrangement of punching horns and resounding piano chords as the Andantes—and Marvin himself—harmonize with his vibrant lead vocals. On "Wholly Holy," penned with Benson and Cleveland, Marvin slows the pace considerably, offering a lovely, simple hymn of praise to God, built on saxophone pirouettes and sweeping violin lines as he says Jesus "left us a book to believe in," and that with his love, we "can rock the world's foundation."

In "Right On," written with percussionist Earl DeRouen, Marvin duels amiably with a transcendent flute that weaves in and out of the busy rhythmic traffic. He nimbly sketches a utopian vision of social harmony that embraces both "those of us who simply like to socialize" and those "who tend the sick and heed the people's cries." (*Rolling Stone* critic Vince Aletti misjudged this song when he wrote in his review that "'Right On' the longest number, misses"; Aletti overlooks how the song perfectly sets up "Wholly Holy" with a saucy jazz kick.)[23] On the album's remaining two songs—both of them, along with "What's Going On," were released as singles—Gaye goes cosmic and gets critical. "Mercy Mercy Me (The Ecology)" is among Gaye's most forward looking songs, in tune with environmental justice at a time when it had hardly darkened the cultural agenda. On a bed of percussion, reeds and strutting guitar licks, Marvin builds a tract of concern for the disappearance of "blue skies," overcrowded land, the poisoning of the air, "[o]il wasted on the ocean and upon the sea" that leads to "fish full of mercury," and radiation that kills animals and birds. It was if Rachel Carson had caught the gift of song to warn the world about ecological devastation.

Gaye closes the album with "Inner City Blues (Makes Me Wanna Holler)," written with James Nyx. From the song's spare opening piano chords, thudding drum beats, conga strokes, and rubbery bass, the ominous tone is set for what is to come: Gaye's strongest indictment of America for the suffering black ghetto. His opening lines take the government to task for probing outer space while leaving the poor to fend for themselves. "Rockets, moon shots/Spend it on the have nots," Marvin begins, doubling his own voice for harmonic and dramatic effect. Besides criticizing the military's draft of the poor ("Send that boy off to die") Gaye grieves over the forces that make the ghetto economy especially harsh: mounting bills, dwindling resources, inflation and heavy taxes—even as he confesses he can't pay his own. When he cries, "Makes me wanna holler/Throw up both my hands,"his anguish seems real. (Throughout my teen years, I thought Gaye was saying, "Makes me wanna holler/Throw up on my hands," deeming it a nasty but effective symbol of social disgust!) The album ends with a curious but prophetic coda. Marvin repeats a line—more slowly, and with a piercing vocal—from "What's Going On," except this time he switches gender, striking the phrase "Father, father," and chanting instead, "Mother, mother, everybody thinks we're wrong, but who are they to judge us/Simply cause we wear our hair long." The first words on the album are, "Mother, mother, they're too many of you crying."[24] Marvin comes full circle, closing the loop of affection around a woman who loved and cared for him until death. While Marvin may not have intended the coda to signify his love for his mother, we can't ignore his parental relations in divining its meaning in his life. It is perhaps poetic justice that Marvin rhetorically displaced his father on wax—something he failed to do in the flesh, a failure that cost him his life.

Gaye's album expressed elements of urban realism and the more venerable tradition of social and personal expression in the blues. As musicologist Joanna Demers writes, throughout the album, "Gaye decries the ghetto as a purgatory for lost souls forgotten by society at large. Repression from without (through racist governmental policies) as well as degradation from within (through black-on-black violence and drug sales) conspire to change once-thriving urban centers into ghettos."[25] But Robert Hilburn perhaps best captured the connection between *What's Going On* and the blues tradition.

It was that album that underscored Gaye's most significant role: our most radical and influential link with the vital American blues tradition...Gaye made a far greater contribution by applying the introspection and social commentary of the once rural blues tradition to modern sounds. Gaye didn't employ the established blues structure or instrumentation, but much of his most involving post-'71 music reflected the spirit of the blues: from the frequently confessional tone to the constant sense of struggle and searching...*What's Going On*, which mixed the anguish of the blues and the prayerful yearning of gospel music into a classy, sophisticated pop package, was as dramatic a fusion as Bob Dylan's mid-sixties merger of folk's social protest and rock's energy... Gaye's post-1970 music detailed a personal, often tormented search for salvation—a search that reflected the tension of the blues tradition."[26]

What's Going On also consolidated the black soul music market, the intellectual aspirations of the pop musician as poet/performer, and album-based American radio. As musicologists Larry Starr and Christopher Waterman argue, Marvin—and Sly Stone, Stevie Wonder, and George Clinton—was able to

connect long-standing aspects of African-American musical traditions with elements from rock, including the notion of the musician as an artistic mastermind and of the LP record album as a work of art...Marvin Gaye's commitment to a socially responsible aesthetic vision, surpasses any measure of commercial success. Along with Stevie Wonder and Sly Stone, Marvin Gaye showed that soul and R & B albums could provide artistic coherence that transcended the three-minute single, managed to bridge the divide between AM Top 40, FM album-oriented radio, and the soul music market, and help open the possibility that popular music might still have something to do with social change, as well as money making and artistic self-expression."[27]

While it's important to recognize that chosen soul artists played off the intellectual identity of the American pop artist, it's a mistake to see their efforts as somehow derivative. Some critics even relegate towering figures like Marvin Gaye to the shadows of the Beatles, denying the distinct quality and sources of black art.

A typical error of rock critics is to assume that, after the Beatles, all musicians in the Afro-American idiom took their cues from rock. From this perspective *What's Going On* is merely soul music's answer to *Sergeant Pepper*. But, as anyone in the field of jazz knows, soul musicians in the 1960s got their inspiration from other sources, notably a new kind of spirituality in jazz…as when Ellington began in the mid-1960s to compose full-length concerts of sacred music."[28]

Marvin's inspiration, and his outrage, moved beyond his album. In a radio interview, he eloquently phrased his disgust at social conformity and indicted a government that didn't have its citizenry's best interests at heart. His words illumine his moral mission on *What's Going On*: to stir our civic conscience and to make us aware of our political surroundings.

You know what bothers me? It bothers me tremendously to see *us* sit around and look at the people virtually destroying us, and pretending that it's okay. I cannot understand how we human beings can let a few powerful men in the world treat us like cattle, and insensitive people, and robots. We're programmed, we're sensitized, we're Big Brothered, and we're police stated. We have no fight; we seem apathetic. It's horrible. I don't see why so many people in the world are allowing a few men to destroy our civilization…Stand up and say, 'We people who love to live the simple life, who love the sun and the air and the birds and the bees, whom you people don't seem to have any regard for…' Somewhere, somehow, it has to be stopped, or we're gonna all be destroyed and very soon, perhaps in my lifetime."[29]

In my teen years, Marvin's songs, especially "Inner City Blues," fed my hunger for social justice. It also helped me to grasp my ghetto roots, much as Claude Brown's forceful *Manchild in the Promised Land* helped me to understand young black men trapped by social neglect. I suppose Gaye's album at points might be seen as the smoother musical complement to Brown's brutally honest book. Gaye's vision grew from one great and troubled black metropolis—Detroit—while Brown tracked the terrain of his origin in Harlem. Like Marvin—in his music and in his personal woes—Brown seemed fated to narrate the story of his troubled generation of black men. Brown was born and reared in Harlem, the mythic heartland of black America. His father was an alcoholic railroad worker who beat Claude and his siblings, much as Marvin's father beat his brood. Like Marvin's mother, Brown's mother was extremely devoted to her son. But Claude's mother sought in exasperation to send her son to juvenile-delinquency programs because, by the time he was eight, he'd already begun a life of crime. Brown was a gang member, a thief and a drug dealer. When he was a teenager, a drug addict shot him in his stomach. Somewhat miraculously, he eluded the designed-to-fail circumstances of his upbringing with the help of reform school. Eventually, at 22 he enrolled at Howard University, where he met Toni Morrison, a young writing instructor who encouraged and assessed his early literary efforts. Six years later, in 1965, he published his searing masterpiece, *Manchild in the Promised Land*, an autobiographical novel that has sold more than 4 million copies.

Brown says that the people he wrote about are "sons and daughters of former Southern sharecroppers...the poorest of the South, who poured into New York City during the decade following the Great Depression." I first read Brown's book when I was 12 years old, the year Marvin Gaye's *What's Going On* was released. My mother and father had been swept to Detroit in the great migration of Southern blacks, in their case, from Alabama and Georgia. "I want to talk about the experiences of a misplaced generation...in an extremely complex, confused society," Brown wrote. "This is a story of their searching, their dreams, their sorrows, their small and futile rebellions, and their endless battle to establish their own place in America's greatest Metropolis—and in America itself."[30] These words plumbed my chaotic and violent urban existence and allowed me, for the first time, to interpret my experience as the child of two Southern souls wrenched from their native soil. It was the secular, though no less inspiring, literary twin to Malcolm X's autobiographical tale of redemption as self-invention. When I listened to *What's Going On*, I gained insight into the spiritual desires and social hopes—and the disappointments and stunted dreams—of black folk who toiled in obscurity away from mainstream acceptance or understanding. Marvin also made the social gospel I'd heard from time to time preached in my home church compelling, immediate, relevant.

Of course I wasn't the only beneficiary of Gaye's gospel grandeur. On *What's Going On* Marvin made the logic of black Christian love accessible to millions who may have otherwise dismissed its most ardent believers as parochial or irrelevant or dangerously naïve. He took his tunes to church and baptized them in the swelling currents of love of God and fellow man that washed over him as the son of a Pentecostal preacher. Even more striking, Marvin made it clear that social justice is what love sounds like when it speaks in public. He glossed a hundred theology books and gleaned the gist of a thousand sermons when he tied God's love to love for children and poor people and for the environment and in defense of peace. Parts of Marvin's album were a soulful update of the Negro spirituals, or the sorrow songs of the slave, plumbing the depths of black spiritual resistance to social despair and personal hopelessness.[31] Other parts of his musical homily were drawn from Biblical models of grieving for the vulnerable and victimized—for instance, in the book of Lamentations, where the prophet Jeremiah weeps over evil instead of celebrating the destruction of the unrighteous. Marvin's prophetic vision drew on chords of empathy and disappointment, a sign that one has neither given up the music of community nor ignored the discord of one's own shortcomings. As the critic Mark Anthony Neal argues, Marvin's album should be seen "as one incarnation of the nonviolent mass civil disobedience Martin Luther King, Jr. demanded shortly before his death."[32]

Just as striking is how *What's Going On* elicited several features, many of them accidental, which figured prominently in Marvin's future art. The themes that tie the album together emerged as Marvin and his fellow creators blended brain and heart to fashion a lucid and compelling *artistic* statement. It happened that at the time of their collaboration, questions of social justice in various guises dominated their thoughts. To be sure, the way Marvin carved and crafted the words of his collaborators stamped their art with his unique style, and to a degree, with his moral ambitions. He had become fed up with making music that failed to address the world around him, a world that seemed to lurch into catastrophe in the newspapers he read and in the stories he heard from friends and family. He yearned to be more socially relevant in his art, to reflect in his music the hopes and terrors that seized his soul. But the decision to blend the album thematically—and to allow the music to bleed from one song to the next—happened on the ground, as things developed, and not in advance of the project's conception. Marvin worked with what he had—musicians, writers, songs—and drew his inspiration from the mix of talents and ideas in the room. It was a case of *bricolage*, of making do with what is at hand.[33] It was not a planned artistic pregnancy; it was one of those accidents of timing that produced great results from the heat of the conceptual moment. The circumstances of its creation do not deny the power of the album's intellectual core; it simply underscores how the conceptual web that united *What's Going On* came to be.

Accident played a role in the potent vocal layering that Marvin pioneered and mastered as well. His experience in the

Moonglows gave Marvin intimate knowledge of the construction of vocal harmonies from every voice. His doo-wop background helped to develop his unique registers, especially the three distinct voices that Marvin mastered in his repertoire of vocal articulation. "I have a very sensitive voice," Marvin said in 1983. "It doesn't record the same as most people's and I have to be extremely aware of my technique when I am recording…I have three voices: a very rough voice, a falsetto, and my natural and smooth mid-range."[34] His duets with Mary Wells, Kim Weston, and Tammi Terrell were so compelling because they captured one of Marvin's real strengths: blending even disparate voices with arcing, subtle harmonies. Marvin put his vocal knowledge to excellent use on his work with the Originals, and most gloriously, on his own recordings, beginning with *What's Going On*. Marvin was able to bring all three of his voice ranges and styles to bear in multiple tracks of his vocals that were replicated in layers and amplified to sound like a chorus full of Marvin Gayes. Thus, he locked into a technique that essentially refines and adapts Coltrane's "sheets of sound" to the pop vocabulary.[35] But it was the result of a mistake made by an engineer on the single for "What's Going On." "That double lead voice was a mistake on my part," Ken Sands told journalist Ben Edmonds. "Marvin had cut two lead vocals, and wanted me to prepare a tape with the rhythm track up the middle and each of his vocals on separate tracks so he could compare them. Once I played the two-track mix on a mono machine and he heard both voices at the same time by accident."[36]

Marvin seized on the mistake and integrated it into his artistic vocabulary and into his stylistic and recording repertoire. As critic Stanley Crouch says:

His is a talent for which the studio must have been invented. Through over-dubbing, Gaye imparted lyric, rhythmic, and emotional counterpoint to his material. The result was a swirling stream-of-consciousness that enabled him to protest, show allegiance, love, hate, dismiss, and desire in one proverbial swoop. In his way, what Gaye did was reiterate electronically the polyrhythmic African underpinnings of black American music and reassess the domestic polyphony, which is its linear extension. The upshot of his genius was the ease and power with which he could pivot from a superficially simple but virtuosic use of rests and accents to a multilinear layered density."[37]

Mark Anthony Neal sees political and social importance in Gaye's vocal layering, noting how it "metaphorically and aurally reconstructed the various communities of resistance which undergirded black social movement" in the seventies, and that it mimicked "the diversity of communal voices" and "popularized a dominant black social paradigm" at "the moment when communal relations" were fracturing.[38] Both Crouch and Neal tap into critical dimensions of Gaye's layered vocal landscape. Crouch helps us to understand how Marvin's manipulation of multiple voices extended and informed black musical tradition by stressing its varied rhythms and intellectual purposes. Neal highlights the parallel between Gaye's art and the social conditions that it both marks and, in some instances, mediates. Marvin's engineer, Art Stewart, sheds light on how Marvin's craft was guided by conscientious attention to artistic merit. His multiple voices were unleashed to enhance his music and not merely to display or abuse technical developments in the recording studio.

"The multiple tracks were brought about by the technological advances," Stewart explains. "But he was able to take it and not misuse it. I'll give you an example. When I started at Motown, they had come out of the eight-track and had just started with 16-track machines. When we moved to the west coast, we're now up to 24. And another technological happenstance came along, and that was the ability to sync tracks with the tone, where you can now have ad infinitum tracks. You can have 120 [tracks] if you want. Along the way, some people took that and abused the system. In other words, using those tracks for the sake of, 'I have them, so let me use them.' So now we start getting away from taking a little and making a lot. Now, because we have a lot, we begin to bastardize what we're doing. So rather than have an artist to sing the song down one track the whole way, we now put him on 24 tracks."

"And plug in this mistake with this take?" I ask Stewart.

"That's right. Marvin's background was with the Moonglows, and singing with groups. And in order to be in a group, he said he learned that a lot of times you had to interchange the voicing in a group. Let's say if the tenor didn't show up—because back then you had an alto, tenor, soprano, you had guys who actually sang in those ranges, unlike today. Everybody don't really know what that means. But, at any rate, he could demonstrate how he could do all these voicings. So he took that skill that he learned and began to sing the background parts to his songs. And he didn't do that just so he could come back and find out which note he sang right. He actually put the parts down. He put down the bass, and whatever note he wanted to sing, rather than using 24 tracks for the sake of, 'Well, I can't make up my mind...'"

"So the technology was dictating the process as opposed to the artist using the technology to get to his or her end?" I asked.

"Yeah. He put those tracks down; they had a purpose. He didn't do it because he had the ability or the territory or the space to do it."

In light of how fortuitous mistakes played a role in the recording of *What's Going On*—not only the conceptual grid and vocal layering, but the famous opening saxophone riffs on the single were culled from a warm-up session, after which the musician, Eli Fontaine, was sent home—it is not overreaching it to suggest the presence of what anthropologist Melville Herskovits termed "the deification of Accident."[39] Herskovits observed in African cultures, and in black American life, a social trait of weaving into the fabric of the culture events that appeared accidental, but which were subsequently viewed as an extension of the culture's ideas and survival. The coming together of *What's Going On* seems the perfect example of such a black cultural habit, one that, to be sure, is unavoidably modified in different social and creative circumstances.

It was this confluence of events surrounding *What's Going On*, and some of Marvin's other albums from the seventies, that sparked Harry Weinger's curiosity about what other stories—of origins, process, accidence and magic—that the vaults might yield. "Marvin is a never ending source of artistry and fascination," Weinger says, "because everything is great. Everything. And you read the books, you hear stories about his struggles with women, pushing against Berry, and going with the flow of the sixties, using his craft and his skills, and then he starts to push a little. What comes out of that? His songs that are autobiographical, the songs that are outward looking, the songs that are inward looking, it's all extraordinarily fascinating. And then to find out how deep it goes—to find out *What's Going On* was done in ten fucking days! I think it's important for us to be amazed with that. I love to be able to have exclamation points at the end of these things [and] not take these things for granted. To put on *What's Going On*, and whatever record, and listen to it, and go, 'How did he ever get there?' It's a miracle he got there, and then what he did with it!"

Weinger underscores the point that Marvin's genius could not have been as forcefully expressed without his gifted collaborators. "The creativity of Marvin Gaye is something to always be amazed by, and to feel honored that you're there, and to be in awe. The human side is that Marvin couldn't do any of this without collaborators. Marvin's best work was always with collaborators. What are his great vocal [performances] of the sixties? Norman Whitfield, baby, pushing him. *What's Going On*, it's Obie Benson, the Funk Brothers, David Van DePitte. And they segued the record together. Then there's the engineer who mistakenly came up with the idea of combining the vocals." But Weinger acknowledges the reciprocity of Gaye's collaborations and how his genius benefited his artistic colleagues. "I think we should also be fascinated and amazed by the fact that Marvin's artistry gave those people permission to say to Marvin, 'Sure, we can do that. Let's try that. I've got an idea. Let me do that.'" Weinger insists that Marvin inspired his fellow artists and producers by his willingness to stretch his vision and test his own talents in the studio. "They'd say, 'Damn, Marvin's playing percussion, let me get in there. Let me do something with that.'"

One of the advantages of poking around in the tapes vault is that one may stumble upon treasures and have a moment of luminous accidence oneself. Some of the things Weinger stumbled on have already added to what we know about Marvin Gaye's artistic habits, how and when he created what he did. Plus, Weinger unearthed some nuggets that have now been sonically archived. "When you look at *What's Going On*, and what's around that record, you find stuff. We came up with a live version of that record." As Weinger writes in the liner notes to the *What's Going On* deluxe edition, Gaye's apprehensions in live performance—he hadn't been on stage since Tammi's death—left him "terrified. He hasn't performed in nearly four years...A hectic schedule means there is little rehearsal. The show gets a cruelly late start...Yet despite the chaos and the pain and the time away, Marvin is sweet and supple. Marvin is real. He leans on the confident grooves of the original Funk Brothers and his friends the Andantes, flown in specially from Detroit. He embraces the audience. He trusts his own voice. At the end of a long day in his honor, Marvin Gaye delivers the word."[40]

Louvain Demps tells me that the Andantes didn't want to travel with Gaye to Washington. "It was a hard thing, because I wanted to go, and the rest didn't. We didn't usually travel much. We went out on the road with Kim Weston...but actually getting out there and working with the other artists, we didn't do that. And [Marvin] got on the phone and talked to me and tried to get me to get the girls to go. And after a little verbal battle with the girls, they agreed to go. Marvin told me, 'Oh, baby, I'm just scared.' I told him, 'I tell you what you do. Do not smoke, do not do anything. I'm going to be standing closest to the piano, so what you do is, when you come out, and you feel yourself really sacred, look up at me. I will be there. And I'll be praying.' And of course, he did not look up. And I guess he was high. And it was something, because he sat down and I guess the fear kind of gripped him. And we had the orchestra [from] Washington, but we took the basic rhythm section with us. And Maurice King, the great director, was there. And Marvin got so nervous that he turned two pages at once, and he skipped over [many songs]. And therefore the orchestra was playing something and he was somewhere else. But the rhythm section kept on. So Maurice King stepped out, and then he said, using his great big voice, 'Oh yeah, yeah, what's going on? Yeah!' and just made it like it was part of the act." The deification of accident indeed. The May 1, 1972 concert, presented as part of "Marvin Gaye Day" in Washington, D.C., documents Gaye's jazzy voice in live performance of his sixties material, and captures an artist who is still ascending in the freedom of self-production.

Ironically, it was a more personal case of accidence that spurred Weinger to dig deeper into the vaults for new insight into how Marvin made *What's Going On*. Journalist Ben Edmonds, a Weinger friend and American editor of the British magazine *Mojo*, phoned Harry to tell him he was writing a piece on *What's Going On*. "Well, that's interesting," Weinger recalls telling Edmonds. "I was still feeling a little proprietary because we have recording logs and dates and song titles in here. They're numbered; we go to the session book and look up the date." Weinger told Edmonds it would take a little time, since he'd have to look up the recording dates in the microfiche. "I gotta spend all this time looking up stuff. So he kept bugging me. Finally, it was about 5:30 at night, and I push my chair down the hall [to the room with the microfiche], look it up, and I start seeing this picture. I said, 'Shit!' I discovered when it was recorded, how it was recorded, what they did. They basically recorded the whole album in sequence." The 30th anniversary of the album was approaching, and Weinger pitched the idea to his bosses of an expanded edition, and the deluxe edition was born. "It came out of somebody going, 'When? How?'"

In his astute and assiduous investigations, Weinger ends up as a rather scholarly, if posthumous, Gaye collaborator. Without his extraordinary diligence, key parts of Gaye's recording history would remain a mystery. As I sit across from him in his Manhattan office—a thin, prematurely gray, tall, boyishly handsome and ultra-hip middle-aged white man—his enthusiasm levitates the room. He describes, in flowing, even musical hand gestures, and with animated facial masks, just how and what he learned, and the barriers he had to overcome to give the public a clearer vision of Marvin's art. "It's a cliché, but *What's Going On* still resonates in the culture. The feeling about it for 30 years was, it's sacred, you can't touch it. 'Cause even before I delved into this, people who had the job before me knew that the B-sides [to the singles] are different versions. 'God is Love' is different. 'Sad Tomorrows' is a different version of another song. The single of 'What's Going On' is a completely different version of what's on the album." Still, Weinger says the feeling around his company was, "the album is the album," with little incentive to add to it or to change it in any way. But *What's Going On*'s 30th anniversary and Edmonds' article inspired Weinger to press on. He meticulously combed through the tapes, and learned a lot about the technical features behind Marvin's creation, especially how the engineers formed the final album through inventive measures. "They overdubbed onto it the multi-tracks being edited together. They didn't record all the stuff and then cut the pieces together. They recorded onto 16-track—the rhythm tracks—then the engineer spliced the two-inch tracks into side-long suites. The horns and strings recorded on top of the edited pieces, so they could react to the changes. And that's clearly on the tape. You can see the splice. So I learned that technical aspect of it that helped Marvin and David Van DePitte create the final version."

Weinger discovered that there were no outtakes from *What's Going On*, but there were, besides the B-sides to the singles, at least ten mixes of the single "What's Going On." He speculates that the engineer may have generated so many different versions because Quality Control was rejecting different takes, and he was unsure of what version they'd go with. Harry made the choice to wade through *all* the tapes, not just the singles, a considerable cache of Gaye's history all collected in the vaults. It would prove to be a task of sorting and sleuthing. "I said I'm going to look at every tape that says 'Mercy Mercy Me', or 'Ecology,' or 'What's Going On,' or 'What's Happening,' or 'What's Happening Brother,' or just 'Brother.' You just do your due diligence. The title cards tell me that 'God Is Love' was called something else. Is 'Sad Tomorrows' a different session than 'Mercy Mercy Me'? What does it mean? We can look it up. 'Sad Tomorrows' was something else. 'Flying High In the Friendly Sky'—what was that called in the sessions? It must be called something else. I've got to find that. And I came up with a master. In my business we always like to find the primary master, the pre-master master, because records issued from vinyl are thinner than what we can accept on CD. We want to have a full dynamic spectrum. I found a tape that looked like the pre-

master. And we played it, and it's a completely different mix of
the album, which told us a whole 'nother story. And that whole
other story was that Marvin mixed the whole record in Detroit,
and went to L.A., and said 'Here, Berry, here's the record,' and
went to L.A. to work on a movie."

By now, Weinger is even more wound up. He leans closer to
me and gesticulates more dramatically as he recounts what happened next. "He gets to L.A., he calls up Steve Smith (a
Motown engineer) in Detroit, and says, 'Send me the tapes
again.' He mixed the record all over again!" (The Detroit mix,
a rougher, more rhythmically intense version that Gaye envi-
sioned for a late-night party—in contrast to the version that
was ultimately released, a softer, smoother mix that Gaye imagined would be played at an intimate dinner gathering—is
included in the deluxe edition). "That's the record that came
out. And that's why, if you listen to the album and read the
lyrics, some of the lyrics are different. So some of us went
through it, and started editing the notes, the lyrics that are
printed. And then I went back and listened to the Detroit mix,
and said, 'Time out. Do *not* edit those lyrics.' We found out that
Marvin Gaye dictated the lyrics over the phone to Georgia
Ward at Motown. And that's what's printed in the booklet. But
he dictated what he remembered from the mix. When he went
back and remixed it, he changed it. Not the vocal, but he
punched some things in and out. So we restored the lyrics. We
wouldn't have found out that story if someone had not edited
the lyrics, if someone had not taken the extra step to say, 'Well,
let's at least make the lyric content that's printed match what's
on the record.' And somebody else in the next step said, 'Well,
let's be sure,' and discovered these two versions are really differ-

ent. Not just in terms of whether the percussion is loud, or whether the 'Hey, baby, what's happening' isn't at the front or the end, or whether there's an extra five seconds of 'God is love.' Unless somebody raised their hand and said, 'Let me check,' we don't get that story from Georgia Ward. See?"

Harry stands up, hoists his lanky frame to the file cabinet and back to his seat, pantomiming the motions of discovery for me so I can truly get the picture. "And then there's reels and reels of tape that say 'Mercy, Mercy Me,' 'God Is Love,' 'What's Going On.' And it says what looks to be 'DEN AUD.' Denver Auditorium? I call up somebody and ask, 'Did Marvin ever play Denver Auditorium? 'No, no, it's KEN...Kennedy Auditorium. The Kennedy Center.' What?! And I play it—and Motown had a reel-to-reel machine, so when the tape runs out they have to put up another reel—and there's a song or two missing. But if you don't play that tape, if you just assume, 'I already have 'What's Going On,' what do I need to play this for?' you miss out. I play the tape and go, 'It's live? It's live from when? Is this the correct date? Does it match? Well, let me go back and read....oh, it's that show! It's eleven o'clock at night. He's stoned and mixed up. Listen to how he drags. Then you call up Jack Ashford (of the Funk Brothers), call up the Adantes, and find out about Marvin's late night phone calls, worried about how he was going to sound, that he didn't wanna do it. You know? He's going home to see mother and father, and going back to the school where he sang in the choir. All these stories start coming out because you decide, 'Maybe we should just play that tape.' And then you're amazed all over again."

If Marvin's work on *What's Going On* was amazing, it was due in large measure to his artful melding of politics and piety, and to his explicit embrace of a black aesthetic. As Joanna Demers writes, most "ghetto-themed songs featured nominally African or African-diaspora percussion, such as conga drums and wood blocks. As an aestheticization of black music, the ghetto sound was a musical manifestation of Afrocentrism, an attempt to valorize African roots and African-American culture." [41] Marvin's album also helped to create a sonic storm of social protest and political expression that reflected the brave example of artists who publicly identified with the black freedom struggle—including Mayfield, Harry Belafonte, Ray Charles, Isaac Hayes and Nina Simone. [42] Sly and the Family Stone released *There's a Riot Going On* six months after *What's Going On*—almost as if in response to Gaye's poignant question. Before soon, the work of Mayfield, James Brown, the Temptations—and the Promethean offerings of Stevie Wonder—poured forth in a stream of politically and racially charged R & B.

Marvin managed an extraordinarily difficult feat that, with the possible exception of Stevie Wonder, arguably has not been duplicated since: he mined black cultural styles and social complaints while tapping a vein of universal spiritual awareness. "He's in a world of his own," observes Rona Elliot, a former *Today Show* entertainment correspondent who interviewed Gaye a year before his death. "He opened doors that I don't think have since been opened, that will not be opened. When he opened the door to consciousness—and I'm not talking about what Curtis [Mayfield] was singing about, because that was a different thing, that was cheerleading for black power, which I don't want to diminish because the guy was incredibly talented. But Marvin was waking up to what was going on in the world in *What's Going On*. And there hasn't been an artist since, or before…I don't see it, and I don't hear it. I don't hear the wake up that he brought."

Marvin's political and racial awakening—and his musical experimentation and growth—carried forth in his next project, although not in nearly as obvious a fashion. In 1972, Gaye released *Trouble Man*, the soundtrack to a blaxsploitation film of the same name.[43] The album's eponymous title track is a moody, sexy exploration, through Marvin's tangy falsetto, of the lead character's machismo. Released as a single, the track's minimalist, cool aesthetic—with its famous line, "There's only three things in life for sure, taxes, death, and trouble" echoing the T.S. Elliot quote he loved, "Birth, copulation and death. That's all the facts when you come to brass tacks"—garnered Marvin another top ten hit. But most of the album was instrumental—a sparkling, tasty, introspective probing of the pop dimensions of hard-bop and soul jazz.[44] On *Trouble Man* Marvin deepened the jazz vocabulary first spoken on *What's Going On* while emulating the art of composers like Gershwin.[45] Across a spare aural landscape, Marvin sketches sweet and spicy saxophone riffs, pungent, tinkling keyboards, airy strings, plangent drumming, hard-hitting horns, and interspersed snatches of song and first tenor scatting and wordless articulations—almost like speaking in tongues to musical accompaniment—set off by the psychedelic, synthesizer-drenched funk and haunting tones of the Moog synthesizer. Marvin's art was equally edifying, if challenging, in the recording studio.

"Without realizing it, he had scored the movie in such a fashion he had not rendered it for easily sliding in, taking a track, then compiling an album," engineer Stewart tells me.

"And so what he had to do was make songs from what we call stings—what we call short background music."

"Stings?" I ask.

"Yes. In other words, you may hear in a movie a dramatic piece, or a stencil piece, right? (Stewart hums a few bars.) Next piece had nothing to do with that. Now, he had heard it, so he had to build songs from pieces like that. And what he would do, as we were going through the material, he would say, 'Okay, I want to use the phrase I just gave you. Art, I want to start right here—and I want a hand right here...' And I'd say, 'What do you mean?' In other words, some of those tracks did not have a drum beat, did not have a click, or didn't have anything you could key in on as to where he wanted to start this piece and where he wanted to end it, so you could make a clean cut. It mostly had to do with feeling, which was something Marvin had to transfer to me, because if you don't have 'one, two, three, four,' you know, you don't know where to cut."

"So how did you get that feeling?"

"You gotta listen. And the whole time that I would listen to this music, I'd say, 'Okay, okay, stop right there.' Well, 'stop right there' is fine. Now when you stop, okay, now where am I? Okay, I'm stopped. Now cut it right here? Yeah, cut it right there. Well, I can't, so you rock the tape back and forth looking for something to cue in on, and if you don't have a definitive sound on there, it is hard to do that. And strings and light-weight instruments do not emit a sound like a drum beat, a thump or a bump. So we'd have to go back and forth. I'd cut it, and Marvin would say, 'No, that's not it.' And I said, 'Okay, Marvin, you gotta let me see what you're feeling. Let's just go over this thing two or three times.' So I would get with him, and finally I could catch on to exactly what he was hearing, and make the job a little easier."

"So you two had a symbiotic relationship? You were dependent upon one another; you learned each other's language and grammar of music and sound?"

"That's correct. In other words, I had to learn from him what he was trying to get. I had to get with him, and get that. But that's how it was done. I mean, to put this in words, the only way I could describe it is if you're trying to put something together, you need a definitive beat, or something definitive to go from. And when you have a basically airy sort of piece, it's hard to find exactly where to cut. Anyway, that's how we put a lot of those songs together. Now, once we've keyed that, and we have a length of music that we consider three minutes, three-and-a-half, however long he wanted to go, you've got to add musical instruments if you're so inclined, to make this piece work. Remember, now, you're basically dealing with strings—in a lot of places with horns—and it's very hard to do a song with just strings and horns. So you need some kind of drum beat or some kind of mood, or something to make this thing viable. That's when I realized this man was a true genius, in that he took this music from this raw conception—you know, the piece that we put together—and added to it as he saw fit, to make it what it turned out to be. In other words, he did that all from his head and from his heart. And working with him on that was an incredible experience, to see you could do that."

"And people don't often realize how difficult that is, because if you've got something already set, where both the lyrical or melodic structure is in place, the harmony is in place, then it's much easier to create, isn't it?

"Right. Music is math, and wherever you have the math notation, wherever someone is clicking on the 'one,' or the 'one' and the 'two,' doesn't make any difference where it is, as long as it's constant. You can be on the upbeat or the downbeat, that's only one end, or two ends—it doesn't make any difference. As long as there's a definitive marking there, you can always get it and do whatever you want to do. That's the difference, having that definitive sound to work with.

"Well, that's a gift from God, I suppose, that Marvin had?"

"Yeah. Very few people have it in that sense, or could do it that well, and have it come out the way it did. Because, remember, I started with the raw piece and then heard the finished product, and when you heard the finished product, you know where it came from. You could appreciate it more so than the guy who only heard the finished product. He doesn't know what it cost, or what you did to achieve this end. All he knows is, 'Hey, I like it.'"

Although the album enjoyed critical praise and popular support—it rose to number 14 on the pop charts—*Trouble Man* has not been widely understood as an embodiment of Gaye's musical and political evolution. One critic, who praised the album as "not a lot of fluff wrapped around some images and obvious themes," but as "sweet and churning jazz that abstracts the action rather than decorating or interpreting it," nevertheless concluded that "it doesn't take his music a whole lot further (than *What's Going On*) and certainly sidesteps the problem of how to follow up a sweeping life statement."[46] Even a cursory listen to the album—especially in light of Stewart's comments about the technical genius behind its creative expression—suggests that Gaye delved deeper into the bop music whose innovations "were rhythmic as well as harmonic and thus had a direct effect on the quality of social action with the black culture, as rhythmic advances have been seen to be both a cause and a function of social freedom."[47] On *Trouble Man*, Gaye was stretching aesthetically and politically by embracing jazz forms that were associated with progressive ideas and social struggle in black communities. Gaye's ties to black vernacular art was also expanding; his soundtrack took its place among works by gifted musicians whose art was often superior to the films they scored—including Isaac Hayes' 1971 soundtrack for *Shaft* and Curtis Mayfield's score for *Superfly*, released the same year as *Trouble Man*. These soundtracks, which stood free of the films they accompanied, were full-blown works that "commented upon rather than merely illustrated the film's action."[48] All three works "offer genre blending fusions of soul, funk and contemporary jazz."[49] Each soundtrack took up themes of black urban existence: the blighted city landscape, drugs, underground economies, political malfeasance, black-on-black crime and persistent racism. Thus, each composer seized the soundtrack art form to express and expand the language of urban realism.

Interestingly, Mark Anthony Neal argues "the narrative silence" of *Trouble Man* "evokes the ghastly silences that accompanied the smoldering ashes of riot-torn Detroit." Neal says that Gaye's decision to "create an instrumental recording to address black urban life both on film and reality, is a logical response to state sponsored attempts to silence such narratives, through both covert and overt means, among progressive elements within the black protest movement and a reflection of the general demise of a communal spirit of resistance." Neal contends that the first-person narration of his "Trouble Man" single highlights "Gaye's ability to conflate the personal with the communal." Finally, he maintains that Gaye's relative silence on *Trouble Man* "represented a conscious retreat from" social protest influenced by market forces since the album, lacking words and other singles, "could not be reduced or manipulated by mass market sensibilities." It shouldn't be surprising that *Trouble Man* "prophetically anticipated the even darker urban terrain that hip-hop artists" explored a decade after Gaye's recording, and that it "remains one of the few Marvin Gaye recordings that have been sampled by contemporary hip-hop artists." [50]

Perhaps Gaye's active silence on *Trouble Man* is amplified when one listens to his passive silence in the face of social turmoil. Gaye admitted that his failure to directly engage in black protest resulted from his lack of readiness to "sacrifice my life for a cause." Marvin was ashamed that his art was quarantined from social suffering, a fact, perhaps, that led him to take up arms on wax in *What's Going On*.

I remember I was listening to a tune of mine playing on the radio, 'Pretty Little Baby,' when the announcer interrupted with news about the Watts riot. My stomach got real tight and my heart started beating like crazy. I wanted to throw the radio down and burn all the bullshit songs I'd been singing and get out there and kick ass with the rest of the brothers. I knew they were going about it wrong, I knew they weren't thinking, but I understood anger that builds up over years—shit, over centuries—and I felt myself exploding. Why didn't our music have anything to do with this? Wasn't music supposed to express feelings? No, according to BG [Berry Gordy], music's supposed to sell. That's his trip. And it was mine."[51]

If Gaye expressed social resistance through prophetic silence on *Trouble Man*, he would reclaim his active voice in one of his last, and most famous, live appearances—one that subtly blended art and protest. On February 13, 1983, Marvin was slated to sing the national anthem at the National Basketball Association's All-Star game, held that year at the Forum, the Los Angeles Lakers' arena in Inglewood. Marvin had been on a serious coke binge, and already fearful of live performance, he failed in his desperate efforts to get singer Luther Vandross to take his place. Marvin huddled with his musician brother-in-law, Gordon Banks, who doubled as the director of his touring band. The day before the game, they used a drum machine and guitar to create a background tape for the anthem that Banks refined in his home closet. The song was a reggae rhythm that sounded like a slowed-down version of Marvin's 1983 hit, "Sexual Healing."

At the Saturday rehearsal, for which he was hours late, Marvin performed a four-and-a-half minute version that spooked Lon Rosen, the Lakers director of promotions. Rosen was responsible for getting celebrities to sing the anthem at the team's home games. Lionel Richie had been Rosen's first choice, but when he called the NBA for its approval, they replied, "Who's Lionel Richie?" After fielding recommendations from the players, including Magic Johnson, Rosen had settled on Gaye. At the rehearsal, it was not only Marvin's style that caused concern—"That's not the anthem I learned in grade school," Rosen said—it was the length. He explained to Gaye that since CBS was broadcasting live, he could only have two minutes. Marvin refused to speak to Rosen until basketball superstar Julius "Dr. J" Erving mediated. Marvin relented and accepted the two-minute limit, and agreed to return on Sunday morning to practice. He didn't show, and by noon, when he hadn't appeared, Rosen asked his regular stand-in, a Forum usher, to be prepared to sing at 12:25 p.m., five minutes before CBS was slated to go live.[52]

This wasn't the first time Marvin had performed the national anthem for an important sporting event. He sung the anthem in New Orleans at Super Bowl V in 1971. He sang it again before the September 29, 1979 Ernie Shavers–Larry Holmes heavyweight championship fight, after a fighter in whom he had a big interest, Andy Price, had suffered a crushing first-round knockout to welterweight champion Sugar Ray Leonard. On that night, according to his biographer David Ritz, his deep disappointment spurred Marvin to deliver "a soul-searching rendition of the national anthem, turning a hymn of hope into a cry of despair."[53] A decade earlier, Marvin sung the anthem before game four of the 1968 World Series in Detroit. Tigers' announcer Ernie Harwell, who chose the singers, said that the teams' front office asked him to speak to Marvin before his performance. "They were worried about Marvin because of his Motown connection," Harwell remembers. The riots had ripped through the city a year earlier. "They told me to go to him and ask him to sing it a little more traditional than he might ordinarily. He complied to that and sang it very straight."[54]

The next day, the gifted, blind Puerto Rican singer Jose Feliciano, armed with an acoustic guitar and following the lead of his guide dog Trudy, had his turn. He shocked the 53,634 fans at Tiger Stadium with a gospel-laden, heart-thumping, Latin-Jazz version of the anthem. He also enraged many in the viewing audience of 50 million, 400 of whom placed irate calls of protest to NBC. Later, Feliciano said that Gaye disappointed his people with his straight rendition of "The Star-Spangled Banner." Marvin was incensed. "Feliciano is a magnificent artist," Marvin said. "Original, dynamic and controversial. I respect his rights to do his thing with the national anthem, even though some people say he did it to attract publicity and sell albums. I don't agree that he disgraced our country's song; he simply sang it as he felt it. But I do think it's wrong of Feliciano to say that in singing the national anthem straight, I was letting my people down. If he means by 'my people,' the black community, I know he is wrong. I am proud to be black. My fans know this, and they show it by accepting my records and albums today more than ever. My style called for interpreting 'The Star-Spangled Banner' the way I did. And from the hundreds of phone calls and letters and telegrams I have received, I know most Americans, black and white, like the way I did it. So did the Detroit Tigers. And so would Francis Scott Key! Sure, I agree with Feliciano that a lot of things need changing in this country, and it's up to us young people to do the changing. But, his remarks about me were uncalled for and unprofessional. I'll challenge Feliciano any time, at any concert, on any stage and on any TV show, to a battle of soul songs—the real thing—and let the people who know soul best, be the judge."[55]

When Marvin showed up at the Forum for the 1983 All-Star Game, barely five minutes before CBS's national coverage was to begin, he was decked in mirrored aviator glasses and a dark double-breasted suit. He made his way down the Forum's steps and handed Rosen a cassette. When Rosen asked if it was two minutes, Marvin nodded, and Rosen rushed the tape to the arena's studio engineer. After sportscaster Dick Stockton announced him, as the first beats of Gaye's track bled into his introduction, Marvin launched into his soulful, deliberate version, laying behind the beat in his opening phrase. "Say, can you *se-e-e-e-euh*," he gently, but passionately sang, bouncing the word "see" in delicious melisma. The crowd cheered, and Marvin, buoyed by the response, enlivened his lilting version even more. When he got to "broad stripes," he emphasized *stripes* in rigorous staccato. He dragged out "stars" to at least nine syllables! The crowd was all his. He punctuated "through the perilous fight" with a gospel echo—"Oh Lord,"—and then repeated the phrase, "Whoa, the fight," and gently exclaimed, "Jesus."

On top of the reggae beat, he "took the song to church": he gave it spiritual intonations and the subdued fervor that marks vocal performances in black religious circles. By the time he got to "the rocket's red glare"—he capped glare with a red-hot sprint to the top of his natural tenor range—Marvin emphasized the phrase with clenched fists and bended knees. As he proceeded sweetly to his conclusion, the crowd joined in, clapping on beat. When Marvin articulated, "and the ho-o-o-me of the…home of the bra-a-a-a-ve, Oh, Lord," the crowd erupted in applause. Although he sang for his fellow man, Marvin had managed to transform the anthem into a song of personal triumph. After all, given his trepidations and trials, it was an act of bravery for Marvin to perform. But there were social and racial dimensions that he explored as well. Perhaps Feliciano's remarks 15 years earlier, buried deep in his heart, fed his courage to embrace the lyric with soulful abandon. Predictably, his version provoked controversy, but that didn't dampen broad enthusiasm for Marvin's spectacular performance. Whatever else his inspirations, Marvin's stirring performance was rooted in black style and spirit. By tying "The Star-Spangled Banner" so explicitly to his gospel origins, and to a distinctly black sound, with its blend of rhythms, he reaffirmed the value of his people's culture—and the struggles that made that sound possible. He had come full circle around the loop he began twelve years earlier with *What's Going On*. Between that classic 1971 protest album and the national anthem he remade in the image of his blackness, Marvin explored the often tense but exciting relationship between sexuality and spirituality. The three great themes of Marvin's art—social justice, sexuality, and spirituality—were always in conflict. But for the balance of the seventies, and the rest of his career, the pursuit of the last two would lead him to great art, profound heartbreak, and terrible confusion.

CHAPTER THREE

"Somethin' Like Sanctified"
Sexuality and Spirituality

In its inspired advocacy of social and environ-
mental justice, Marvin Gaye's *What's Going On* revealed his
surprising love of politics. On 1973's *Let's Get It On*, Gaye
proved equally adept at espousing the politics of love. In erotically charged anthems ("Let's Get It On," "Keep Gettin' It On,"
"Come Get to This," and "You Sure Love to Ball"), songs of
intense emotional yearning ("Please Stay" and "Distant Lover")
and elegiac evocations of love's possible and real loss ("If I
Should Die Tonight" and "Just to Keep You Satisfied"), Marvin
drew a bracing portrait of romance that rivals some sociological
tracts.

Still, *What's Going On*'s unique place in pop music history
has unfairly obscured the complex and high-quality work
Marvin did in its aftermath. Critics concede that Marvin Gaye
made some very good—and occasionally brilliant—music after
What's Going On. But too many think that Gaye never again
approached the political engagement, conceptual rigor or musi-

cal elevation of his 1971 classic. Such a judgment may be over-drawn. On several albums, Gaye displayed conceptual mastery and sublime musical achievement. *Let's Get It On* and *I Want You* are concept albums of inspired sensual music that are often lyrically poignant. The two recordings also make rousing social statements in their sexual frankness. It's remarkable that within the space of two years, Gaye managed to amplify the ambitions of two cultural revolutions: the struggles for social *and* sexual liberty.

"Although there was a 'conscious' revolution, there was also a great sexual revolution in the late sixties and early seventies," says rapper and actor Q-Tip. "I think [*Let's Get It On*] was Marvin wanting to make commentary on what was happening. I think there was a big 'love-in' that was going on. And with him quoting T.S. Elliot [in his liner notes, that life amounts to "Birth, copulation and death"], and the young lady moaning [on the album], we hadn't heard that before. That was another first, as well as him capturing erotica like that, and weaving it into the music the way he did; it was mind blowing. I think it was a natural progression, because we were having a revolution with our minds, and then with our bodies at that time."

Q-Tip's observation suggests that it may be a mistake to remove *Let's Get It On*—and other erotically charged Gaye albums like *I Want You*—from the political trajectory of *What's Going On*. To be sure, the subject matter of the two albums is largely, though not completely, different. (As David Ritz writes, *Let's Get It On* is "a serious inner monologue on matters philo-sophical and spiritual, although the title...misled his fans and critics into thinking the subject was strictly sexual.")[1] But if one listens to *Let's Get It On* in the context of the era's sexual mores, it is just as socially aware and courageous as Gaye's earlier masterpiece. Producing an erotically explicit and emotionally vulnerable album as a *black* man in 1973 resonated politically. Along with the wildly uneven depictions of black male sexuality in blaxsploitation films—which both embraced and crushed racial stereotypes—Gaye's album introduced a voice that vibrated libidinal liberty. His voice also soared with spiritual yearning. Marvin undressed in plain language the carnal cravings that earlier mainstream soul singers had to drape in suggestive metaphor. Marvin's sexual liberty also drew from the same political energies he championed on *What's Going On*. One of the goals of black freedom was the right to live free of the erotic constraints imposed by dominant society.

But the male-centered quest for black power in the early seventies also had negative consequences on black music. There was a shift in tone and approach to sexual politics in seventies R & B. It reflected the aggressive stances of black men in pursuit of social and economic equality. Unfortunately, a desperate machismo was now linked to racial struggle. In some cases they became indistinguishable.[2] Of course, the harsher view of women held by some black male R & B singers found its roots in some blues lyrics. Also, the strident sexism of the culture seized the imagination of some artists. To be sure, male soul artists "had always combined dreamy romance with raunchy desire; fidelity, understanding and respect, with infidelity, sexual objectification, bitter recrimination and poisonous suspicion."[3] Although Marvin Gaye's explicitness was a leap within mainstream soul music (raunchiness, after all, is relative, as testified to by comparing Gaye's lyrics to much of contemporary R & B), it nevertheless held in tension erotic desire and mutual respect.

Gaye was perhaps more in line with another strand of sexual politics advocated in black culture: patriarchy within the nuclear family. His lyrics on *What's Going On* confirm it—in the constant reference to fathers, mothers, sisters, and brothers, and their particular roles in the home and society. And his lyrics on *Let's Get It On* and other albums extend patriarchy into the bedroom: although his view of romance is tender to the erotic touch, his occasional frustration with women grows from their failure to behave appropriately. That appropriateness, of course, is determined by rather rigid gender beliefs. Still, Marvin mostly refrained on record from exploitative visions of eroticism. Some of his spiritual values were in conflict with his chauvinistic views.[4] Critic Brian Ward captures the impact of the era's sexual politics on soul:

[M]ale Rhythm and Blues from the late 1960s to the mid 1970s continued to deal with every conceivable human emotion and activity relating to domestic and sexual relationships. Within that continued diversity, however, there was a marked revival of the sexism and sexual hostilities which had been so much a part of R & B before the birth of the modern civil rights movement, but which had been far less conspicuous between Montgomery and Selma. Sadly, as a progressive movement fuelled by radical equalitarian ideals splintered, a form of retrogressive entrenchment took place. Frustrated, angry and increasingly desperate and alienated, black men, particularly the masses who failed to escape into the black middle class, where they could practice a different, more mainstream, form of patriarchy and sexism, sometimes took refuge in a peculiarly intense form of racial and sexual chauvinism. The revival of black macho and the myth of matriarchy in soul were cultural manifestations of that phenomenon."[5]

Marvin's sensual romp was also sparked by resistance to the status quo in other quarters in the late sixties and early seventies. Bourgeois morality came under attack from hippies and feminists. Marvin embraced the sexual revolution's flaunting of conformity in the effort to reclaim erotic control of one's life. Sex was no longer seen as nasty duty; its beauty was extolled. Brave individuals and groups challenged negative views of sex propounded from pulpits and political campaigns. Therefore millions of ordinary Americans experienced greater sexual freedom. Many people no longer saw marriage as the only source of sexual intimacy for consenting adults. Thanks largely to the birth-control pill, procreation was not necessarily viewed as the primary reason for sex. Millions of women—and not a few men—were relieved of the sexual guilt and fear that burdened earlier generations. They felt empowered to explore passions they had been discouraged from acknowledging in a sexist society. Despite his lethal chauvinism, Marvin's music reflected many elements of this new attitude.

On *Let's Get It On* and *I Want You*, Marvin was carrying out an even more personal rebellion. In his erotic exultation, Gaye struck a symbolic blow against sexual prisons built on narrow religious belief. As the son of a strict Pentecostal preacher, Marvin had plenty of cells to unlock. He was reared in a branch of Pentecostalism that wed elements of Jewish orthodoxy to Christian theology. Marvin's father was a minister in the House of God, the Holy Church of the Living God, the Pillar and

Ground of the Truth, the House of Prayer for All People. The House of God describes its theological roots in the Old and New Testaments:

> Hebrew Pentecostal, denominationally, teaches the relevance of both the Old and New Testament principles pertaining to proper religious practices and current day worship. This designation proclaims that we are the descendants of God (Elohim) through the covenant he made with Abraham the Hebrew. This covenant included the promises of both natural and spiritual blessings. By believing God (Elohim), Abraham became the father of faith. Jesus (Yahshua) is the promised seed of Abraham. Our faith in Jesus (Yahshua) brings us into harmony with the promises of the covenant...The House of God, is Hebrew Pentecostal because the foundation of our doctrine spans the scope of the both the old and new covenants. The commandments, statutes and judgments of God (Elohim), which were the foundation of the first covenant, have been removed from the stones. The Holy Ghost writes them in our hearts. The promise of the Holy Ghost was fulfilled on the Day of Pentecost."[6]

Hebrew Pentecostalism's adherents, of whom there were relatively few in the 1940s, were distinguished from other Pentecostals by their beliefs. These included keeping holy the Sabbath on Saturday, the following of orthodox Jewish dietary restrictions (no pork or seafood), no celebration of Christmas, and the observation of Passover. Like other Pentecostals, Hebrew Pentecostals also advocated speaking in tongues, heal-

ing and tarrying for the Holy Spirit.[7] "Our church was a very
spiritual church and we were a very chosen people," Marvin
Gaye told a journalist in 1974. "The body was small, but the
spirit was intense, and very evident to anyone who passed by or
came in. It immediately encompassed them. And there were
very strong people who seemed to bring the spirit forth. When
they spoke in tongues, the words were foreign, but they were
almost clear to me. I was frightened because of how the spirit
came forth. I wondered why the spirit had such disregard for
their bodies, making them bump into things and fall on sharp
objects. Or when they tarried, which is saying, 'Thank you,
Jesus,' over and over again until you know you have changed. It
becomes evident, physically, that they shouldn't do it that long.
And yet the spirit is there and their mouths begin to foam and
that's part of it. I never tarried that much. But I am a pray-er."[8]

Their Hebrew Pentecostalism meant that Marvin and his
three siblings—including sisters Jeanne and Zeola, nicknamed
"Sweetsie," and brother Frankie—were to a degree alienated
from both secular blacks and mainstream black Christians.
Marvin showed early artistic promise, and from the age of two,
sang in church on the religious circuits with his father. "I used
to travel and do evangelical work," Rev. Marvin Gay, Sr. told
Rolling Stone in 1974. "Marvin, when he was five, went with me
to Kentucky for a convention of the Church of the Living God.
He sang 'Journey to the Sky,' and that was probably the first
time I realized he could deliver a song and that he had a unique
style. After that, when I traveled with Marvin, people would
always want him to sing."[9]

Later, he became the pianist in his father's church, which
met at first in their home, and never grew to any significant

size. Yet, the church remained central to the Gay home, and the Bible was the source of Rev. Gay's stern, even brutal, discipline of his children, and his rigid religious practice.

"[Marvin] was very spiritual," Martha Reeves says. "You knew, when you heard him sing, that his father or somebody had been a minister, or that he would soon be one. Because he always had the Lord in the forefront of anything he delivered or anything he sang. I'm not sure a lot of people realized how sensual and how sensitive Marvin Gaye was as a person. But I always recognized his spirituality and always respected him as being a child of God on a mission. Some of his songs indicate that. I'm not just talking from what I don't know. He always had Jesus or God in his lyrics. And he said 'Lord, have mercy' so beautifully he had girls screaming and saying, 'Lord, have mercy!' He had trials and tribulations here on this earth, and having survived a lot of them, I know that Marvin was a true lover of people." Kim Weston sees how Marvin's spiritual upbringing shaped his style of performance. "He was shy; he was timid. He was a nervous wreck before he would go on stage. I remember the time they were telling him, 'Man, you've to move [on stage], you've got to do something.' And he just wouldn't do anything, and I think that was because of his spirituality."

Marvin's Pentecostal roots stamped his secular art in many ways. His ability to play music by ear, to play multiple instruments, and to improvise, was nurtured in his father's church. As musicologist Teresa L. Reed notes:

The musicians in [Pentecostal] churches are often expert improvisers. They usually play by ear rather than by written music, and their accompaniment of the intensely animated singing, preaching, and shouting is skillfully rendered. Because they must be able to accompany any worshipper singing in any key, the musicians are flexible and creative and may even be described as virtuosic. These churches also incorporate a variety of instruments in their ensembles, the most common of which are piano, Hammond organ, drums, bass and lead guitars, saxophones, and tambourines."[10]

Marvin gained in church a profound sense of the spirit's presence, especially as the spirit showed forth in the rhythms of the music. "I try to sense the spirit, feel the spirit, be aware of signs of the spirit," Marvin said in 1974. "I try to sense the spirit in a gust of wind, or in a bird chirping, or in a drop of rain. I think that somewhere down the line, God owes somebody a favor. If I do my job well, then God will smile on my offspring and on their offspring."[11] It can be argued that Marvin was not only influenced by doo-wop harmonies in crafting his background vocals, but that the angelic sounds he generated reflected the spiritual ecstasy—the spirit possession—that he experienced in the Pentecostal church. Reed explains Pentecostalism's influence on black secular music:

The specific contribution of black Pentecostalism, however, was that it specialized in preserving the ritual of spirit possession and the whole collection of African rhythms, sounds, and gestures associated with it. In addition, black Holiness/Pentecostal churches, to a greater degree than others, also approached music not simply as an avenue for devotional expression, but also as a means for inciting spirit possession. In particular, the shout was accompanied by a feel and style of music that marked rhythm and blues and its descendant forms."[12]

Marvin also inherited his father's theological aptitude. "He had a quicker grasp of Scripture," Rev. Gay said in 1974, referring to Marvin's superiority to other Sunday School students. "And sometimes, as a small boy, he almost sounded like a grown man, a minister."[13] He even exceeded Rev. Gay in using religion to interpret events, explain reality, or justify his actions. Marvin was obsessed with God throughout his life. Although he never attended church regularly once he joined the Air Force at 17, Marvin's outlook on the world bore the imprint of his spiritual upbringing. His beliefs helped him to cope with crisis and self-doubt—or, by their intensity, to increase them. This was especially true as Marvin negotiated the tension between sexuality and spirituality in his life. He was willing to indulge his sexual fantasies with zeal, and yet his religious past robbed him of uncomplicated erotic joy. He dabbled in sadomasochism, yet he felt an inner restraint that tagged such excesses as sin.

The tension between the flesh and the spirit gave Marvin's music a sensual glow that never faded in the dark chambers of his conflicted psyche. Marvin praised God as the source of all love. In fact, it might be argued that Marvin's greatest love, his magnificent obsession, his undying attachment, his longest affair, was God. On the original version of "God Is Love," which was the B-side to "What's Going On," one can hear clear evidence of Marvin's passionate love for God. The song, dripping in doo-wop harmonies, is a splendid testimony to Marvin's fusion of sensuous style and spiritual sentiment. Marvin means the song, pure and simple, as a love song to God. It is every bit as delicate, sensuous, and arguably, theologically erotic—which draws from the unapologetic love for God as friend, soul-lover and caregiver—as any secular song could hope to be. When he demands that we "don't go and talk about my Father," there is a sense of special kinship bequeathed through intimate association.

At the end of the song, Gaye ad-libs the ecstatic glories of God, proclaiming God's love is "wonderful" and that "He makes the wind to blow, He makes it rain, he makes the snowflakes fall yeah." And he grabs hold of the evangelical theology whose proselytizing fervor never left him, and declares, "I know there is a God, don't deny him," as his voice fades out. This is the gospel baptized in the sensual articulations and erotic phrasings that are not foreign to the black church. The gospel music tradition sings in the sublimely ambiguous interface of erotic intensity and religious passion. They are hardly distinguishable at the moment of their execution. And while the two are defined by their divergent ends, their useful blending in worship service is one of the unconscious draws to a people hungry for physical affirmation of their blighted black bodies.

On many of his recordings throughout the seventies and early eighties, Marvin engaged his sexual appetite. Still, he insisted that erotic delight be rooted in romantic norms that had religious sources. That's why he could declare on "Let's Get It On" that love "gives you a good feeling, something like sanctified." For Marvin, sanctification was the ideal against which even sexual congress had to be measured. Similar to the boy in C.S. Lewis's account who, when told of the delights of sex, asked if it were as good as chocolate—since that was the height of his pleasurable experience—Marvin viewed religious sanctification as the ideal form of union, in this case, between humans and God. Rona Elliot, the former entertainment journalist, sums up Gaye's outlook in a memorable phrase he gave to her when she interviewed him. "I've been quoting this now since 1983 or '84," Elliot says, "which is: 'Life is a paradox between Jesus and pussy.'"

His sensual strivings took on political meaning because they decried the spiritual claustrophobia that smothered erotic freedom. Marvin insisted that sexuality could be transcendent; he preached that sensuality could be spiritually motivated—and useful. On *Let's Get It On; I Want You; Here, My Dear* and *In Our Lifetime*, Marvin held on to the best of his religious background while discarding the worst. He preached what critic Craig Werner termed *spiritual sexuality*—an eroticism informed by religious sentiment and the passions of romantic love.[14] Moreover, spiritual sexuality is concerned with more than carnal relations. It is attuned as well to the treatment of our bodies. Spiritual sexuality attends to the psychic elements that affect human sexuality. It is conscious of how sensuality is shaped by social forces.

"I don't think being religious means you can't have sex," Marvin told *Rolling Stone* in 1974. "I think that you can do it and still be good. I think it's ridiculous to say you can't be a priest and also screw. People are supposed to say, 'If he's giving up the Supreme Goodie, then he must be a good man.' Why shouldn't a religious man have the Supreme Goodie and be an even greater man? If he is intelligent enough to be a priest, he ought to be intelligent enough to handle the goodies. I think sex is great. I think sex is sex and love is love. I think they can be and are separated. I think they are beautiful together, but they are two separate things. I'm a fantasy person myself. I think there is a point where you can live out your fantasies and not go over in pervertiness. Is that the word? Perversity. I think society makes people creep and crawl about and it only accentuates perversity. I suppose that makes it more fun for the pervert, though. Who wants to be perverse if everybody says, 'Okay, go ahead, we don't care.' I don't know, I just think we're all too uptight about sex. All of us." When Marvin was asked why he concentrated on "the tender, romantic aspects of sex" on *Let's Get It On*, he replied "that's the way I would like to be presented. If someone were to say, 'I wonder how he is,' then they could listen to the album and tell.'"[15]

Rona Elliot thinks that Gaye's blending of sexuality and spirituality was connected to his vulnerability and his willingness to share his pain. "He fuses, from my point of view, spirituality—I'm not talking about the black gospel church—sensuality, sexuality, pain, restraint," Elliot says. "It's the restraint that he brings to it that creates this unbelievable tension. And there are very few people—I think Tina Turner is one of the other ones—who allow you to get in touch with that without your mind getting in the way. It's just a physical, spiritual transformation that takes place. At least for me. I'm sure other people listen to Marvin Gaye and just want to get laid. This is not what happens to me. It's that he brought that spirituality and that longing and that fear and the humanity to the table like nobody else. It's his humanity that I think made him so vulnerable within that context. When he's up there saying, 'You sure do love to ball,' that's real. I don't think he's making it up."

Q-Tip agrees. He thinks that the authenticity of Gaye's artistry set him apart. "He was no-nonsense in telling people how he felt musically," Q-Tip says. "He wasn't guarded or pent up about that. Now he may have been like that in his life, but when the mic was on, and the piano was there, or the drums or whatever, he would so effortlessly get to it and ask questions. And you'd be right there with him. You didn't feel like he was being jive when he was telling a story, or when he was thinking of Jan, his second wife,or Anna. You knew that was where he was at, where he was coming from. And I really appreciated that." Q-Tip also believes that Marvin's religious bearing brought feelings of vulnerability that gave his music heft and power, and made it appealing to listeners. "He had a dichotomy that existed in the struggle with God and sexuality, being the son of a preacher who was an abused child. So his mom was getting abused [as well]. There were a lot of complexities there. And the fact that he may not have had the answer, so he always gave it up to 'Father, help me.' And that could have been taken as the Omnipotent, or his father in the flesh. And he wasn't ashamed to show his vulnerability. He was probably the most vulnerable recording artist of the past fifty, sixty years. And people could really connect to that. They just opened up."

Tragically, Marvin fell prey to sexual energies every bit as harmful as those of his repressed religious tradition. He engaged in sexual gamesmanship with both his wives. They cheated on each other in merciless fashion. They also hurt each other's egos in manipulative sexual behavior. Gaye made regular visits to prostitutes. Marvin revealed his philosophy of sex and marriage to *Ebony* magazine in 1974. "I don't believe a man should live his life with just one woman, or vice versa," Gaye said, a year after he'd met Jan. "I'm not challenging any concepts or principles. It's just a gut feeling. Well, actually not a gut feeling. God has said, 'Hey—I've given you all a neat goodie; as long as it's pleasurable, there will be kids born. But, hey, how do you control it? How about one woman to one man? But that's a fallacy. It's like a suit or a pair of shoes. They may be really nice but you want some new shoes every now and then. They may be comfortable as hell and nice and everything, but you look into a shoe store one day and say, 'Hey, I'd like to try that pair on for size.' In some countries, a man can have as many wives as he can afford. I think that's a pretty good system. There are two types of world, the flesh and the spirit. I think God meant you to be *in* the world but not *of* it. For a spiritual man, one woman is enough. But the flesh constantly calls. You work hard to hold things to a minimum while you build on that spiritual thing. The thing is not to go hog wild."[16]

Marvin was always conflicted about embracing explicit sexuality. "I don't know how long I can keep up this sex image stuff, but I'm not going to do it much longer," Marvin told Nelson George in 1983. "I think my approach to sensuality and sexuality is that of subtle exhibitionist. I can't deal with the raw fact. I'd rather be teased by a woman before I get it. That's the French way: You make a person think you are going to do something, but never do until you are ready."[17] When George asked him if *Midnight Love* had overcome the tension in his art between sex and love heard on *In Our Lifetime*, Marvin was clear. "No conflicts are resolved."[18] Marvin was always torn between sex and salvation—or seeing sex *as* salvation. He sought to rid himself, unsuccessfully, of the desires of the flesh. "I would really like to reach the state of a Buddhist monk, the mind and spiritual link that Buddhist monks have," Marvin told *Ebony* in 1974. "But you must be devoid of ego for that, of thinking that you want a steak or a diamond ring or a car or whatever we have brainwashed ourselves into thinking we need. If I can relieve myself of this yearning for the flesh, then I will be happy."[19] Still, his emancipation on *Let's Get It On*; *I Want You*; *Here, My Dear*; *In Our Lifetime* and on *Midnight Love's* "Sexual Healing," proved liberating for millions who cheered his healthy eroticism. Not everyone thought that Marvin's erotic experiments on record brought out the best in his art or the soul music tradition. Martha Bayles argues that Gaye's transition from spiritually grounded secular prophet to "love-man" vitiated his artistic powers:

> We've seen how performers with religious backgrounds like Gaye's tend to be highly unstable, either retreating back into the church to seek forgiveness, or plunging into celebrity hedonism with the conviction that they're already damned. This instability got worse in the 1960s, when large numbers of whites either ignorant of or indifferent to the religious background of soul perceived its enthusiasm to be wholly erotic, and many black performers did their best to reinforce that perception…In a desperate attempt to shake his sexual guilt, Gaye transformed himself into a circuit-riding preacher in the new 1970s religion of liberated sex."[20]

But it was the way Marvin's erotic gospel joined sexuality and spirituality that entertainer and television host Arsenio Hall, who saw Gaye's last tour, found attractive. "It seemed to me that Marvin was really about the two most important things," says

Hall, "spirituality and sexual healing." Hall is referring to Gaye's last hit, "Sexual Healing," an entrancing reggae-flavored rhythm whose lyrics celebrate the medicinal effects of good sex. "When Marvin sang about sex, he was singing about one of the greatest gifts God gave us. *We* created football and a lot of fun things, but *God* created making love and procreation, and made sure that if we chose not to do it, the world would come to an end. I'm not sure why people are afraid of the combination. I don't think porn goes with spirituality, but full creation—it's God that put all those tendons in the genitalia to make it so sensitive. I think that the toughest brothers can say, 'Oh, no, as bad as I am on the gridiron, or as much as I wrote a song like 'Sexual Healing,' I am about spirituality. That's what takes toughness. See, it's hard to have condoms from the Pleasure Chest, and then, after you finish making love, you say, 'excuse me baby, I have got to say my prayers.' It takes a real man to get off the pussy and say your prayers."

Rona Elliot theorizes that Marvin's conflicted feelings were rooted in his own sex appeal and figuring out what to do with it. "He was beautiful. He was sexy, and he was confused by all of it. He did grow up in the church. And we all know what that did to a lot of different artists. And it made for a lot of conflict. But he had a gift like nobody. Curtis [Mayfield] had that gift, but it was really quite different. It didn't make you want to fuck your brains out, or go to church or have a relationship with God. Or put you in touch with your own feelings. And with Marvin, the longing was always simultaneous. It was, 'I long to sleep with you and I long for God.' He wanted all of you. 'Let's Get It On' and 'You Sure Love to Ball,' that was outrageous at the time, but it wasn't funky and ugly like these guys are singing now."

It was his tortured psyche that opened Marvin to addressing gender in an insightful if flawed manner. Spiritual tensions roiled his sexual identity. He won from his battles, at least on record, a level of mature self-awareness that may be foreign to many hip-hoppers. Many of them revel in the explicitness of Gaye's music—though often in a far raunchier fashion—without taking his introspective tour of gender's complex landscape. "I think he accepted the duality of his masculine side," says Q-Tip, "and I think that's the thing that made him most masculine. He was able to show the vulnerability, whereas today, we look at that as a sign of weakness. But once you ignore your feminine side all that does is put you in a weak situation, because you're one dimensional. And you don't accept the side that the Creator snuck in on you. You might as well pay attention to that, because that'll help you figure things out. And that's why I think, when I look at hip-hop today, it's homoerotic in a way. It's like a boy's club, a bunch of men trying to beat their chests: 'Now I got money, so you can suck my dick.' Anybody can be a brute. I think that was the thing about Marvin: he embraced that duality. But you've got to be of a mind to navigate those borders, or you wind up in some nasty spiritual bags."

Two theological writers think that Gaye ended up in nasty spiritual bags. Orea Jones argues that, despite his faith, Marvin was "captive to a cocaine-riddled body, and his life's passions oscillated between the extremes of sanctification and narcissism."[21] Jones says that Gaye couldn't escape the tension, and attempted to "synthesize the two extremes to form an existential theology that was erroneous and therefore never fully able to sustain him." For Jones this is illustrated best on "Sanctified

Lady," (originally titled by Gaye as "Sanctified Pussy") a song on Gaye's posthumously released *Dream of a Lifetime*. The song borrows a page from eighties soul group Zapp, which pioneered computer electro pop through its vocoder talk boxes, artfully distorting leader Roger Troutman's voice. The opening chorus of the upbeat funk tune "Sanctified Lady" is distorted through a vocoder talk box, repeating the staccato chant "sanctified, sanctified, sanctified, lady, lady," three times before giving way to Marvin's erotic tenor. On the song, Marvin details female promiscuity, begging for a "sanctified lady," who "goes to church," a "good girl" to keep him "warm" and to keep him "home." Jones says that Gaye's original title of "Sanctified Pussy" is an "oxymoron." Marvin's attempt to merge "the extremes that 'sanctification' and 'pussy' signify" was the "precursor of the theme of 'sex as salvation' in the music of Prince."[22] Jones argues that Gaye's conflict was not unique to him.

> Like so many musicians who have carried the spirituality of their religious upbringing into their secular world, Gaye was split between his fundamental love for God and his preoccupation with the worldly opiates of drugs and sex. It is possible, for instance, that the notion of 'sexual healing' at *midnight* is somehow derived from symbols gleaned from his religious background, namely that in the sullen quiet of the midnight hour, when life seems darkest, relief comes, the prison gates burst open. Such oscillation between the religious and the sacrilegious is not uncommon among a large population of Christian believers. Even Gaye's faith in the deliverance and transcendence of sex was not nonfaith.

Rather, his love for God was partially displaced by his need for sexual love."[23]

Jones says the high incidences of teen pregnancies and sexually transmitted diseases proved that many agree with Gaye that "in this hedonistic and narcissistic age of lovelessness, 'sexual healing' is the nirvana needed to maintain sanity."[24] Jones writes that 'sexual healing' "was, and remains, a frightfully realistic statement of a principal form of idolatry in contemporary American society."[25] Jones dissects the lyrics of "Sexual Healing," suggesting that it could be "Gaye's subconscious' existential cry in the darkest hour of his life for extrication and salvation, that the voices crying 'get up' and 'wake up'[which are heard in the song's introduction] was his spiritual self (his soul) subjugated within an afflicted body and mind."[26]

Jones provocatively interprets Gaye's theological beliefs and the contradictions in his life between his spirituality and sexuality. Jones's grasp of the elements that might send Gaye into turmoil—the need for sanctification pitted against the pursuit of pleasure—is right on. But one wonders if Jones misses Gaye's challenge to black religious beliefs: there are huge tensions in reconciling sex and spirit, but the alternative is not harsh denial of the flesh. If Gaye sometimes moved too far in one direction—self-destructively blurring the tension between the flesh and the spirit—the core black church has perhaps remained stuck in unhelpful rigidity. Gaye's art, and even his errant practices, were in some measure a criticism of black theological Puritanism and spiritual inflexibility. Too often, the answer of the black church was to either pretend the body didn't exist in sexual modes, or to cut it off at the genitalia. Marvin's honesty, even when it lead him to the hurtful extremes Jones catalogues, was at least ethically refreshing—not necessarily in its practice, but surely in its intent.

Marvin's quest for "sanctified pussy" can be reasonably endorsed in black religious circles, if the point is to form relations with others who have our best spiritual and sexual interests at heart. One can't expect Gaye's explicit phrasing to be widely adopted in such circles. But the will to sexual mutuality and erotic protection that he expressed certainly can be. Finally, Jones ignores how some of Gaye's missteps came from an unhealthy, unrealistic religious vision of black sexuality. The sexist, homophobic impulse—one that Gaye embraced with unfortunate zeal—is never mentioned in Jones's list of Gaye's sins. That's because most black religious traditions have denied the erotic acceptance of all black folk. Hence, an unspoken tension is hardly addressed: the conflict between a love ethic that affirms human beings and an impatient moralizing that targets some for special disdain.

Writer Graham Cray observes that since the time of the Second Great Awakening in the early nineteenth century, black music has been interpreted in narrow, dualistic terms. Unlike earlier times when all black music, sacred and secular, was influenced by West African roots, a "sharp divide" separated gospel music and the Devil's music.[27] This created tension in artists who came out of the church to sing secular music, including Little Richard, Sam Cooke, Al Green, and of course, Marvin Gaye. Graham believes that Gaye's life and music is caught in two inseparable conflicts. The first is "between his confusingly legalistic Christian upbringing and the license offered by the classic pop star indulgence in sex and drugs."[28]

The second conflict is "between his resentment of his father and his deep need for his father's love."[29] Cray focuses on both *What's Going On* and *Let's Get It On* to examine Marvin's theological beliefs. He concludes that the former "called for love and justice in the name of Jesus, respected the ten commandments, and set out the vision of being 'wholy holy,'" while the latter "justified adultery in the name of the Spirit [Gaye's relationship with Jan while he was separated from Anna], walked out on a marriage, rejected 'moralistic philosophies' and renamed sin as sanctification."[30]

Cray uses Gaye's music and life to think about Christ's temptations. Because Jesus resisted satisfying his earthly desires, he is a contrasting figure for Gaye, who not only capitulated, but who traded his theological birthright for a mess of secular pottage. Cray says:

> Marvin maintained his fame and commercial success ('Let's Get It On' was the biggest hit of his career) for the price of changing his beliefs. Having justified his lifestyle morally his theology was modified to fit his chosen way of life. Moving away from the theology of his childhood he embraced increasingly New-Age-style beliefs. He maintained the view from 'What's Going On' that the world was in deep trouble, but abandoned it to its fate. He imagined himself as 'part of an elite who were evolving towards a higher consciousness and who would escape the eventual destruction.'"[31]

Viewing Jesus' temptation experience as his model, Cray cast an eye on Gaye's theology, and finds it wanting. Jesus saw a personal devil, embodied evil; even in the theological variations among Christians, Cray says, most maintain that evil is "something more substantial than a force within individuals, and that it is a power which impacts the lives of individuals from the outside."[32] Marvin's music proves that he sees his conflict as an internal one, not having to do with external forces outside his life. As a result, Gaye appears "unaware of the power to which he was yielding himself by turning from the commandments."[33] While Marvin grasped social evil, his failure to understand its personal dimension left him vulnerable. Cray also contends that unlike Jesus who invoked the Spirit to carry out God's will, Marvin "invoked the Spirit to justify his abandonment of the Ten Commandments."[34] Also, Cray argues, Jesus grew to spiritual maturity from his temptation crisis. But Marvin shrank, being consumed by "paranoia, addiction, laziness and fear of public performance."[35] Finally, Jesus showed trusting obedience in his Father; Marvin hated and distrusted his father, while craving his love. Cray says that when "resistance to temptation becomes costly, the critical issue is the trustworthiness of the Father. The cost is bearable if the Father can be trusted."[36] Cray concludes his essay ambiguously:

Marvin was shot dead by his father. He was the victim of his father's rejection. Jesus gave up his life for us according to the will of his Father who was at work through his death ('In Christ God was reconciling the world to himself,' 2 Cor. 5:19). Father and Son were united in their love for us and in their action for our redemption. The Spirit was the gift from the Father who enabled the Son's loving act of recapitulation. It was this which the tempter tried to abort."[37]

Cray is right to point out the conflict between Marvin's rigid, repressed upbringing and his indulgence in drugs and sex. And he's right that Marvin's desperate desire for paternal love, and his father's refusal to give it, caused resentment and pain for Marvin. When he says that Marvin embraced love and justice in the name of Jesus on *What's Going On*, but spurned his lesson on *Let's Get It On*, Cray fails to see how he's rooted his contrast in the sort of harsh duality that Marvin sought to overcome. After all, Marvin's vision of holiness and his respect for the Ten Commandments, which Cray praises, was nurtured in the same household that Cray calls confusing and legalistic. It makes sense that Cray might on the surface have problems with Marvin's philosophy and theology on *Let's Get It On*. As Cray points out, the album was performed by a married man who had walked out on his marriage but was in love with a teenager. Hence, Cray says, Gaye turned sin into sanctification.

But it's all a bit too neat. If Cray would look past the obvious sexual and theological dimensions of *Let's Get It On*, he'd at least find moments where Gaye embraces strong spiritual values and the absolute need for love. On "Let's Get It On," Gaye invokes sanctification, not simply as a come-on, but as a means to suggest a transcendent purpose to romantic love. On the tune, Marvin appealed to Christian beliefs about sacrificial surrender and uplifting reciprocity. As David Ritz argues, on "Keep Getting It On," a continuation of Gaye's "Let's Get It On" found on the same album, Marvin had transformed the song.

Suddenly the message evolved. The come-to-bed conceit was gone. Rather than address a woman, Marvin started preaching. He contrasted making love to making war, recommending the former, finally calling out the name of Jesus, explaining that this was an attempt to 'tell the people'; we must 'get it on' in the name of Jesus. The meanings had changed. To 'get it on' now carried the significance of loving fully, and had the blessing—indeed the mandate—of the Lord of Love himself.[38]

Marvin's views were certainly contradictory and conflicted. But those views deserve serious consideration, especially since Gaye both embraced and rejected elements of the theology he inherited. It is true that Marvin failed to live up to many of the religious views he espoused. That would make him no different than many Christians who admit they have "fallen short of the glory of God."[39] But Marvin was also rethinking and recasting his theology as he matured. Cray's attempt to suggest Marvin's spiritual immaturity by calculating how faithful he was to Jesus' model misses Marvin's inspired irreverence. Or, to put it in traditional religious terms, Marvin was exercising the prophetic prerogative. He also proved to have imagination as he interpreted scriptures and Christian belief. Cray seems to ignore all of this.

As for Gaye seeing evil as an internal battle, and not the actions of an outside force, Cray has made two errors. First, he seems to be splitting theological hairs. If Gaye acknowledges evil and seeks to name and oppose it, even if it's inside him, he makes no claims that it necessarily originated there. Second, he hasn't listened very closely to Marvin's music, which is full of profound and striking meditations on good and evil, God and the Devil—especially on his neglected masterpiece *In Our Lifetime*. It may also prove that Marvin wasn't bound like Cray to literal interpretations of scripture. It's clear, as Cray admits, that Marvin understood evil. He saw its shape-shifting anatomy, and fought it as best he could, whether in his own mirror, or as it careened in from the world around him. It is true that Marvin was open to non-Christian literature, ideas and religions. But that doesn't prove his theological corruption; it may suggest his strength of belief, which wasn't upset by engaging other traditions. Or it might mean that Marvin was seeking to leave behind the narrowness and rigidity he had come to associate with his religious background, even as he held tenaciously to central, essential tenets. Like the love of Jesus. Even at his lowest, when, according to Marvin, self-destruction was in his hand, or up his nose, he still called on Jesus' name to save him, even from himself. He said on the liner notes to the last album released when he was alive, *Midnight Love*, "I still love Jesus." Still is the critical word—after all the paranoia, drug and sexual addictions, bouts with suicide and near insanity, he *still* recognized the sovereignty of God and its clearest manifestation in Jesus.

Cray's handling of Gaye's father is curious. It may also, inadvertently, help explain how some of us Christians cherish religious belief and interpretations of scripture more than the people they're meant to help. Cray sees the obedience to and trust in "the Father" as the key to Jesus' faith. But he comes dangerously close to conflating earthly and heavenly fathers. Neither does he offer theological criticism of Rev. Gay's murderous actions. He simply ends by citing the trustworthiness of God as Father, and hence, contrasts that, implicitly, to Gaye's father. What about the Father protecting Gaye from his father? Perhaps Gaye's "sinning" left him unprotected in Cray's theol-

ogy. Maybe Marvin's sins—his drugs, sex, and decadence—lead
to his unavoidable death in Cray's view.

In any case, Cray fails to turn as critical a lens on Rev. Gay as
he does on Marvin. That suggests that theological doctrine—
God as Father—is used to obscure the obvious violence done in
the name of God as Father. Feminist theology has been especially good at pointing out the difficulties of calling God
father.[40] That language often overlooks the theological and
physical violence that victimizes women and children. Marvin
was a victim on many counts. Rev. Gay's vicious whippings of
Marvin as a boy found Biblical support. Marvin endured the
symbolic violence of associating God with rigid belief. And he
experienced the violence of being asked to yield to a brutal,
unloving father out of reverence for the Ten Commandments.
Ironically, Marvin's submission to that principle, and his resistance to it on the last day of his life, was a source of suffering.
Cray has nothing at all to say on this score.

Besides being a victim of drug addiction, Marvin Gaye was
genuinely God-intoxicated. On his funk drenched, self-com-
posed *In Our Lifetime* album—over whose release Marvin left
Motown, arguing the company put it out without his permission and without allowing him to finish it—Marvin Gaye
dipped again in Pentecostal waters to state his love for God.[41]
He struggled brilliantly, mightily, with the war between the
flesh and the spirit, between God and the Devil, and between
good and evil. On "Praise," a buoyant, up-tempo dance song
built on percussion, bass, and infectious, interweaved Gaye
background vocals, Marvin aims to transform the dance-floor
into a holy sanctuary of praise to God. He riffs on an extended
chorus of "Praise Hims": when "you go to work," when "your

feelings hurt," when "you're feeling glad," and by "the love you give," the "way you live" and "whether rain or shine, shine, shine." On "Life Is For Learning," Marvin adopts a seductive, grinding funk groove carved from sax and vibes to tell a story of how the artist "pays a price so you won't have to pay." He tells of the "songs from wisdom" and the "songs from Satan," the songs "from lust," and those "from pain." Gaye sings that the "Devil has his special plan to make hot songs for sinners," while God will turn it around and "make good songs for winners."

On "Love Party," Marvin funks up a disco vibe full of radiant bass lines to remind his listeners that "Revelation's prophesy [is] nearly fulfilled," and since they are "blessed to experience a changing world," they have to "love before our fate is closed and sealed." Gaye tells his aural congregation to meditate and sing and pray. On "Love Me Now Or Love Me Later," Marvin offers a philosophically acute reflection on the nature of existence, good and evil, and the strife between "a God of love and a God of evil." As his chorus of Gaye voices float through the song's slow-funk bass rhythm, Gaye brilliantly explores the internal thoughts of the God of love and the God of evil, using this trope to broadcast the theological struggle of human beings subject to forces beyond their creation. "I got what the soul desires—for mankind's flesh," the Evil Lord said, while the Good Lord said, "I'm in your soul, your decision is free."

Marvin Gaye eloquently summarized his views about the struggle between spirituality and sensuality in a television documentary in Ostend, Belgium.

If you really want to live so that you experience life as a human embryo should experience it, you have to be on a spiritual plane. And you have to stay there, and you have to have a great deal of faith in something higher than yourselves, and myself. And then you have to give in to that power totally, and that power will take care of you. And then and only then will you breathe and feel the way you should feel. That's living. People who accomplish great physical and personal disciplines, you have to start off as a child almost, and be taught a certain way, to have the strengths that you should have to overcome the flesh, and the material desires, and the desires of my wicked soul. I'm human, too. I think I do as well as anybody, but I think I could be a lot better, and I want to be a lot better. And I wish I were all pure and holy and righteous. People hate that kind of person, too, you know that. I mean they can't stand to be around a person like that. I didn't cuss, and I would never take a drink. I wouldn't smoke any pot or whatever else I might do. I wish I didn't like chicks a lot, the ladies. I wish a lot of things. I wish I were a monk. I wish I could be strong enough to give up all of the flesh. It's all so difficult sometimes. The flesh, this stupid flesh."[42]

Marvin Gaye struggled his entire career to reconcile sweet flesh and sustaining faith. The tension between sexuality and spirituality lead him down troubled paths in his personal life— and to artistic glory. His willingness to say what was on his heart and mind produced music that inspired millions. His courage as a child of God to claim his erotic birthright proved both exhilarating and shocking. Marvin helped many black Christians and American souls tell the truth about their own sensual desires, even as he stumbled in his own relationships.

He struggled with loving women—secretly and in the open—whose passions left marks all over his art. In the span of a decade, Marvin produced two classic albums that defined an erotic era in black pop music. Those albums, *Let's Get It On* and *I Want You,* carved a niche of black love in the musical universe.

CHAPTER FOUR

"How Sweet It Is to Be Loved By You"

Black Love and Secret Romance

Marvin Gaye's efforts to tap the sensuous inter-
face of spirituality and sexuality proved to be commercially
appealing. He exploited the credo of the feminists he opposed:
the personal is the political. Marvin disregarded how women's
private lives and personal choices were shaped by male
supremacy—after all, he was an avowed, if clumsy, male
supremacist. Instead, Gaye mastered the politics of erotic
expression just as the love ethic that fueled civil rights workers
and peace activists faded from view. Marvin ingeniously
reworked elements of charity into a menu of sensual expression.
He didn't seek to displace public love but to harness its energy
to his erotic agenda. Marvin managed to elevate eroticism
while not dismissing politics involving the equal distribution of
resources and goods—the resource was spirit, the good was
romantic love.

This is not to deny that Marvin's transformations of love—
he went from promoting love *as* public (good) on *What's Going*

On to love *in* public on later recordings—lacked either cultural resonance or political effect. Martha Bayles thinks that seventies "love men" reeked of narcissism and, to paraphrase Carly Simon, showed that the love song really wasn't about their women, but themselves. Bayles also argues that the genre's racial politics played off of implicit distinctions between white rockers and black soul stars:

> From a business point of view, the [love song] promised to win a niche on the pop chart by offering an old-fashioned type of masculine sex appeal that was clearly missing from hard rock and heavy metal. The assumption was that any woman in her right mind would prefer the love man's smooth-talking, satin-sheets-on-the-waterbed approach to the ear-blistering screeching of white boys with roadkill hair…Was love really the point? From a woman's point of view, there is something unconvincing about the sound of a man so enamored of his own powers of seduction that his partner is reduced to a faint chorus of orgasmic chirps…The exemplary love man is not sadistic like the headbanger, but he is no less self-absorbed. All alone in his dream world, he may express trembling passion and profound adoration for his sackmate, but that doesn't make her any more real than the pliant victims of the heavy-metal stage. In both cases the agenda is not really sex between man and woman. For the headbanger it's aggression against society, and for the love man it's a not-so-veiled put-down of the white boys."[1]

Bayles is right to draw attention to a marketplace that sought to capitalize on racial differences in black and white musical genres. Packaging black men as romantic balladeers capable of seducing women does have resonance. But that's not only because they're seen as comparing favorably to white rockers in musical terms. It clearly plays into stereotypes about black male sexual superiority, a point Bayles may imply but doesn't address. As for speaking from a woman's point of view, Bayles is brave but bounded—by class, by taste, maybe even by race. Millions of black women warmed to Marvin's—and Teddy Pendergrass's and Barry White's—erotic charms. For black women who hadn't been acknowledged or addressed in many quarters of the entertainment world—much less in the general society—the love they got from artists such as Marvin meant that their existence was affirmed. True enough, the acknowledgment was somewhat paradoxical, tied to an imperfect marketplace that exploited black women's desire for recognition. And some of the love men's sexual and gender politics left a lot to be desired. Still, black women were utterly overlooked in the broader cultural arena—not only among white men, but white women as well—and naturally harkened to the velvet voices of black love men.

Until the 1970s, black women comprised a huge market that went largely ignored by the mainstream music industry. This is not unlike the early '90s "discovery" of a massive and untapped black female reading audience when novels by Toni Morrison, Alice Walker, and Terry McMillan hogged the *New York Times* best-seller's list at the same time. Although Marvin Gaye certainly wanted to break free of the R & B ghetto and achieve pop stardom, he never aspired to leave behind the core audience that loved him and brought him fame. He merely wanted to extend his musical reach. He also wanted to show the tremendous intellectual, spiritual and erotic vitality of black art. "No one really takes the soul form seriously," Marvin said. "Putting deep messages over a funk groove gets those folks mixed up. We ain't supposed to be sayin' nothing. Keep the lyrics simple and just keep everyone dancing—that's all they want."[2]

It's hard to argue with Bayles' insight about black masculine strategies in seventies music. Black soul stars may have indeed showed off their erotic wares and irresistible appeal. But these stars worked at a deficit not faced by their white rock peers: white male jealousy of black male sexuality. Ironically, black stars operated in a culture that didn't seem to mind exploiting their sexuality in the marketplace, as long as it was in the name of making money and selling albums. Marvin was on the cutting edge of brokering acceptance of the erotic ambitions of black men. His music fought conservative white cultural values and political ideologies that portrayed the black male as a threat. In that light, Bayles' observation that the real agenda of the love man is a put-down of the "white boys" may reveal more than it intended. It taps a vein of resentment of the alleged sexual superiority of black men. For a long stretch in the seventies, Marvin was the best example of the soul artist whose gifts could provoke such fears and jealousies.

Marvin's erotic art projected the musical values and aesthetic beauty of the vulnerable black male voice with his haunting falsetto torching his erotic recordings. It is a splendid and representative artifact in the sonic archive of tender black male expression. The black male falsetto came into its own in the gospel music of the early twentieth century, a great deal of which wasn't heard for a long time in mainstream culture. Its pure tones and soaring reach conjured the celestial climes to which it spiritually aspired. When the falsetto migrated beyond the sanctuary, its baptism in the currents of black secular culture meant that a wider range of hearers had access to both its artistic merits and its moral intensity. The falsetto's political meaning was partially derived from its willingness to reach for notes—like reaching for freedoms and privileges—far beyond the pale. Thus, the aesthetic quality of the falsetto mirrored the moral intent of black community: to shirk imposed limits and gain a higher register of achievement.

Nathaniel Mackey captures the social meaning of the falsetto in his novel, *Bedouin Hornbook.* In this passage the narrator responds to an essay he received and uses it to reflect on the black male falsetto, especially Al Green's:

Would it be going too far to say that in your essay the black falsetto has in fact found its voice? (Forgive me if I embarrass you). In any case, the uncanny coincidence is that the draft of your essay arrived just as I'd put on a record by Al Green. I've long marveled at how all this going on about love succeeds in alchemizing a legacy of lynchings—as though singing were a rope he comes eternally close to being strangled by...One point I think could bear more insistent mention: What you term "the dislocated African's pursuit of a meta-voice" bears the weight of a gnostic, transformative desire to be done with the world. By this I mean the deliberately "false" voice we get from someone like Al Green creatively hallucinates a "new world," indicts the more insidious falseness of the world as we know it. (Listen, for example, to "Love and Happiness.") What is it in the falsetto that thins and threatens to abolish the voice but the wear of so much reaching for heaven? At some point you'll have to follow up this excellent essay of yours with a treatment of the familial ties between the falsetto, the moan and the shout...Like the moan or the shout, I'm suggesting, the falsetto explores a redemptive, unworded realm—a meta-word, if you will—where the implied critique of the momentary eclipse of the word curiously rescues, restores and renews it: new word, new world.[3]

It is a new world of black erotic hope that Marvin strains to create through his eerily arching falsetto. In his guttural cries, his hectic moans, his elliptical ejaculations and his plaintive whispers, Marvin explores the healing and redemptive dimensions of black romantic love. He serves as a voice piece for the millions who identify with his ethical intent: to claim space in the heavens, whether it is social or erotic. He speaks as well for those who hunger for his poignant vulnerability. When Marvin inaugurated his erotic quest through his falsetto's affecting pitches and elastic range, it appeared he had found a new style as well. That much is true. But thematically he was returning to familiar romantic territory. At the beginning of his erotic era, Marvin Gaye was coming full circle: having once chafed at the role of sex symbol, he now embraced it, at least for a spell, with enthusiasm. He brushed aside the youthful innocence of his uplifting '60s duets. Instead, he imbued his philosophy of lust, love, and longing with a darker, perhaps less idealized outlook. If his views were chastened, they were still hopeful, lending urgency to his music. It drew to him millions of listeners who identified with his exhilarating if frustrated quest for intimate fulfillment.

Let's Get It On makes this clear: the world of spiritual sexuality has the imperfect joys and stunted desires of the society he found wanting on *What's Going On*. *Let's Get It On* was the first album Marvin made in Motown's studios in Los Angeles. Marvin finally settled there in 1972 after filming the forgettable biker film *Chrome and Hot Leather*, which he began shooting when he completed *What's Going On*. By the summer of '72, he had separated from Anna. Marvin was also more loathe than usual to get into the studio. It wasn't until February of 1973 that he began to make the album *Let's Get It On* after the single hit big. It was a sense of déjà vu since it nearly followed the same recording pattern of *What's Going On*. The difference was that Motown was solidly in his corner.

On the first single "Let's Get It On" (cowritten with Ed Townsend, who had a 1958 pop hit "For Your Love")—which claimed the top slot on the pop charts in June 1973—Marvin lets his lover know of his pent up emotions, exhorting her to join him in erotic license built on mutuality. "And if you feel like I feel, baby, then come on," he growls above bass grooves and guitar licks deliciously distorted by a wah-wah pedal. "Let's get it on." Gaye doubles his voice in beautiful harmony to suggest a similar unity in his erotic and emotional desires, since "giving yourself to me can never be wrong, if the love is true." He enlivens his sexual sentiments on "Keep Gettin' It On," an extension of the groove of its parent which grows looser in sound, more lush in its harmonic streams, but gains gravitas along the way. "Wouldn't you rather make love children, as opposed to war?" Gaye asks in a soul holler, refusing to separate the bedroom from the picket line.

"Come Get to This" thrives on sweet anachronism: it sounds like a hyped-up '60s mellow soul track, full of jutting saxophone lines, swirling harmonies, and strutting rhythms. Marvin brightly celebrates a lover who's come back from being away, telling her "I want you hear, I want to do, somethin' freaky to you." This infectious song was the album's second single, rising to number 3 on the R & B charts and snagging the 21ˢᵗ spot on the pop charts. On "You Sure Love To Ball," Gaye goes for the erotic jugular. This was the album's third single, reaching number 13 on the R & B charts, and number 50 on the pop list. Riding a lilting rhythm made of sparkling guitar riffs, sprightly percussion, and soothing strings, Marvin dips into the vernacular to exclaim his desire to give love around the clock while taking delight in his lover's high sexual energy—the fact that she loved "to ball." Gaye's explicitness—including the distinct female moaning in the background—is cushioned by the song's equally sensuous groove, speaking his desire with his mouth and his music.

Marvin turns more traditional lover-man on another song he wrote with Townsend, "Please Stay (Once You Go Away)." On the affecting ballad, wisps of his tight but airy multiple-background vocals hug the poignant plea for his lover not to leave him because "I won't be able to sleep peacefully in bed without you beside me." It is the song's sheer repetition of sentiment that finally drives its message to emotional and musical climax. "Distant Lover" is, besides "Let's Get It On," the album's best known tune, in part because of the thrilling live version of the song that appears on *Marvin Gaye Live*—drawn from the first full-fledged concert Marvin gave (in the Oakland Coliseum on January 4, 1974) after Tammi Terrell's death. The live version of the tune was released as a single later that year and became an R & B hit that peaked at number 28 on the pop charts.

The album version is equally powerful. The smoldering ballad—cowritten by Gwen Gordy and Sandra Greene—is a blues lament over the physical and psychic spaces that separate lovers. Marvin reflects on the vicissitudes of a love affair: time spent together, promises made, daily letters, and then, its sudden end. Marvin registers the anguish of a spent affair, and the tender emotions and loving memories that linger, in a passage that seemed to rip from a personal hell of tortured love. "Please, come back baby," Marvin utters. Then he voices a startling passion that prompts him to strip away his feelings—leaving him emotionally naked. "Somethin' I wanna say/When you left you took all of me with you," he fairly shouts at the top of his natural tenor. The song's composition counterpoints his agony with sweet harmonies; his wounded spirit is punctuated with beautiful blasts of trumpet. Marvin closes the song wondering if his departed, distant lover wants to hear him "scream, plead, and plead, *ple-e-e-ase*"—Marvin recruits cognates to do his bidding—"Oh please baby, come back home to me girl."

"If I Should Die Tonight," written with Townsend, is a shudder of recognition that one has been fortunate to meet his ideal love. With gentle flutes and precious vibes tickling his words, Marvin transforms a philosophical paradox into soulful testimony: he finds the pure meaning of love because he knows he may lose it. Marvin tells his lover if he should die—and he admits it would be tragically premature—he won't "die blue, sugar yeah, 'cause I've known you." He extends his meditation by questioning, "How many eyes have seen their dream, oh, how many arms have felt their dream?," completing his thought by asking "how many hearts, baby, have felt their world stand still?" He answers himself in the serene assurance that he beheld what others only imagine, because millions "never, they never, never, and millions never will, baby, they never, will."

"Just to Keep You Satisfied," written with Elgie Stover and Anna, is Gaye's sad reminiscence about a woman who was "my wife, my life, my hopes and dreams." Although they are no longer together, bittersweet memories play on his mind, especially the power of making love. "I stood all the jealousy, all the bitchin' too, yes I'd forget it all once in bed with you." The song has a symphonic quality: doo-wop harmonies echo across the soundscape and strings bleed through the crevices of his aching, mournful words as he queries, "Oh darlin', how could we end up like this?" In an endearingly modest, even coy, moment, Marvin substitutes a nearly onomatopoeic phrase for lovemaking to conjure the passion he felt: "And when we, wo-oo-o-o, we'd stop the hands of time, you set my soul on fire." Because of that, he pledges to be by her side should she need him, even though "the many happy times we had, can never really outweigh the bad," he confesses "I'll never love nobody like I loved you baby." As David Ritz notes, this song should be seen as part of Marvin's brilliant meditation on marriage and its complications in *Here, My Dear*.[4]

Let's Get It On perched at the second spot on the pop charts, which was even higher than *What's Going On*, which topped out at number six. *Let's Get It On* was a commercial and critical triumph for Marvin, especially since he seemed to have successfully answered the question of how to follow up a classic album. He simply made another. But the question of why Marvin Gaye abruptly turned from social justice and spirituality to sexuality lingers to this day. Some of the explanations are speculative, even intensely intellectual. Others are supremely practical. But all are revealing.

Critic Dave Marsh in 1983 suggested that in "the disintegration of his marriage, and his eventual divorce, Gaye seems also to have experienced a separation from the social concerns that fueled that music, and as a result, his themes have narrowed: eroticism, on the one hand...and an obligatory, somewhat desperate nod to Jesus."[5] Critic Mark Anthony Neal argues that *Let's Get It On* represents Gaye's willingness to "reconstruct himself as a sexualized patriarch in the guise of the black superstud...a character that gained mythical status in the black community as an agent of empowerment in black celluloid fantasies like *Truck Turner, Shaft in Africa,* and *Superfly*."[6]

Gaye's biographer David Ritz maintains that on *Let's Get It On* "Marvin was arguing with his Pentecostal upbringing."[7] In that light, *What's Going On* might be viewed as the positive public expression of Marvin's religious beliefs: that God is love, that justice should prevail, and that human beings should treat each other with respect. Marvin's Pentecostal church roots and Christian ethics fueled his loving critique of the world. But Marvin's learning in the world allowed him to return the favor: his experience beyond the church doors allowed him to reshape his religious beliefs. *What's Going On* was outward looking; it cast a searching spiritual eye on social relations. *Let's Get It On* was inward looking; it gathered data from the erotic sensibility that had been repressed in his religious life. If Marvin delivered perceptive analyses of social injustice and political failure on *What's Going On*, he was equally prophetic in rejecting the punitive aspects of his Pentecostal bearing. But he vividly brought to life its insistence on the spiritual character of sexual union. As Ritz says, Gaye was also "arguing with his liner notes," which touted the separation of sex and love, because "Let's Get It On" "concerned the union of love and sex," and in spite of his "chauvinistic posturing, his art elicited a powerful desire to wed feeling and flesh."[8]

Then, too, it may be that Gaye had not engaged in the necessary spiritual inventory needed to produce the kind of work he did on *What's Going On*. When journalist Nelson George told Marvin in 1983 that the times seemed to demand the sort of commentary he provided on his 1971 jeremiad, Gaye was reflective. "It seems to me that I have to do some soul-searching to see what I want to say," Marvin said. "You can say something. Or you can say something profound. It calls for fasting, feeling, praying, lots of prayer, and maybe we can come up with a more spiritual social statement to give people more food for thought."[9]

Another explanation for Marvin's transition from the social to the sexual sphere lies in his restless creativity and his fierce desire not to repeat himself. "I've made it a point not to follow in my own shadow," Marvin told the *New York Times* in 1983. "Repeating yourself is boring. But being a bit, let's say, 'far out,' I do tend to shock people with my albums and singles. It's been that way since I became my own man, when I recorded *What's Going On*."[10] As the critic Robert Palmer argued, Marvin reserved his greatest shock for fans who elevated him as a musical prophet. "[J]ust when Mr. Gaye's followers were getting used to the idea of their favorite soul singer as the conscience of contemporary pop, he shocked them again by making some of the most sexually explicit hit records in pop music history, beginning with 'Let's Get It On.'"[11]

Marvin's desire to shock aside, the reason for his shift from spirit to sex may be less esoteric than previously thought. When I ask Art Stewart, Marvin's engineer, if he can help me grasp this change, his answer is direct.

"Well, no, I can't really," he says, but then he does just that. "Because I think what happens is that times change, moods change, and it depends upon the material that's presented. I think when Ed Townsend brought 'Let's Get It On' into play, I think that sort of set the mood for the rest [of the album]." That's already a big leap that helps to clarify Marvin's motivations: it was another case of bricolage, of him using the material that was at hand. But Stewart has even more surprises for me. "And see, a lot of the songs were comprised of music and collaborations that Marvin had with the Originals. When Marvin produced 'The Bells' on them, my understanding is that he had recorded a lot of music for them, and a lot of that music ended up on *Let's Get It On*, with Marvin reworking the lyrics and doing the music himself."

"Nothing was wasted for Marvin, then?" I ask.

"No. Not really. One thing led to another. From 'Let's Get It On" to 'Let's see, what else do I have in my bag?' 'Ohhhh! I did this song on the Originals. Hey, let me bring that in and see how this fits into this thing.' That, I believe, is how the album came about. It wasn't necessarily designed to be what it turned out to be. 'This is the material that I have, and since I have this particular song, what do I have to compliment that? From this, where can I go?'"

"The theme was driven by circumstance?" I clarify.

"Right. You go from 'Let's Get It On' to 'Distant Lover,' to whatever other songs [are available]. Then he says, 'I can make this work.'"

"So the pattern emerged out of what was at hand, and then what was at hand helped to shape the theme that's adopted on the album?"

"That's right. A lot of the music that came from him came because of the circumstances in his life. That's what he was feeling at a particular time."

If Marvin shaped the album from the music he had available—much like he did with *What's Going On*—then his collaborators had as much influence on him as social events. In this case, at least for three of the songs, his collaborator was Ed Townsend, a singer-songwriter-producer who had worked with artists such as Brook Benton, Connie Stevens, and the Shirelles.[12] Marvin had crossed paths with Townsend out on tour in the '60s. The prospect of working with Townsend had lured Marvin back to the studio. Ed had gone to his house to play him six of his songs.[13] Marvin chose three: "Let's Get It On," "Please Don't Stay," and "If I Should Die Tonight." Marvin agreed to record them if Townsend would produce him.

There are even more intriguing reasons to explain Marvin's course: the failed attempt to repeat the conscientious politics of *What's Going On*, and the fact that some of the songs on *Let's Get It On* were of earlier vintage than the '73 sessions.

When I ask Harry Weinger about the transition, he, too, resists seeing Gaye's career and music in those terms.

"I don't think it's a transition," Weinger tells me. "I think it's just what happened. I think Marvin certainly struggled with the results of *What's Going On*. He did 'You're the Man' a year later, and that was his attempt to follow it up. You say, 'Well, that [*What's Going On*] was a hit; might as well try it again.' And it didn't work."

"You're the Man"—a stinging indictment of political deceit accompanied by pleas for more jobs and less taxes—rode a funky soul-jazz beat. Marvin employed an eerie falsetto reminiscent of Curtis Mayfield's work on *Superfly*. "You're the Man" was a top-ten R & B hit in April '72 but failed to command the pop charts, peaking at 50. As a result, Marvin had serious doubts about pursuing political commentary in his music. "He worried that he could no longer count on social issues for sales," writes David Ritz.[14] Critic Brian Ward sees the failure of "You're the Man" to crossover in the context of the era's racial politics and the quirks of white liberal ideology:

> Gaye followed up the innovations of *What's Going On* with 'You're the Man,' a stridently militant single which failed to cross over into the white pop charts despite the fact that Gaye's stock in the progressive white rock audience had increased greatly as a result of *What's Going On*. Perhaps this failure also revealed something of the limitations of white liberal support for black demands. *What's Going On*'s essentially humanistic globalism was acceptable, but a song which in the election year of 1972 called for a candidate who would end inflation, cure chronic ghetto unemployment and support busing seemed too much."[15]

"Because 'You're the Man' wasn't a hit, he said, 'I've got no reason to finish an album,'" Weinger says of Gaye's lack of motivation to follow up his latest single. Weinger also provides a glimpse into Marvin's psyche, and how he drew on fan appreciation to craft his work. "'Let's Get It On' was rushed out as a single [in 1974] because that's all Motown had. The B-side is 'I Wish It Would Rain'; it's not from any 'Let's Get It On' session. If that's not an immediate smash, does Marvin go back and finish the album? He did, but Marvin had to be shown that people loved him and wanted him before he'd do what he did. Because you can imagine what it takes to do what he did. He's going to do it all the way, baby! He's going to layer those eight voices. He's going to get Ernie Watts to come the day before the record's supposed to ship and do a flute solo. You know?"

Even more revealing is that Marvin had recorded the tracks for several of the songs for *Let's Get It On* before he recorded most of *What's Going On*. In that light, it's hard to conclude that Marvin made a shift in his musical vision that was based primarily on philosophical will or sustained reflection. As was true for *What's Going On*, it doesn't deny the ingenuity of Gaye's art, or the profound effect it had on the culture. Neither does it suggest that Gaye didn't intend to express his emotional, erotic, and philosophic beliefs. After all, he chose and crafted the songs he placed on the album, leaving others aside. The themes he resonated with guided his selections. Neither does it rob him of the luster of auteur. Rather, this new information highlights the role of collaboration and the play of circumstance in deciding an artist's direction—at least Marvin Gaye's.

It has been reported that Marvin said he wouldn't record after Berry Gordy initially refused to release the single of "What's Going On." But that turns out not to be true. "You find out he did record," Weinger says. "He recorded 'Distant Lover'

and 'Come Get to This' and 'Just to Keep You Satisfied'—
pieces of it, not the whole thing, not the final result. But the
basic tracks are done; the background vocals are done. In fact,
'Just to Keep You Satisfied' was cut with vocals from the
Originals, and he went in and changed their vocals, one version
at a time, since there are many different versions of the vocals.
[The Originals version, and others, is included on the deluxe
edition of *Let's Get It On*.] One version is disco. He goes back in
and he starts recording more vocals to all the stuff that became
the *Vulnerable* album. He didn't *not* record; he recorded for *himself*. But he wasn't making assembly-line material for Berry
Gordy. He was using the system for himself."

There are even more revelations that throw light on the
process with which he created albums. Gaye transformed the
meaning of Townsend's lyrics, which were initially conceived as
an exhortation to get on with life; they did not promote the
spiritual sexuality that Marvin had in mind. "I know there
should be peace and love, we all talkin' about it, let's get it on,"
Marvin sings on Townsend's original version. It's included in
the deluxe edition of *Let's Get It On*. Later, he extends the
song's social themes by encouraging his listeners to act on positive beliefs. "Understanding and brotherhood, everybody ought
to try to do some good." (Marvin obviously rewrote the song to
match the themes of romance and spiritual sexuality he had
explored on the tunes he had recorded in Detroit. This proves
that Marvin worked dialectically with his collaborators. He
edited and expanded their work to fit his interests and worldview). Townsend's sentiments grew from personal battles with
addiction. "Townsend was saying if you want peace and love,
well let's do it," Weinger says. "Don't march about it; don't talk

about it. Let's get it on! And he wrote that out of his rehabilitation from alcohol." Townsend's original version also makes clear that "Let's Get It On" and "Keep Gettin' It On", intended as a single song, were later divided into two on *Let's Get It On.*

As Weinger sorted through the tapes vault, he was bewildered by the huge amount of material. It became clear that Marvin had many false starts and pursued a number of directions—and even another album—before settling on the songs that became *Let's Get It On.* "Sometimes, I swear to you, the *Let's Get It On* deluxe edition almost didn't happen. I'm confused because there are all these disparate elements. There's stuff with the Miracles, there's instrumentals, there are things with Willie Hutch. I said, 'Forget it, let the album stand on its own.'" But Weinger's methods prove that even sophisticated thinkers depend on help beyond the rational realm. "The guiding voice walks in the room, spiritually speaking, and says, 'But you know, it just needs to be heard. It's Marvin!' Let the segues be confusing, let it be kind of mixed up, because it *was* mixed up."

"Was it mixed up because of poor bookkeeping, or was it mixed up because Marvin was mixed up?" I ask Weinger.

"It's because he said, 'Yeah, I'll do the track. No, I don't wanna do another one.' It's a great idea, and then the idea is gone. Or, 'Yeah, You're the Man, that's cool.' Then he does two different versions of the track. Was that for an album? So there was a sense that the album is the album."

"But in trying to parse that out, aren't you getting inside his confusion? Aren't you actually tracking what he went through to try to get there?"

"Yeah. And I'm not doing it pretending I know Marvin personally. I'm doing it just by looking at the dates, just by looking at the pieces of paper. The evidence is all there. I told David Ritz, 'Your book did not have any of the information that I'm turning up, but your book is still correct, in terms of the timeline.' Yes, Marvin was confused. But it's interesting. I'm just providing more. It helps you appreciate the records more."

The information Weinger turned up helps to clarify what Marvin did to complete the album. It also throws light on other projects he participated in around the same time. Motown made many efforts to get Gaye into the studio after *What's Going On* and *Trouble Man*. Motown was so desperate that it convened an A&R panel—including Berry and Motown VP Suzanne DePasse—and got Marvin to agree to join in as they auditioned producers for him. They heard from the Mizell brothers (Larry and Fonce), Freddie Perren, Pam Sawyer, Gloria Jones, Willie Hutch, and Hal Davis. Many of the producers did tracks with Marvin, some of which are included on the deluxe edition of *Let's Get It On*. Gaye jibed well enough with Hal Davis that he agreed to do another duets album—this time with Diana Ross. Berry Gordy selected the songs. "Clearly, Berry Gordy is saying, 'Well, let's at least do a record we know will sell,'" Weinger says. "'Just do some covers, don't think about it, don't worry about it. Do 'Pledging My Love,' 'Don't Knock My Love,' 'You Are Everything.' We know these tunes. Knock it out.' And that's what he does, most of it before *Let's Get It On*, although it comes out later."

Diana and Marvin was released two months after *Let's Get It On*. It only reached number 26 on the pop charts, proving to be a commercial disappointment. Its critical reception was hardly better, even though there are highlights on the album, including "My Mistake," "Pledging My Love," "Love Twins," and the biggest hit single, "You're a Special Part of Me." In 1973 Ross vaguely suggested the intense atmosphere of the album's creation when she told a *Rolling Stone* reporter that "I've loved Marvin for years and wanted to record with him. We did a great number of songs together during the last year and a half, so many that I didn't know which one was the single until you told me."[16] The manner in which the album was produced suggests, Weinger says, that Motown "was hedging their bets."

It's become clear as well that Marvin was experimenting with instrumental music during this period. Of course, this was discovered by accident. When Weinger consulted with David Van DePitte to restore his credit to the deluxe edition for arranging three of *Let's Get It On*'s songs—it had been taken off the album's earlier reissue—he learned more about Marvin's work of the period.

"Whatever happened to that album I did with Marvin?" Weinger recalls Van DePitte asking him.

"What do you mean?" Weinger replied.

"You know, he was off living in the desert with Jan."

"So in going through the '72 and '73 tapes, there are all these sessions: 'Cakes,' 'Song #3,' 'Song #4.' It's on the *Let's Get It On* deluxe edition. And I sent it to Dave, and he goes, 'That's Herbie Hancock on the grand piano.' I said, 'Are you sure?' He said, 'He was standing next to me.' So there's another story."

"Song #3" is, not surprisingly, a mellow but upbeat piano-driven soul-jazz ballad that features the crisp, striking tones of Hancock's keyboards, melodic strings, and the entrancing guitar licks of Melvin "Wah Wah" Ragin. "My Love Is Growing" is a bit more up-tempo and funkier, and features the same musicians seamlessly interweaving with Marvin's natural tenor and pleading falsetto. He meshes his vocals, at times half-scatting, within the song's melodic fabric, proclaiming his growing passion for his lover. "Cakes" returns to a sinuous, soulful jazz groove. The song takes off on the rhythms of the glorious percussion, scintillating vibes, vibrant bass, and plaintive trumpet chords. All three songs were co-written by Marvin and Van DePitte.

The deluxe edition contains even more instrumentals from another Gaye session. "He wanted to do a funk record with Michael Henderson," Weinger says. Henderson played bass for several Motown acts in the mid-sixties before finding fame as a singer in collaboration with Norman Connors, Jr., and as a solo artist who made some well-received albums in the late seventies and early eighties. "I called Michael Henderson, and he said, 'My Afro couldn't fit through Marvin Gaye's front door. I was 19. Marvin Gaye, are you kidding me? It was like working with Miles.' Well, I said, 'I've got the recording date in front of me. When did you work with Miles?' And I went through my Miles books, and I said, 'You went from working with Miles to walking into Marvin Gaye's living room?' So everything leads to another story." Besides Henderson, the 1971 session—featuring two versions of "Running From Love," and "Mandota"—also included guitarist Ray Parker, Jr., who gained acclaim in his group Raydio, and as a solo artist, and drummer Hamilton Bohannon, who had a big hit in 1978 with the propulsive funk jam "Let's Start the Dance."

But it was perhaps Marvin's interactions with Ed Townsend that had the greatest impact on his album—and his life. Not only did Townsend bring three songs that they transformed into some of the best of Marvin's career—all of them, arguably classics—but he pushed Marvin to dig deeper and find his best performance. "Ed Townsend, who came from the old school, told Marvin, 'You're punching it and punching it and punching it,'" Weinger says. [Punching, pioneered at Motown, was a technique that allowed a vocal or instrumental solo to be raised or lowered or covered over by a new take. In its early history, the easiest way to punch was to cut the tape; for safety, two tapes were usually made.][17] Townsend did a bit of punching himself, except the target was Marvin's ego. "No wonder you can't play Madison Square Garden, because you're afraid to sing!" Townsend said. Weinger says that goaded Marvin to respond with a classic performance. "Marvin took off his shirt, sang at that microphone for eight minutes, and said, 'How's that?' And that's the record, 'Let's Get It On.'"

Townsend elicited another moving performance from Gaye, this time on "If I Should Die Tonight." When Townsend initially played the song for Gaye, he said he couldn't sing it because he had never felt that way about a woman. When Marvin asked, Townsend told him the story behind the song's creation. He had finally met a very beautiful woman he had dreamed of for a long time. After their blissful encounter, she repeated to him a variation of the folk wisdom that "we can't build our happiness on the unhappiness of others"—especially since they were both married. When Townsend agreed with her and prepared to leave, she asked if that was all he had to say. He replied, "No. Let me tell you this: 'If I should die tonight, Lord before my time, I won't die blue because I have known you.' Marvin said to me it was a lovely story but he couldn't feel like that."[18]

Nothing Townsend did could remove that feeling. Then, one night, Townsend's lady friend, Barbara Hunter, visited the studio with her 17-year-old daughter Janis Hunter. That night, March 22, 1974, Marvin was cutting his lead vocals for "Let's Get It On." He had recorded his "demo" version on March 13, adhering faithfully to Townsend's sentiments of getting on with one's life. But after meeting Janis Hunter, Marvin was immediately smitten. On the spot, he recomposed the words to Townsend's song and gave them the spiritually sexual overtones for which it became widely known. Marvin essentially viewed Townsend's words as a jazz musician might view chords: as the building blocks of a composition that would expand through improvisation. He improvised a hugely uplifting and erotically engaging song from Townsend's lyrics, and forever stamped soul music with his romantic ambitions. Although the feat is standard in jazz instrumentals, and perhaps common among the best of hip-hoppers who generate lyrics in elegant freestyles, it is a rare feat for a singer. As Ben Edmonds points out, "few moments in all of pop music can compare with what Marvin Gaye pulled off with 'Let's Get It On.'"[19] Almost as if a double portion of his romantic spirit fell down, Marvin embraced the lyric for "If I Should Die Tonight" with renewed energy. "After meeting Jan," Ed Townsend said, "he turned around and said, 'Ed, get that tape. I can sing that son of a bitch now.'"[20]

In a sense, one can chart Gaye's career—besides referring to big social changes and political events—by calculating the state of his love life. As David Ritz says, in the sixties, Marvin was singing to Anna, and in the seventies, he was singing to Jan. That is largely true—and led to some of Marvin's greatest art, including the remarkable and underappreciated *I Want You.* But there is another woman that Ritz, and all other writers, has left out: Tammi Terrell. Like everyone else who has written on Marvin Gaye, I have been told by countless people that his relationship with Tammi, while undeniably full of good feeling and deep emotion, was purely platonic. That is until now. During the course of my conversations with Brenda Holloway and Martha Reeves, the truth came out.

Holloway was Motown's first West Coast artist, recording for the company as a Los Angeles–based solo artist from 1964 to1968. She was an extremely gifted singer, songwriter, and violinist. Holloway released five singles during that period—including "When I'm Gone," "Operator," and "You've Made Me So Very Happy," which she wrote, and which later sold two million records for *Blood, Sweat and* Tears in 1969—and an album, *Every Little Bit Hurts*. She was also very beautiful, outspoken, and a fashion trendsetter. Holloway was such a talented vocalist, and her words so clearly enunciated, that Berry Gordy had Marvin Gaye and Diana Ross listen to her tapes to learn from her clear diction.[21] Holloway only lasted four years, leaving Motown and show business entirely, feeling that the company did not properly promote her. (Berry Gordy had signed Holloway himself. But after 1967, when Gordy had ceased being involved in Motown's day-to-day operation, Holloway slid through the cracks). In search of some spiritual rejuvenation and direction, she turned to the church.

Holloway was at a distinct disadvantage as a West Coast artist years before Motown relocated to Los Angeles in 1972. She has been described by journalist Nelson George as "the most beautiful woman ever signed to Motown. Her skin had a striking bronze hue. Her hair was bouncy and straight, with curling ends that highlighted oval, almost Oriental eyes, and full, sensual lips. In any dress, but particularly the tight gold and silver sequined outfits she often performed in, this Atascadero, California, native was a head-turner."[22] When I met Holloway, now 57, she was still plainspoken, radiant, warm, and beautiful. Holloway replaced Tammi Terrell and sang with Marvin in several concerts after the songstress had taken ill. In our conversation, I ask her about Marvin's relationship with Anna.

"I don't know if he really loved her," Holloway replies. "I think he really loved Tammi Terrell."

"Really?" I confirm.

"Of course he did."

"Did they ever have a relationship?"

"Of course they did."

"Okay. Right."

I was trying to take all of this in. I was amazed that after all of this time—33 years after Terrell's death, and nearly 20 years after Marvin's—no one had ever spoken publicly about their love affair. It's no surprise that Marvin and Tammi got along famously. Their chemistry onstage carried over to their personal lives. Although she had a big heart, Tammi remained down-to-earth. She had none of the arrogance that sometimes falls on those who receive success early in their career. It's also easy to forget that Tammi was very young: she was only 24 when she died. Thus, Tammi was attempting to establish her own identity, a difficult process for any artist and an especially tough assignment for one in her early twenties. Since Marvin was married to Anna, and Tammi was dating David Ruffin, their relationship was pursued in the typical fashion of most affairs: secret trysts and stolen moments between their professional and personal obligations.

Tammi was a very sensitive and strong listener, a fact that drew Marvin to her even more. A very feminine and strikingly beautiful woman, she nevertheless suffered her own sexual dysfunction.

"She would have sex with people that she met for the first time," Holloway says. "I think she was a nymphomaniac. Actually for the first time in my life I could believe that there was somebody who really fulfilled that term. She was my best friend, but she was promiscuous." (When I spoke to Weldon McDougal, who also knew Tammi very well, he told me that Tammi "was very pretty and she wasn't loose, whatever people say. But she was talented, [and] she had boyfriends.")

Holloway says Tammi was driven by the need to succeed, and thus, freely used her sexuality to achieve her goals. She doubts if Terrell ever experienced true love, except with Marvin. As a young woman, Terrell, like Holloway herself, was just learning who she was and what could make her happy. Tammi proved to be a good friend to Holloway. She was neither possessive nor judgmental. Despite Holloway's troubles with Motown—she didn't get enough recording dates and her material was often passed off to other artists—she bonded with Terrell and got a chance to see Tammi's relationship with Marvin unfold.

"If I was on the road with her, and Marvin would call Tammi, they would talk all kind of smoochy and everything. All of a sudden she said, 'I'm leaving. You can't go.' And she would come back happy. With Marvin, it was on the down low, totally, and you would have to be with her to really know. People could tell, but they couldn't pinpoint it. But it was being done. And if you can be respectful in a relationship like that, then I think they were carrying [it out with] the utmost respect. And they would have to sneak around. It was not blatant, out in the open. It was late at night. I knew she was in love with him, and I knew he was in love with her. But I didn't say anything, because it wasn't my business."

"Very few people obviously knew it for sure, because I haven't seen any references to it," I say.

"It's a very touchy, touchy subject," she concedes.

Since we were on touchy subjects, I asked Holloway about Tammi and domestic violence. I broached the question of her turbulent relationship with James Brown when she was a teen singer in his Famous Flames revue and dating its star. Holloway claims the alleged beating by Brown was because Terrell was promiscuous, although Brenda was careful not to be seen as offering justification for their brutal relationship. Holloway says Ruffin joined in the violence, too, hitting Terrell in the head with a biker helmet in a dispute they had in her apartment. Weldon McDougal spoke to Tammi about the abuse she suffered at the hands of James Brown. He says Terrell didn't believe her violent conflict with Brown caused her brain tumor. McDougal also spoke to David Ruffin about his clashes with Terrell. The singer claimed that Terrell got the best of their exchanges. Elaine Jesmer says that Terrell's problems grew from a sexist society that exacted a severe toll on women with professional ambitions. Moreover, given the era's gender politics, a woman who wanted a serious career in music couldn't afford to alienate the men who controlled the industry. Terrell was caught in the sometimes vicious crosswinds of sexual and professional ambition. It was her rage about how Tammi died that provoked Jesmer to write her novel, *Number One With a Bullet*.[23]

"I couldn't stand to see her just die like that, being so alive," Jesmer says. "Plus, we traded dresses together because we hit it off. She took my paper dress and I took her purple dress. She knew so much more about life than I do to this day. That's why [I wrote the book]. After I talked to her on the phone when she had cancer, I was like, 'No, they cannot do this to you.'"

I asked Jesmer if Tammi and Marvin were involved.

"Their relationship with each other was complicated," she explains. "I could never really understand. I don't know if they slept together. I didn't think they did, but maybe they did. I mean, I don't think Marvin would willingly do this. I don't think he would sleep with someone who was stronger than him."

In fact, Marvin told David Ritz that Tammi was the kind of strong woman he could admire as a friend but not become romantically involved with.

Tammi was the kind of chick who couldn't be controlled by men. That can drive a man crazy—trying to deal with a woman who won't be dominated by anyone. I loved that about Tammi. I knew we could be friends, but never lovers. Independent women hold no romantic interest for me..... James Brown and David Ruffin both had stormy relationships with Tammi, but mine was completely creative. Because she was fun and funny and totally unpredictable, I loved her. Her singing style was also perfectly suited to mine. What we chiefly accomplished, though, was to create two characters—two lovers that might have been taken from a play or novel—and let them sing to each other. That's how the Marvin-and-Tammi characters were born. While we were singing, we *were* in love. The vibe was incredible. The emotions were heartfelt and real. But when the music ended, we kissed each other on the cheek and said good-bye."[24]

When I talked to Martha Reeves, a musical legend, and a beautiful woman as well, I asked her to compare Marvin's singing style in the sixties with Tammi Terrell and his seventies work. Her terse reply confirms Holloway's revelation.

"I don't really know, but I do know that Marvin and Tammi were more than just singing partners."

"You're one of only two people I know to say that," I tell her.

"I knew Tammi," Reeves says. "And you couldn't help but love her. And she couldn't but help love Marvin. They sang so well together. Marvin didn't sing for three years after Tammi passed away. So he dearly loved her. And he made a tribute to her every show he did after that. Tammi was a brilliant singer."

Reeves echoes Holloway in saying that Tammi used her charm and beauty to pursue her goals, affectionately concluding that she was a "bad girl." Reeves says it was the fear of Anna Gordy that kept those who knew from publicly discussing Marvin and Tammi's relationship. But she says their love shows in the thrilling duets they sang.

"You can't hide that. I do know they loved one another. I *do* know that. And I can make that statement boldly, because it shows in the music. It was not legitimate, because they were married. I guess it was a thrill, because she was a very pretty woman [for Marvin], to stand there and smile and to sing a true love song to her. Marvin brought out something in her. I think she matured with Marvin Gaye. She was so much younger. She matured, looking in Marvin's face, singing with that beautiful voice."

I ask Brenda Holloway to describe the effect of combining two good-looking, sexy singers like Marvin and Tammi.

"The shame of it is that with Marvin, obviously he loved

women, but he could have a very shy side. And Tammi Terrell with her promiscuity, [did] not realize her own true value, I guess. So while they were extremely lovely, they didn't see the beauty in themselves."

Holloway's poignant remarks sum up the mysterious search for love. It captures as well the eerie, ironic fashion in which two people who brought such beauty to the world through their art couldn't see it in themselves. Perhaps, however, they caught glimpses of their worth in each other's eyes. I couldn't resist a final question.

"Were they still seeing each other when she collapsed in his arms?"

"I'm pretty sure they were still together. I don't think they ever broke that relationship. I think death broke up that relationship."

Despite pioneering an erotic art that increased the romantic fortunes of millions, Marvin Gaye seemed only to enjoy his love life in spurts and fits. His incredible yearning on *Let's Get It On*, his sense of unfulfilled longing until he met the object of his obsessive adoration in Jan, was fueled by his secret passion for a woman he could never fully acknowledge in his life or art. Death ended his affair with Tammi, giving it a purity, perhaps an artificial durability and illusionary perfection that can only be achieved when a relationship can't be tested in open. Marvin's relationship with Jan, which also began in secret but didn't end there, rode a roller coaster of emotional highs and desperate lows. It also inspired *I Want You*, his greatest album to address spiritual sexuality, a work that did for the erotic realm what *What's Going On* achieved for its political orbit.

CHAPTER FIVE

"Come Live With Me, Angel"
Eroticism and Exodus

For all his sensuous investments and romantic quests, Marvin Gaye acted famously uncomfortable with the women and gays who helped to define erotic politics in the seventies. These two groups forged solidarity to produce a form of music that affected Marvin's standing in the mid-seventies: disco. If *I Want You* is Marvin's erotic classic—his sensual *summum bonum*—it achieved that status by drawing from and rebelling against the styles, sexualities, and politics of disco music. By charting the social and aesthetic roots of disco, and its political uses as well, we better understand the backdrop against which *I Want You* was interpreted and received.

Disco was born in the underground spaces of gay bars and homosexual haunts where interracial audiences embraced black dance music. In post-Stonewall gay culture—Stonewall Inn was the New York City gay bar where a 1969 police raid aimed at enforcing laws against same-sex intimate touching lead to rioting and shouts of "Gay Power!"—political activism inspired increased public displays of homoeroticism.[1] Hence the gay bar and dance club became critical sites where gay sexuality could be expressed as both a political and personal gesture. The music found in such places helped to articulate the homoerotic ambitions of a gay populace in search of social support and cathartic release. Since whites, blacks, and Latinos mixed much more frequently in gay bars than in most places in American society, the music that moved them derived from equally eclectic sources. A new sound was produced that indexed the erotic intensity and rhythmic ferocity of suppressed longing set free. A staple of these settings was a fusion of two styles of early seventies black dance music from which disco drew: polyrhythmic funk pioneered by James Brown and George Clinton, and up-tempo soul music found especially in artists associated with Philadelphia International Records.[2]

In early disco music, live drumming and polyrhythmic beats made it difficult to distinguish the musical pedigree of disco and funk.[3] (As late as 1981, Marvin's funk masterpiece *In Our Lifetime* assembled elements in its sonic stew that winked at early disco's rhythmic brio). As Iain Chambers notes, disco refurbished the sonic interiors of blues and soul and recycled the rhythms in a fashion that created the illusion of timeless repetition:

> Here is the innovative ploy of disco: the musical pulse is freed from the claustrophobic interiors of the blues and the tight scaffolding of R&B and early soul music. A looser, explicitly polyrhythmic attack, pushes the blues, gospel and soul heritage into an apparently endless cycle where there is no beginning or end, just an ever-present 'now.' Disco music

does not come to a halt. It just fades out of hearing...The power of disco...lay in saturating dancers and the dance floor in the continual explosion of its presence.[4]

In disco, as with other forms of black music, the body was central to expressing the genre's aesthetic priorities. The character of the rhythms produced in funk, soul, and disco stretch the body along a continuum of grooves that give dance performance an especially erotic intensity. In fact, the rhythms of black music move the erotic action away from the crotch and redistribute it throughout the entire body.[5] Disco promoted a variety of eroticism that also centered two degraded entities: the gay body and the female voice. It was the gay body in performance to black rhythms fronted by female voices—of Donna Summers, Gloria Gaynor, Grace Jones, and Diana Ross—that gave disco a restorative energy that had political resonance way beyond the boundaries of music. To be sure, the voices of Aretha Franklin, Betty Wright, and Millie Jackson expressed a female sexuality and independence in the early seventies that was virtually absent in other branches of popular music. But the fusion of black rhythms, gay bodies, and female eroticism in disco provided a political lesson in the very existence of the combination. Plus, disco democratized the dance floor because it made the spectacle of performance the star.[6] On any given night, the distrusted, discarded, and devalued bodies of gay, female, poor and working class people could be highlighted under the swirl of lights in clubs, dance halls, and discotheques. And the corporal politics of disco were literally mediated through the percussive textures of the sounds emanating from booming systems that gave the body a visceral charge.

The political effects of disco weren't limited to gay and female cultures. In the post–civil rights era of the seventies—when black power had subsided, black nationalism had waned, black militancy had been killed off in so many police raids, and the upwardly mobile black middle classes had departed the inner city for suburbia—disco provided a web of informal connections between working and poor black peoples as they congregated in social spaces of recreation to reaffirm their humanity. With the rise of post-industrialism, the proliferation of informal underground economies, the spread of violent drug cultures and gangs, rampant inflation, the loss of jobs and shrinking social opportunities, black youth created a politics of recognition from the sonic fragments of black music, including disco, in much the same way they would with a subsequent development in urban music: hip-hop. Thus the assault on disco—which was often homophobic and misogynistic, at many levels racist, given that its major stars were female, black, and/or gay—was often an uninformed attempt to scold youth about their misplaced values or insufficient politics when the music became a means of sustaining hope. As Brian Ward writes:

> On its own Rhythm and Blues had never *made* mass political or social action possible, or even likely, in any direct or simple way. It had always navigated the territory between being a cultural expression of a black insurgency which was organized by other means and essentially shaped by other intellectual, political and socio-economic forces, and being a surrogate for such action. In the late 1970s, in the absence of a viable Movement dedicated to opening up meaningful eco-

nomic, social, political and educational opportunities for the black masses, music, dance and style once again became more of a surrogate, offering a vital cultural mechanism for personal expression and mental survival...The intense energy, creativity, and passion which many young inner-city blacks lavished on a disco phenomenon...reflected the need to escape, however temporarily, the grim realities and mounting frustrations of black urban life. In the process, these dancing...young blacks and their deejays appropriated disco and reinscribed it as a potent cultural, rather than simply a profitable commercial, phenomenon.[7]

None of what I've said denies the late seventies decline of disco into inferior forms of expression that, as with any genre, were often viewed as representative and then roundly attacked. At its best, the music featured neglected voices and bodies—as both performers in the recording booth and on the dance floor—that may have otherwise gone unnoticed. The forms of eroticism that disco unleashed insisted on the pleasure principle as the predicate for social cohesion and individual expression. The erotic often showed up in disco as hedonistic individualism; there was an unabashed sexual energy that was engaged where dance floors of throbbing bodies took on religious overtones of sanctified sensuality.

By the time Marvin Gaye made *I Want You* in 1976, early disco had made its mark; later, more standardized studio production of the genre did not yet rule, but its day was fast approaching. Enough, in fact, that Barry White's heterosexual boudoir bravado and elaborate orchestrations were viewed as of a piece with bohemian rhapsodies spawned in homoerotic fields of play. Not surprisingly, Gaye resisted disco, not because he didn't respect many of its artists, but because, as he said, Motown was demanding that he embrace the music, and he resisted.[8] Still, one suspects that Gaye's struggle against being in any way gay-identified—he did change his surname from Gay to Gaye—plus his male chauvinism, may have had something to do with his resistance to the music's homo-and-gynoeroticisms. But he could totally resist neither the genre, nor obviously, the hyper-eroticism he shared with its gay and female artists. Marvin argued that the erotically pulsating "Got to Give It Up" was his single concession to the form. But, as critic Martin Johnson argues, *I Want You* "straddles jazz funk and a restrained variant of disco."[9]

Other critics also spotted disco's influence on the album, though not in nearly as charitable a fashion. Although the album was a big commercial success—it sold over a million copies—it was panned by many critics. Their tenor is captured by Vince Aletti, who, writing in the *Rolling Stone*, views *I Want You* as a symptom of the schlock that was ruining soul. "With Barry White on the wane, Marvin Gaye seems determined to take over as soul's master philosopher in the bedroom, a position that requires little but an affectation of constant, rather jaded horniness."[10] Aletti's first line only sets him up to literally play Marvin's *Let's Get It On* against his latest erotic effort. "The pose has already been established in *Let's Get It On* (1973), on which Gaye was hot, tender, aggressive, soothing and casually raunchy—the modern lover with all his contradictions. *I Want You* continues in the same vein but with only the faintest traces of the robust passion that shot through and sustained the earlier album."[11] Aletti says of one song ("Feel All

My Love Inside") that the urgent lyrics are "undermined by the laid-back passivity of the vocals and a production (by Leon Ware) too pleasant, low-keyed and subtle for its own good. As pillow talk this is entirely too limp..."[12] Of one of the album's greatest performances, "Soon I'll Be Loving You," Aletti opines that "Gaye pleads and cajoles—'Baby please let me do it to you'—but too often he ends up sounding like a little boy whining for candy."[13] Aletti says that all of this might have been acceptable to a lesser artist than Gaye, "but after a landmark album like *What's Going On* one expects something with a little more substance and spirit," and that "there's no fire here, only a well-concealed pilot light."[14]

While Aletti was right about Gaye's earlier classics *Let's Get It On* and *What's Going On*—actually in his review of *What's Going On* he missed on a couple of singles and admitted that he was surprised that Gaye could produce such a work—he and many other critics missed the boat on *I Want You*. This "restrained variant of disco" with a jazz funk pedigree is a work of extraordinary accomplishment. Part of the explanation for Gaye's critical drubbing rests in response to the lush, symphonic sounds that bathe the album, and the dense harmonic backgrounds that show Gaye at his aural zenith, manipulating and multiplying his voice with a dexterity surprising even for him. His ambitious and fully realized orchestrations and percolating percussive textures—and yes, the background moaning and ubiquitous eroticism—seduced critics into believing that he had simply produced another mindless make-out album. Or, perhaps, disco without discretion. To be sure, its hormones were in high-gear, but the album is much more than a pit stop at adolescent horniness. *I Want You* is Gaye's classic work of his erotic era, on par with *What's Going On* as a superb example of existential utterance yoked to artistic genius. It is a concept album rooted in the vagaries of sensual pursuit, and yet its spiritual bona fides resonate as both the subtext and the sky of the erotic universe Gaye conjures.

As with his earlier classics, Gaye didn't generate the album alone. Perhaps more than any work Gaye produced, this album emerged from a creative symbiosis between two masters whose singular visions and soulful voices are even more remarkable looking back than when they first appeared. Marvin's partner for the album, his guiding light of sensual philosophy, was Leon Ware. Ware (and a couple of co-writers) wrote all of the songs on the album before he met Marvin; when Marvin transformed them through his erotic alchemy, he and Ware had produced a work of lasting beauty. *I Want You* is as much a product of Ware's ideas—and Art Stewart's brilliant engineering—as Gaye's romantic fury that swept them for a season into his libidinal and romantic orbit. Harry Weinger's archival curiosity on the deluxe edition of the album has clarified even more why this work stands as a classic of its kind.

I Want You is also unmistakably a work of romantic and erotic tribute to the woman he deeply loved and would marry shortly, Janis Hunter. Gaye's obsession with the woman barely out of her teens is nearly palpable in the sensual textures that are the album's aural and lyrical signature. Their relationship was relentlessly passionate and emotionally rough-hewn; they played up each other's strengths, and played off each other's weaknesses. The volatile mix started almost immediately. "Ed Townsend introduced us," Janis told a radio interviewer in 2002. "He was working on *Let's Get It On* with [Marvin]. And

he asked if I wanted to come down to the studio and listen.
And I said, 'Sure.' And my mother and I went down and sat on
this little couch. And Marvin was in the glass booth doing his
vocals. And he looked at me and I looked at him. And my
mother was, like, elbowing me in my ribs, like, 'Would you stop
looking at him like that. You're much too young and he's much
too old.'"[15] Janis later recalled that meeting Gaye was "the most
wonderful night of my whole life."[16] After his scorching performance that night on "Let's Get It On," it didn't take long for
Gaye, separated from his wife Anna, to establish a relationship
with Janis. "[T]he first time he and I had a chance to be alone
together," Janis told a journalist in 1994, "I was absolutely
scared to death. I was only 17 years old, and he was 33. There I
was with this superstar singer who was paying attention to me
and I was like, 'Oh boy, what am I gonna do? I hope I don't
have pepper stuck in my teeth, I hope I'm not drooling'—I was
a nervous wreck. I mean to me, Marvin was just an absolutely
gorgeous man. Marvin's one of the most classically chiseled
men to walk the face of the Earth. He was just incredible."[17]
Janis's father was Slim Gaillard, a noted black jazz entertainer.
However, she was reared alone by her white mother Barbara in
Los Angeles.

After they began seeing each other, Marvin retreated with
Jan to Topanga Canyon, not yet ready to show his newest love
to the world. "He went to the desert not long after that," Janis
said in a radio interview. "He said he needed time to himself, to
think about things, because he was still married to Anna at the
time. And he was trying to work that out with her. And when
he came back from the desert, we started seeing each other and
that was it. I moved in with him, and it went on from there.

Didn't make my mother very happy; four months after I met him I was pregnant and still in high school. It just wasn't what she had seen for me."[18] Jan had a miscarriage, but not long after that, she got pregnant with Nona Aisha Gaye, who was born in September of 1974. A year later, in November, Janis gave birth to their second child, Frankie Christian "Bubby" Gaye, who was born a day after the uncle for whom he was named. After Gaye's divorce from Anna in 1977, and with pressure from Janis, he married her in October of 1977. It wouldn't be long before he and Janis were headed for divorce as well. "We got married in New Orleans," Janis told a reporter in 1994. "We had planned to wait until we got back to L.A., but we both loved the city of New Orleans. We have good friends who live there, Andy and Laura Brown, so we got married at their home."[19]

In a 2000 documentary on Marvin, Janis described the rather unromantic circumstances in which they were married. "Around the time that he and I decided to get married—it doesn't sound very romantic—but there were some tax problems. And his manager had decided that if we got married, that it would help to alleviate some of his problems. So he came to me with this idea; we talked about signing prenuptials. I said, 'It doesn't sound very romantic. It sounds like we're dooming the marriage before we even get started. I don't want to get married under those circumstances.' And he pretty much left the concept of the prenuptials alone. We got married...this is after having been together for four years...our children were at the wedding. And like I said, it really wasn't as romantic as a person would like to think their wedding would be. We spent our honeymoon with his extended family: his manager, a few of his musicians, my children. Just wasn't what my idea of a honey-moon would be. But it was a commitment that we had to each other."[20]

After Marvin and Janis were married, their relationship quickly deteriorated. Already suffering the pressures of their lifestyle—plenty of drugs, the attempt at an "open" relationship full of affairs on both sides that led to bitter recriminations and mutual jealousies, Marvin's suicidal bouts—their marriage couldn't save their relationship. Marvin and Jan would sepa-rate, then divorce, and attempt numerous reconciliations over most of his remaining years, sometimes on foreign soil during Marvin's 3-year exile from the States. They made each other outrageously happy and insanely angry, often at the same time. As Janis said, she went "back and forth across the ocean, around and around the planet, just chasing this relationship that never worked. But I was never willing to give up and nei-ther was he."[21]

One of the most beautiful and enduring artistic monuments to their relationship is preserved in *I Want You*. Along with *Trouble Man*, this was Gaye's favorite album.[22] And it was the first album that Gaye completed in his "Marvin Gaye Recording Studio," which he had built in 1975 in the heart of Hollywood. *I Want You* is an album stitched together by the conceptual thread of romantic pursuit. It hangs together on a marvelous erotic conceit: that romance is the core of sensual truth, its surest revelation, and that sex is merely the commerce of a higher spiritual economy. "It's an opera about a relation-ship," says Gary Harris, a prominent music business executive. "Love found, desire, desperation, the absolute 'I got to have her.' He meets her, gets her, loses her, sees her at the party and tries to get back with her. It's all interwoven in this dramatic way." The opening song, "I Want You," states the album's thesis: desire built on sustaining mutuality. The capacious feel of the tune is evoked by the lush orchestration of its individual elements—congas, horn ostinatos, descending stinging guitars, thumping bass, and the luxurious interplay of Marvin's angelic and earthy vocals. The song is aural foreplay, the dance of seduction—and by its mellow, fusion jazz disco beat, that's quite literally the case. Marvin foreshadows in the structure of the song its function: the more-than-a-minute long lead-in is a gesture of sonic foreplay. The introductory build-up climaxes in Marvin's declaration—breathtaking for the swiftness with which it pleads its case—that "I want you the right way I want you, but I want you to want me too." That's the song and album in a nutshell: to love, and give love in return. Marvin's desire floats through the song as nimbly as his vocals tear at the gently swaying wall of sound. But if he has phrased his desire in sensual terms, his bottom line is an old-fashioned commitment: "Don't play with something you should cherish for life." But our romantic hero must overcome resistance, since he acknowledges that "you don't want me now, but I'm going to change your mind, someway, somehow."

The wooing continues on "Come Live With Me, Angel," as Marvin baldly declares his wish: "I wanna be your lover." Marvin assures his lover a pleasing return on her erotic investment: "Three times a day in all the ways, baby." Throughout the album, Marvin is emphatic about the cherished light in which he views his lover: she is called "angel," and "precious," monikers for the sweetly devoted. The music is relaxed and airy, a muted trumpet signifying his desire and matching Marvin's mood and pace. This is a mature man promising his young lover—Jan, literally—that they will be "locked up for days." And wisps of female moaning feather the serpentine groove. "After the Dance (Instrumental)" foreshadows the love to come, after the love has been won and lost and won again. It's almost as if it's an assurance to Marvin that things will turn out all right. It's a musical down payment on love that makes sure it'll stick around long enough, as the old spiritual says, "to see what the end is gonna be." Its tones rise from a Moog synthesizer played by Marvin with verve and sounds bordering on the timbres of the human voice, as a flute provides melodic counterpoint. "Feel All My Love Inside" is an impossibly sensuous document. Even before the song truly begins, Marvin declares, "Let's get naked." The song is an ethnography of lovemaking, as Marvin starts in process, announcing, matter of factly, "Now we're making love." After repeating his opening line three times, he asks his lover, "Where'd you get such sweet sugar?" Marvin is so hot on the song that it climaxes several times, usually capped by descriptions of "stroking" and "kissing," as he confesses that "I love to hear you make those sounds." Marvin passes judgment on his lover, and finds her "the best in the world." At the end, as a spare bass slinks through the soundscape, Gaye pleads, "Live with me, baby, in luxury." He's already tied his erotic desire to fidelity: "cause I want you baby, for my wife."

"I Wanna Be Where You Are" is one of the most exquisite touches to the album: Marvin wishing his children and wife goodnight. Bright, punching horns frame his farewell—which was not noted on the original LP and closed out side one. It's a vamp on the Leon Ware tune originally sung by Michael

Jackson. Michael's interpretation was high octane and furiously declarative, while Marvin's is much more subtle and rides a syncopated shuffle for little more than a minute. Marvin's style here and throughout reflects Leon Ware's influence. "Leon had this kind of dispassionate California cool," says Gary Harris. "It was a California soul thing that was going on. It wasn't about shouting. It wasn't about the filed holler. It was really more urbanized. Every time I hear a Leon Ware record, more often than not I think I'm in a pool hall somewhere." Marvin unveils the familial context of his erotic ambitions. For all his discourses on free love in other places, here Marvin exults in the ties that bind. After a twenty second blast of the instrumental version of "I Want You (Intro Jam)"—it's both a reprise of the first song, and a foreshadowing of a longer song to come, but in any case, it's a brief reminder to his beloved that he's taken three shots to tell her he wants her—Marvin forgives his unfaithful lover who's flown the coop because, even though she's "promiscuous," she's still "the best lay in bed." On the song, Gaye gives the blues a shot in the arm and transmutes the "she done me wrong" convention into a defiantly joyful embrace of his spurning lover. The memory of her love is so strong that it erases all complaint and persuades Gaye that he must be indirectly responsible, as he declares her "bad, but I must like you like that." All the while, his chorus of voices deliciously sprinkles his glee at her return and finger snaps and percussive rhythms keep his mood upbeat and hopeful.

"Since I Had You" is the story of two former lovers who meet by chance at the neighborhood dance. Marvin rises to the top of his tender, yearning falsetto to plead to his ex to rekindle their romance. Since we are still friends, Gaye argues, let's make love again. Obviously of critical importance to his persistent love is that they've remained friendly, implying that friendship is the basis for true and lasting romantic connection. Marvin also confesses that "since I had you, honey, there hasn't been, no other woman." Her love was so completely unrepeatable that it sent him into celibacy in her absence. Here, and throughout the album, Marvin shows his remarkable vulnerability by saying things most men are loathe to admit. The ballad puts us in its hold precisely because Marvin is in her hold, and his telling of it only strengthens his artistic grip on us. His doo-wop chops hit hard in the background and the composition's busy crosscutting of strings and horns bestow a dramatic affect.[23]

On "Soon I'll Be Loving You Again," Marvin's vocal layers are ethereal as they constitute a poignant rhythmic backdrop to his dream of his lover's presence. "I played D'Angelo that record," says Gary Harris, who was the A&R man who helped the singer with his groundbreaking *Brown Sugar*. (By his own admission, Harris had *I Want You* in mind as he helped the young singer craft his first album). "With the opening, with the congas and the strings: it's like the sun is rising. It's a very cinematic approach to the whole thing. It shows a thing Quincy Jones called 'ear candy.' The voicings and the arrangements convey not only mood but probably time, place and image. He's talking about 'dreamed of you this morning.' It's crazy. The other thing about Marvin and the song is he always, no matter what he was doing, how many risks he would take, he was a radical traditionalist and always held onto his doo-wop upbringing. Those background harmonies, no matter what he did, no matter how increasingly percussive he got, how funky, the background vocals were always steeped in that tradition." On the song, Marvin realizes that when dawn came, his dream of his lover's presence was just that. He claims the strong need to "love you everywhere," saying he's never done it before, but "there's always a first time, you know."

For the third time, the opening theme reappears, this time as "I Want You (Intro Jam)," a gentle but insistent reinforcement of the essential unity of Marvin's purpose and the rearticulation of his conceptual rigor. It sets up the gloriously funk-jazzy "After The Dance," where one of Marvin's first asides is spoken in a low rumble, "What a freak." The song's undulating rhythms snuggle up to Marvin's soft confession of his desire, which bleeds through his pure and self-contained falsetto. "What she needs is me," he says confidently, although his lyrics at the end aren't nearly so conclusive, since he asks, "Why don't we get together after the dance?"

"*I Want You* is one of my favorite records, one of the top three records that I've ever heard," says Gary Harris. "It's just so pure. And it combined that working class sensibility, that street edge, eroticism, romance, the whole idea of spirituality at the highest level and the struggle between those two poles, a sense of community, a sense of family, a ballad and an ode to his children. I mean, in many ways Marvin Gaye embodied most of what you'd want to be as a black man, in terms of various ways to express love toward family, community, women, art, the moment. The whole idea about he meets this girl at Big Daddy Rucker's, [which he mentions on 'Since I Had You'] and it's the sense of a fish fry, and that's a tradition you can go anywhere in the United States on Friday night and that's going to be the down spot."

Leon Ware's voice and vision are crucial to Gaye's achievement on *I Want You*. I visited Ware in his Marina Del Rey apartment in California not so much to get the lowdown on the making of the album as to probe the philosophy of sensuality he has refined over the last 30 years—and which came to fine fruition on *I Want You*. Ware was a gifted and prolific song-writer who wrote classic tunes like "If I Ever Lose This Heaven," (later covered by the Average White Band), which he sang with Minnie Ripperton on Quincy Jones's 1974 album *Body Heat*. Ware also co-wrote much of Minnie Ripperton's superb 1974 LP *Adventures in Paradise*. His own *Musical Massage* was released in 1976, though it never received the support it deserved from Motown, where Ware recorded the album and had served as a Jobete staff writer. That album, re-released in 2003, is now judged a soul classic.

Ware is a not-quite-short, tightly muscled dark brown fount of wisdom—consider him, at age 63, a chocolate Yoda. He sat in his reclining chair, and I copped a spot on a backless seat in front of him to hear that gentle voice—much like Marvin's—reiterate his worldview. Speaking to him is like catching a thinker *in medias res*, the conversation already informed by webs of connection to other ideas that bubble up almost in random fashion—except they illumine their subject in cumulative spurts.

"I'm known for my music and my talents, but now, at this point in my life, I have such a serious message for the world that me and Marvin delivered, from *I Want You* to "Sexual Healing," Ware says. "A few months ago, when I was in London, I got onstage and said, 'You can consider me your sensual minister.' A year before that, in a place called the Jazz Café, a gentleman who works for *Blues and Soul* magazine remarked, 'Almost 30 years ago, you thought sex should be a religion.' And I said, 'Yes, and I still not only feel that way, I now understand what I was saying.' Now I realize—with Marvin and myself, Barry White, Luther [Vandross], James Ingram, Jeffrey Osborne—that all of us are ministers of love. Soldiers of love that are sending messages to the hearts that listen. Me being a male, I want it to go to the women, but it's also for the men, so they can send a message to their women. The beauty in it is that now I can validate every innuendo, every sigh, everything that I ever put on a record. And I know that it was my ministry that I was emitting to the community, the world that I live in. It was a very honorable emission, and a very honorable place for me to come from."

Ware obviously understands that there has been huge criticism of the erotic tendencies in black music, and that he and his comrades suffer the charge of hypersexualism. In its extremes, their "art" is viewed as what one writer termed "pornoglossia"—the verbal equivalent of pornography.[24] But his message is not simply about sex. In his mind he is embracing the mysterious origins of humanity. Ware leans back and closes his eyes as if imagining the mysterious source of human existence, as if he had formed its vast, shapeless energy in his sensuous imagination.

"Now you would've thought that out of all of the 'isms' we have embraced since we've been on this planet—from Buddhism, Catholicism, and the rest—that sensualism would have been the first."

He smiles wryly, poking rhetorical fun at the philosophies and religions that have prevailed while taking satisfaction in his discovery of their source. He argues that his philosophy doesn't take its subscribers to an external deity—say God or Buddha—but to the internal source of creation in love, which finds it potent origins in the sexual act. Without making love, there is no possibility for love to be known. Our ignorance about our species shows up in a nefarious manner, especially in the bigoted ways we refuse love's presence in whatever ethnic or racial form it comes to us. Just as Ware insists that there's but one race, the human race—clichéd, to be sure, but still somehow compelling when it falls from Ware's lips—his attractive Italian wife Carol pops in to ask if I want some tea. "Yes, ma'am, that would be nice," I reply. After I grab hold of my glass, Ware picks back up without missing a beat.

"We have different cultures, white, Asian, whatever. There's only one race—mankind and womankind. I don't consider myself brilliant. I'm just reminding people that this"—meaning the sensuous, sexual spaces that spawn human existence—"is where we come from. As you get on your knees to pray to God, remember, if you really want to embrace your origins, it's sex."

As if that weren't a bad enough bashing, though pleasantly delivered, of religious sentiments that hold out for higher purpose to genitalia, Ware waylays the assumption even more. He suggests getting on one's knees at night and praying to every erotic attitude one might conjure. Ware looks at me, perhaps remembering I'm also a Baptist preacher, and retorts, "I'm having fun with this." Then he stares me down to let me know that, despite the humor of his approach, he's dead serious. He is in no way opposed to religions, which he sees as cultural systems of organized thought that attempt to express the values of its advocates. As such, they should all be respected. But Ware is skeptical of the claims of exclusivity that each proffers. Only the profoundly insecure have to wage war to defend their religious beliefs. Likewise, he thinks the same insecurity haunts heterosexual men who are unnerved by gay men. For Ware, the bottom line is mutual respect and a sense of love that flows from our sensual recognition of the other.

"Every man that wakes up in the morning wakes up to magnify the other. The whole purpose for being here is to magnify your best qualities, to see all the rich possibilities you have in your space. We have not come close to that on this planet. We have not had many leaders that looked at power as being what power really is: not oppression, but power is what the sun does—makes everything grow, gives oxygen, breathes life. From Martin Luther King, Jr., to Mahatma Gandhi, the leaders who wanted to see us do what we're supposed to do for each other have been eliminated."

Ware's philosophy is certainly humane, but I ask him how one can translate the philosophy of sensualism into principles to guide the behavior of young people. He claims that he freely tells his five-year-old granddaughter that his religion is sensualism, which he defines as the love of the spirit of sex, romance and eroticism. To underscore his point, Ware leans over to me and repeats it softly but emphatically.

"The *spirit* of it, not just the touch. It's going to be a humongous challenge to make this message really clear, because there's such a massive misunderstanding of what sex is. We've been taught to look away, that it's naughty, and not a place where you get on your knees and seriously pray."

Of course, that brought me to Marvin Gaye, who seemed to struggle with the tensions between sensuality and spirituality in a way that don't exist for Ware because of his religious neutral-

ity—except, that is, the religion of sensuality. How did he and
Marvin get along given their varying approaches, at least philosophically, to the issue of spirit, body, and sex.

"When we did *I Want You*, that was the ground, it was the
nucleus, of what I'm doing now. I am now seeing all the things
that me and Marvin got together. It was the most uncanny relationship, because we could look at each other at times and say,
'goddamned.' It's like we knew that telepathy was real. Some
people don't believe it, but it is real. We just have not tapped
into that at this point in our development as a species. There
will be a time when we can talk to each other and we won't
have to open our mouths at all. In fact, we won't even have to
see each other. We will be able to dial each other and just like
that, we'll be able to talk to that person just the way we're talking to each other right now."

The real sadness of such a prospect, I suppose, is that we
won't need music any more either. Then again, music functions
as a kind of moral and spiritual telepathy of sorts right now: it
beams to human beings forms of understanding and commun-
ion beyond the obstructions of language and identity. The trite,
clichéd way of thinking of this is to say that music is a universal
language, but given Ware's futuristic philosophizing, perhaps
that's not as sentimental or far off as it sounds. But that would
imply that sensuality is deeper than the flesh, that it transcends
the very ground of its existence. Wouldn't that mean that sensuality might therefore be an outmoded philosophy for such a
forward looking thinker like Ware? He contends that his ministry is all about the *spirit*. He illustrates his point by presenting
a scenario of two couples who go into separate rooms. One couple is going in to have sex. The other couple is going in to make

love. The couple having sex may stay in for an hour, an hour and a half, then they come out. The couple making love may come out the next day, Ware says, but they're still not finished. For him, love is a dynamic expression of erotic attachment that attempts to divine the spirit of the other. I press Ware on whether one can truly consider sensuality a religion, and if the traditionally religious can attend his church of the erotically spiritual.

"I've been saying for 30 years that sex *should* be a religion. Now I know it *is* a religion. It's not *should be*, it's *has been*. It's a religion we've overlooked. All religions can embrace where I'm coming from. My problem with most religions is that each one of them says they're the right one. I need you to reassess what you're calling 'the one.' I want a church. I don't want to be looked *up* to. I want to be looked *in* to. See, I have a problem with folk who stop growing and think that time resolves everything. Does time resolve? Isn't time continuously moving on? So how dare you think that you're a stronger force, or that your collection of information allows you to resolve anything. I have a problem with folk and their fixations. I understand the input of information can be so strong that they feel so good about it. I'm not resolved. All I can say is this is where I'm at now. I'm in love with the fact that my voice, my attitude, my reason for taking the next breath will be another seed planted in the course of the adventure as far as life is concerned."

Now I believe I've got a much better handle on the philosophical backdrop of *I Want You*, and the keen intelligences and sharp gifts that formed its lyrical web. I end our conversation by asking him about what made him and Marvin click well enough to produce a contemporary classic.

"My relationship with Marvin was special in the sense that we knew of each other before we met each other. I was a successful songwriter, he was a successful artist. And when we met each other, we had heard several times that we talk alike. We had a vocal sound that's very similar. And when we got together Marvin looked at me and said, 'goddamned, you're playing the same chords I'm playing.' Marvin was so gentle on one side and so sincerely sensitive on another. And then there was another Marvin that didn't let go of anything. He was like me. We're sponges. Everything that passes through our space goes in. That's when I realized how important sunshine is, that people can smile even though they're in pain. This surface psychological input is very important for our depth. But our meeting confirmed to me that when two talented people get together, they're supposed to be concerned about the message and the feeling that they're getting ready to emit to the world. I met Marvin through circumstances that proved we were supposed to work together. The rest is history."

I turned to Harry Weinger to explain just how Marvin went about making his masterpiece.

"*I Want You* is Marvin's many voices, and that's where he really developed that ability to overdub on himself in all the different harmonies," Weinger tells me. "It's just extraordinary. There are four, five, maybe six voices and they're all Marvin. Before trying to figure out what the story of *I Want You* is beyond what we know, let's start with what we know. It's about Jan. We know it was going to be a record for T-Boy Ross [Diana Ross's brother], and Leon had produced it, but Berry heard it and said, 'It's for Marvin.' And Marvin wanted the rest of the sessions. We know those stories."

Leon Ware said that Marvin had invited him to his home to work on the tracks, but when he heard the material Leon had for his own album, Gaye told him if he'd give him those songs, he could produce Marvin's entire album. Weinger says that *I Want You* captures the breadth of Marvin's experimentation with his many voices. It is not simply the way he articulates the words, but the manner in which he layers the vocals to essentially talk to himself. Each one represents not simply a harmonic register, but a distinct personality brought vibrantly alive through his sensuous expression. He proposes that we listen to an example. Weinger turns to his compact disc player and cues up the extra disc of material on the deluxe edition, which contains different versions of the seven full songs from the original album. He plays a version of "I Want You," which was the album's lead single in 1976. The song has been stripped of most backing instrumental tracks—except percussion and bass—so that one can hear Marvin's many voices in their multi-tracked strength. His cascading background harmonies dart in and out, while Marvin's lead vocals are doubled, sometimes tripled, playing off of one another. The track illustrates the merger of Marvin's voices into a smoldering soul Gregorian chant, as he subtly limns his ardor and passion for his beloved. "I want you baby, can't you see I need you, baby," Marvin gently pleads. The words now resound in pristine clarity as Marvin's every syllable is caressed and massaged by his supple technique—and by the omniscient wall of sound his voice has created.

Weinger says that since there weren't many outtakes for *I Want You*—unlike the cache for *Let's Get It On*—he focused on the vocal style, technique and process of creation. "So to create something different, again, I felt, well let's just go back to the voices," Weinger says. "And of course, the core of all that is the rhythm and the heartbeat, so I have to have the rhythm and the voices, not just a cappella. Of course, you hear Marvin always cranked the headphones really loud. Every time you hear an overdub, and isolate Marvin, it's as if the band is playing in the room because his headphones are so loud. Some of the doubling voices on the *Let's Get It On* album, we discovered when we went back and listened to tapes, were actually himself and his headphones."

"So he's singing along with himself?" I ask.

"Yes. So he's got it cranked. He's got a previous overdub but his headphones are leaking through to the microphone where he's recording the current overdub. I call it a cappella but there's a little bit of instrumentation."

Weinger says that there are loads of tapes of Marvin doing overdubs on top of overdubs, and then combining tracks. Before the tracks were combined, Weinger found a series of vocal masters of it to show his work in progress, hence the first selection on the second disc of the deluxe edition we've just listened to. I ask him if Marvin had recorded the vocals alone, before the tracks were added. He hadn't. The tracks were done six months before. Then Marvin began the layering process. Weinger insists that the psychology behind that process is something not easily fathomed. There are a few artists who are superb in the art of vocal layering: Al Green and the Beach Boys—especially Brian Wilson. By the time he did *I Want You*, Marvin had mastered the technique. It's all the more remarkable when one realizes that Gaye didn't have forty-eight digital tracks to work with. He had had sixteen tracks. He would have to copy mix over to other tapes. When Marvin had an idea, his engineers would bring the microphone over on top of the board. The track we listened to is a reflection of the original tape where he overdubbed six vocals. Hence, they were laid out in similar fashion on the deluxe edition. When they're mixed into the record over the two-track, the harmonies are combined on one side, and then the process is duplicated for the other side. Then they are blended. On the track we listened to, Marvin created the blend. On the deluxe edition CD we have the opportunity to hear a forty second version of the different pieces, separately, before they were later combined by Marvin.

Instead of turning again to David Van DePitte, Leon and Marvin teamed with Coleridge Taylor Perkinson to write the string and horn charts. Ware took care of the rhythms. Perkinson was a classically trained composer who weaved between jazz, ballet and film work as well. He scored the soundtrack of the 1974 film *The Education of Sonny Carson*, for which Ware sang several songs.

"Coleridge never met Marvin," Weinger says. "So nobody told him what to do. He says, 'I didn't even know where the rhythm tracks were going to go, so I just gave him everything. I figured they would mix in and out what they wanted.' So in 'After the Dance' Art Stewart has the horns and strings all mixed. And Marvin says, 'Your notes are clashing. I don't like what I hear.' The record's ready to go to master. Berry Gordy needs the album. So a week before the record ships, they get Cal Harris [another engineer] to get the moog from Motown, then roll it down the street to Marvin's studio, and Marvin played these lines over the two-track. He overdubbed the two-track and made another master, and that got cut into the record. So then, what I was able to do was I went back to where, yes indeed, strings and horns clash."

"Was Marvin right? What was wrong, and were you able to fix it?" I ask.

"Well, there's this Ernie Watts flute solo throughout the whole thing that's beautiful. Because, according to the dates, Marvin called Ernie in to record some solos. And Ernie, I guess, had as much direction as Coleridge, which was, 'Play everything.' So he solos [on] the whole track. We go to do orchestration, going to the mix, and I was sitting there and the engineer says to me, 'It doesn't work, it doesn't work.' We know Marvin is right, but now maybe, with digital technology we can make it work."

Art Stewart filled me in on just how this happened, suggesting that it shows again Gaye's genius. When they had finished the album, Marvin wanted to pay homage to his children. So he took the Leon Ware written tune, "I Wanna Be Where You Are" and used that to end one side of the album. When they finished recording it, Marvin noticed that on the instrumental version of "After the Dance," the strings and horns were out of tune in a particular passage. Though perhaps hardly noticeable to anyone else, it bugged him. Even though the album was finished, Marvin insisted he had to go back and get it right. Art Stewart tried to convince Marvin that it couldn't get any better, and that they had exhausted all means of creativity. But Gaye wouldn't budge, and asked Stewart how they could fix it. Stewart thought for a moment, then suggested that they call Calvin Harris, a Motown engineer, who had a Moog synthesizer, which could be programmed to make almost any sound one desired. They asked Harris to bring his Moog to Marvin's studio. Given Marvin's extraordinary keyboard talent, he kept experimenting with the instrument in order to fix the song. Stewart played the track back and let Marvin listen to it. Marvin located the notes and quickly played over the clashing passage that annoyed him.

"He played [the Moog] sort of like a lead instrument," Stewart says. "When you think about it—I remember now— the track is spinning and he's playing along with it, whatever he felt. The guy's playing, it's his song, he knows it, he's lived with it, so he plays around with it. It didn't take him long to get it down. Because all he wanted to do, really, was to cover up one spot. But he ended up playing a solo on top of it, which worked well. He gave it another flavor and he liked that too. He got double treasure: He added another instrument, *he's* playing it, and he cleaned up this spot."

I ask Weinger for a specific example of what his investigation turned up that sheds new light on how Gaye shaped his themes and crafted his art in collaboration with another songwriter like Leon.

"You know, this is a situation where you're playing the tape, you're trying to find an extension of 'I Wanna Be Where You Are,'" Weinger replies, in reference to the brief one-minute but melodic good-night that Marvin sings to his wife and children. "You find it. Okay, he says good-night to Nona and Frankie, reaffirms his love for Janis, and repeats [Weinger leans over to me and sings it] 'Jan-is,' in that really evocative way that he says her name. And then the track just jams. So to use it smartly, he uses that piece of it. It's not even indexed. It wasn't until the CD era that the track is noted on the back of the record. The back of the record doesn't say 'I Wanna Be Where You Are.' It's just a good-night on that side. So you begin the investigation. You're playing all the tracks, and you go, 'Wait, that's his vocal on track 11. He's singing 'After the dance we're going to do something instrumental.' Is that a little play on words? Because 'After the Dance' is on the album twice—[as a] vocal and instrumental. 'After the dance we're going to do something instrumental.' What does he mean? But of course it was recorded way before, and he's just playing with words and ideas. He says, 'I will kiss all your secret places.' So he's warming up to all these ideas. What is he saying? I'm going to give you head, and all these things that brothers aren't supposed to....you know, that's the forbidden zone. That you're a 'faggot' if you do this. So he really broke that barrier by talking about it. That chant, 'I'm gonna give you head. I'm scared to do it, I woke up, and should I do it, I gotta taste you.' So I feel he's trying out this concept."

Weinger has solved one of the enduring mysteries on the *I Want You* album: what is Marvin Gaye singing on the background vocals to the song, "Soon I'll Be Loving You Again"? It turns out to be "I'm gonna give you some head." Through his investigations, he has also linked Marvin's extended work on "I Wanna Be Where You Are"—an interlude that ended side-one of the LP, but which Weinger has now discovered existed as a full-fledged song—to yet a third version: a song that uses the same music track, but which supplies different words. This is the track that is entitled "After The Dance (Vocal): Extended alternate mix," included on the deluxe edition's second disc. On the original LP, as Weinger points out, Gaye included a vocal and instrumental version of "After the Dance." Weinger has unearthed a completely different take, one that uses the music of "I Wanna Be Where You Are" but which is not the same as even the extended version of the song included on the deluxe edition. It is that new song where Marvin is trying out the ideas he would adopt on the original LP that Weinger finds barrier shattering: the concept that a black man would admit to performing oral sex.

When I talked to Art Stewart, he tells me that the decision to obscure Marvin's background chant was deliberate—a decision that reflected Stewart's values, a decision with which Marvin cooperated. In fact, Stewart is upset by the decision to clarify Marvin's erotic desire.

"They called me," Stewart says. "I talked to them. I said, 'Harry, don't put out all of this.' When Marvin sang that, I said to him, 'Marvin, you can't do it like this.' I said, 'Harry, have you ever noticed that most folks do not know that those lyrics are in there if you don't put your headphones on? You've got to do a special thing to really hear that. Coming over the speakers, you don't hear it. And it was done that way on purpose.'"

Now I knew why I could hardly hear what Marvin was saying in the background to "Soon I'll Be Loving You" all these years, even as I strained to listen time and again since 1976—first to the LP, then the cassette, and then multiple copies of the originally released CD. There was deliberate sonic ambiguity, a will to muffle in the mix.

"I said, 'If you stumble across it, it's a treat,'" Stewart contines, spelling out how his religious beliefs informed his engineering duties. "You have to have headphones on, a good pair. You have to hear it with clarity. Then you'll go, 'Wow, Marv, baby!' Well, that was done by design."

"You think they're removing the mystery of it?" I ask Stewart.

"Now you put it in print," he says. "I said, 'You guys are killing the guy over again.' Why expose that? Look how long this record's been out. Those who know it enjoy it. Those who find it, enjoy it. You don't hear a lot of talk about that because it's something that people treasure. You say, 'Oh, man, that was a nice little nugget you stuck in there.'"

Since Stewart wasn't a producer on Marvin's album, but the engineer, I ask him how it came about that he could exert his moral influence over the proceedings, especially with two such committed sensualists as Marvin and Leon.

"When Marvin did the 'I want to give you some head' thing, I said, 'We can't leave that stuff in here.' That was my idea to bury it."

"And Marvin went along?"

"Only because I was given license to do that. If you're not given license, you can't take any. You're an engineer, you're not the producer, you're not the writer. It's like, 'What are you talking about?' You wanna get thrown off a project, start putting your moral values up! You gotta pick and choose a battleground. You gotta know when to convince them to do a thing, and you gotta know how to approach a thing to get a person to understand why you wouldn't do it. You can't just say, 'Man, I wouldn't do that.'"

"So when you explained your values to Marvin, that's when the decision was made to bury it?"

"That's exactly right."

"And he could resonate with that because he came out of the same religious tradition?"

"Yes. And see, I liked the idea [of burying it]. I said to Marvin, 'This is something personal you've written for Jan, right? So, now, why put it all out there? Why not let them find the nugget? See, if you're paying attention you'll hear. If you're not into the groove you won't hear.'"

I confessed to Stewart my nearly obsessive hunt for the meaning of Marvin's backgrounds as I've listened for years, and even scoured the Internet for help. I guess my headphones were never of sufficient quality to deconstruct Gaye's erotic irreverence—at least for a black man.

"But, see, that was all by design," Stewart consoles me. "All because of the rapport that I had with the man. He was a genius, but the influence that I had with him gave me the opportunity to say I would or would not do a thing. He would ask. And if you ask, I'll tell you. You want to know my feelings I will tell you how I feel. Now, what you do with that is up to you. I don't have say-so over these kinds of things, other than the fact that you agreed: 'I accept that; let's do it like that.'"

Harry Weinger says he faced views not unlike those of Stewart's as he worked on the deluxe edition.

"I had a female engineer on this," Weinger chuckles. "And I said, 'We're going to listen to this for a while.' She had a similar reaction to Art Stewart, who tried to obscure the mix. She tried to do the same thing. She said, 'It doesn't work.' Thirty years later we have the same feeling—it doesn't work. But I think we brought it up a little to make Leon's point. That was the mantra of the studio. They even had a sign printed up that said, 'Head,' so that would be on their minds all the time."

Weinger discusses another interesting find: the lovely, lilting, "Is Anybody Thinking About Their Living?"—one of two instrumental tracks written by T-Boy Ross and Leon Ware included here that did not appear in some form on the original

LP. Near the middle of the tune—an obvious take that wouldn't be used—Marvin gently utters his vision for the song's possible use on the album. As generous streams of piano, bass, percussion, guitars and vibes wash through the track's mellow smooth jazz groove, Marvin's voice rises above the mix, "You know I hear this goin' out—of the album...to the B-side...this is a strange thing, let me see what happens." And then, as if primed by the music's infectious rhythm, Marvin swirls to the mic and begins a toast of sorts. "Yo mama said if you didn't understand it, you could take your time to try and get it right/Now baby dance, step a little closer, you've got the feelin, so baby let it move ya." Measuring his speech in deliberate rhythm, Marvin paces his lighthearted toast in a fashion that reflected his visit to Jamaica the year before, in January 1973, where he performed in a benefit concert in Kingston for the Boys Club of Trenchtown, also featuring Bob Marley, whom Gaye says he didn't meet that night.[25] In a way, Gaye's performance on the track captures the transatlantic exchange of black ideas and identities, foreshadowing the Caribbean influence on rap music in the United States in the immediate future.

As for Gaye's own future after *I Want You*, it was an uneven path, artistically, commercially, and personally.

"*I Want You* begins a period for Marvin that's kind of the beginning of the end," says Gary Harris. "It's kind of like five years later he's going to be living in exile in Europe. He's going to put out his last great hit with Motown with 'Got to Give It Up,' on the next record, *Live at the London Palladium*. He ultimately goes through a divorce with Berry's sister, Anna. He has to put out, 'Ego Tripping Out' after *Here, My Dear*. And then that's the whole stage where Larkin Arnold from CBS Records will come in and bring him back from Belgium, and he'll put out 'Sexual Healing.' That's like an eight-year period. But people are somewhat confused about what he's trying to do, because he moves into a deeper artistic thing, and really at that point, he makes records with no true commercial consideration. And his best two records were made at that time: *I Want You* and *Here, My Dear*."

Gaye divorced Anna in 1977, and a little while later, he divorced Janis as well. When his personal problems began to catch up to him—alimony, child support, back taxes, and especially his drug addiction—he hightailed in 1979 to Hawaii for several months, living on a beach in a bread truck, part of the time with his son. He moved from there to London, touring and still doing drugs while attempting to reconcile with Jan. When London proved a drain, he was rescued by Belgian businessman Freddy Cousaert, who got Marvin back on his feet, and tried as best he could to head off the hangers on and drug crowds that threatened to help Marvin take himself under. It was while he was in Belgium that Gaye produced the last big hit of his career, 1983's "Sexual Healing." But his success was his downfall. After he left Belgium and headed to America to tend to his sick mother and to celebrate his latest success, neither Marvin nor the world had any idea that he would be drug down into self-destructive paranoia from extreme cocaine addiction, and that he would die at the hands of the man he called Father.

CHAPTER SIX

"Father, Father, Father We Don't Need to Escalate"

Afroedipalism, Corporal Punishment, and the Politics of Self-Destruction

"He opens the door and he's wearing white terrycloth boxer shorts and a white terrycloth robe, with matching white coke rings around his nose," says Rona Elliot of her interview with Marvin Gaye. It took place in his Waldorf-Astoria hotel room before his famed sold-out 1983 week-long run at New York's Radio City Music Hall.

Marvin claimed by then to have been doing coke for nearly a quarter century.[1] That's probably an exaggeration. But he had been doing marijuana for that long, ever since he hit the road with the Moonglows, with cocaine most likely following a few years later. In 1972, Marvin gave *Rolling Stone* a thumbnail sketch of his drug history. "I've been open to grass since I was a kid," Gaye said. "I've also been open to alcohol, cigarettes, uppers and downers, heroin, cocaine, but I mean you know…I dig all of them, too. But what I dig and what's good for me are two different things."[2] It was clear that the increasing amounts of coke Marvin consumed weren't good for him. His addiction merely opened a wider window onto the tortured psychic landscape where his demons hovered. Marvin's demons—in addition to addiction, included suicidal bouts, paranoia, sexual fears, possible bipolar disorder, and violence toward the women in his life—may not all have been of his making. His devilish habits may have been set in motion as he suffered physical abuse at the hands of his father—and alleged sexual abuse inflicted by his uncle. Much of Marvin's troubles also stemmed from a culture that regards corporal punishment as a tenable practice and tolerates violence toward black children—a violence that has its roots in slavery. Except now the hands that deliver the blows are visibly and violently black. That Marvin's father helped at once to create and destroy him symbolizes the twisted Afroedipal logic that harms many black families.

In the beginning, Marvin's drug use didn't have such lethal consequences. As with many artists, Marvin used marijuana to free his imagination from normal constraints. He also smoked it to tap his spiritual energy. "I think he was similar to Bob Marley," Martha Reeves told me. "They prayed even harder when they did get high. It put [Marvin] closer to the Lord." He admitted that he "*stay*[ed] high" and that marijuana ignited his creativity. He told David Ritz, who said Gaye was high during most of their interviews, that:

I respect reefer…In those early days especially, I was trying hard to listen to myself as I sang. That's something I've always tried to do. Herb seemed to enhance that process. I've always listened to natural sounds—like gusts of wind or raindrops falling to the ground—and grass helped me listen closer. In Jamaica I learned that the Rastas use pot for religious purposes, and I can see that. I've had my share of smoky visions. But to be frank, I don't think I started for any of those lofty reasons. I started because I hated drinking—I still do—and if you want to be hip, what else is there? Slowly you see the world through this fascinating filter, and slowly you decide you'd rather live your life stoned than straight. You know it's not good for you, you know it'll cause you to make mistakes, but it's too late. You're a pothead.[3]

As Marvin moved from "herb" to "blow"—and then incessantly switched between them—his love for the pleasure that coke brought seized him in its vicious grip. Cocaine is so utterly addictive because it directly stimulates the brain's reward centers. Usually these rewards require learning. But cocaine's chemistry achieves this automatically and makes no such demands on its users. Within minutes, sometimes seconds, of being introduced into the body, cocaine activates the brain's reward centers and produces the irresistible euphoria in users. That's why the drug exercises such control over the user of cocaine: it is a direct route into the centers of the brain that shape human behavior. When stimulated, these centers function to direct human behavior into pleasurable activities. Cocaine undermines this process by dividing the activity of the pleasure centers from other brain functions—like restricting the pleasure centers' influence on behavior. These constraints are necessary to keep pleasurable experiences—for instance, eating—from ruining the individual in excessive quantities. Regulation is key. But cocaine distorts the ability of the pleasure centers to usefully shape behavior. Cocaine is one of the most dangerous drugs because it affects nerve cells in a uniquely enticing and debilitating fashion.[4]

Characteristic of his brutal honesty, Marvin admitted that he loved the feeling of the coke high.[5] He said it was a "clean, fresh high, especially early in the morning" that could "set you free— at least for a minute."[6] Gaye confessed there were times when "blow got to me" and that it sometimes "built up bad vibes inside my brain." But he saw it as "an elitist item, a gourmet drug." To him, that was "one of its attractions." Speaking rhetorically, Marvin asked himself if his use of coke was corrupting. "Slowly, very slowly," he replied.[7]

The songwriter Ivy Jo Hunter provides powerful insight into Marvin's struggle to maintain his balance and spiritual purpose amidst his heavy drug usage. Hunter explained:

Marvin was at war with an enemy, and he gave bad advice. He can make you hurt yourself. The wrong spirit whispered in his ear. The altered states are not good for you. If you're not yourself, who are you? The use of drugs, any kind of drugs, stems from an inability to cope without assistance…Your remedy for a bad feeling about yourself is to go sit on a bar stool next to another individual that has a bad feeling about himself. Neither one of you did anything but go to your favorite relief station and ply yourself with alcohol so you could feel better. Now it may not be alcohol; your relief station may be cocaine, or reefer…The question is: What caused me to drink?…We lie to ourselves on a regular basis, about things nobody else knows about. We don't even tell God, although He knows, because he keeps trying to show us everyday that there's nothing to be afraid of. It says it 365 times in the Bible—that's one for every day—"Fear not."

When Marvin hit the road to tour, his smoking and snorting routine only increased—he was always fearful of live shows. He was an introverted studio master and highly intelligent artist unnerved by the crass demands of the marketplace. Marvin's performance anxiety extended from the stage to the bedroom. His sexual addiction to pornography and prostitutes provided an outlet for his uninhibited sexual fantasies. At the same time, the aging star battled impotence induced by heavy consumption of coke.[8] Drugs also filled the air in his recording studio as Marvin produced some of his most sexually charged music. It is no wonder that his eclectic hedonism showed in the erotically energized grooves that had a narcotic effect on his listeners.

As Marvin spent hundreds of thousands of dollars on "toot" he also paid the price for his consumption in the mid-seventies: increasing paranoia about friends and colleagues plotting to take his money.[9] Like many conspiracy theories, the truth was more telling than the fears such paranoia generated. Marvin sometimes collected shady associates who increased the likelihood that he would be exploited. In effect, his paranoia was justified, but only because his addiction made him vulnerable to unprincipled hangers on. More and more, his life was a relentless pursuit of pleasure and escape. In November 1978, it caught up to him. Marvin collapsed on stage in Chattanooga, Tennessee during a concert performance. He was exhausted by his fights with Jan. She had filed for divorce even before he had settled matters in his divorce from Anna. He was also a victim of his crazed drug use, which, Gaye admitted, was "as much a part of my day as the weather."[10]

Marvin's existential angst and cocaine addiction made him depressed. "I am schizophrenic," Marvin told *People* magazine in 1983. He was hinting at the vicious mood swings that suggest he may have suffered from bipolar disorder or another mental illness.[11] Speaking of his hiatus from performing, Marvin admitted, "I was a manic depressive. I was at my lowest ebb. I really didn't feel like I was loved. Because I didn't feel loved, I felt useless."[12] His depression occasionally drove Marvin to the brink of suicide. In Hawaii, where he fled in the winter of 1979, Marvin tried to kill himself by ingesting nearly an ounce of pure cocaine in less than an hour. "I was scared," he said. "I called my mama and just said, 'Pray for me, Mama, because I think I'm going to die.'"[13]

Marvin had a violent altercation with Jan when she visited Hawaii. He wanted to kill her. He also wanted to kill himself, but was afraid to follow through.[14] Later, Marvin sent for his mother to help him care for his son Bubby in Hawaii. He was still depressed and feeling increasingly isolated and lonely. "I'd given up," he told David Ritz. "The problems were too big for me. I just wanted to be left alone to blow my brains away with high-octane toot. It would be a slow but relatively pleasant death, certainly less messy than a gun."[15] In Hawaii, Marvin became more socially and sexually withdrawn. He continued down his drug spiral, beginning his days with a shot of potent whiskey, a big joint and some coke.[16]

Even when Marvin left Hawaii to tour in London, he sank deeper into cocaine by hitting the pipe and free-basing. Marvin viewed this as another way of killing himself.[17] He told *Blues and Soul* magazine in 1980 that "I've been through a lot lately...been in a terrible state of depression. The taxman has been after everything I've got. I lost my house and studio."[18] But Marvin wasn't trying to pass the blame. "The trouble is, I'm my own worst enemy. I've never given a shit about where my money goes. I'm not going to change...I feel now that, at last, I'm breaking clear of the bad times. I'm not worried about my financial problems. Matters of the heart are far more important. I just wish I had someone to truly love me for myself."[19] At the same time, Marvin told journalist Nelson George that he was an expatriate because he didn't receive support for his art. He also flashed the conspiratorial thinking that, along with his drugs, clouded his brain. "There was not the kind of love for me in Los Angeles that I was accustomed to," he admitted to George in a phone call from London. "I wanted more love, more respect for me as an artist. There were so many plots and plans against me. People were saying that I was finished. My personality took a horrible beating there. I couldn't work in that kind of psychological hellhole. I won't go back until my tarnished image is repolished by my work. I can't do my best work in American right now."[20] When Marvin left London for Belgium, he was broke and a slave to the pipe. He was a 42-year-old falling star whose future didn't at all appear bright. He was so open in his drug use that he snorted coke in the presence of journalists who came to interview him.[21] Belgian business-man Freddy Cousaert—a promoter and fan of jazz and R & B—rescued him from his precipitous decline and untangled him from his destructive habits. According to Irene Gaye, Marvin's sister-in-law, he cut back on the drugs with the help of

Cousaert. She told me that "Freddy tried his best to keep all the riffraff away." As a result, Marvin rose again to shine in one of his brightest commercial moments: the "Sexual Healing" single from his 1983 *Midnight Love* album.

But when Marvin's mother was hospitalized after being diagnosed with cancer, he returned to Los Angeles in October 1982. He quickly and dramatically picked up his old habits. "This is going to sound crazy, but Marvin had defeated his devil," says Ivy Jo Hunter of Marvin's time in Belgium. "He had come back from really being 'out there,' and when he came back, he had success. If you can take that success and go sit down somewhere and keep working, you can make it. But if that success makes you want to go out and show the world you're back, then you're in trouble. In Europe, that was his medicine: getting back to work. But he didn't realize it."

Hunter waxes philosophical about the moral choices open to Gaye to celebrate his temporary comeback. Ironically, his method of celebration may have ruined his success. "As long as he was making music, he was 'Marvin Gaye,'" says Hunter. "He ended up celebrating the battle but losing the war. If you are going to celebrate a windfall, what would you do? Have a party? Have a drink? Go get some blow? Cop some weed? As the female character says in the film *True Grit*, [when she turns down an offer of alcohol] 'I would not put a thief in my mouth to steal my brains.'[22] Wounded and scarred, that leaves resentment and bitterness. And when you get a chance to demonstrate that you've overcome, if you don't pick the right demonstration, you undermine your position, you lose your progress. Sometimes nothing said is the best demonstration of all. 'Bless your enemies.' That's entirely different; you do not rejoice in his defeat. You don't get off on that. When [God] loses one, He doesn't have a party. He cries."

When Marvin got to Los Angeles, he went straight to the hospital to see his mother. Then he moved in for a while with Marilyn Freeman, his new manager and alleged girlfriend.[23] Marvin was angry at his father for decamping to Washington, D.C. In September 1982, Rev. Gay left for a six-month stay to rehab and sell the family house that Marvin had purchased for his parents. He failed to return to Los Angeles for his wife's operation and convalescence. When CBS threw Marvin a party in late 1983 to celebrate the million-selling *Midnight Love* (it eventually doubled that number of sales) he snorted coke in the bathroom and sang the Lord's Prayer a cappella. He told his audience that although he wasn't known for being "a prolific speaker," to be "honored like this is more than I ever imagined."[24] He also provided a glimpse into his apocalyptic thinking and his troubled artistic soul. "As an artist it's my duty to go to the depths of degradation to find spiritual heights," Marvin said. "I understand now that people are the same all over and that there are two forces in the world—good and evil—and that the world is in very bad shape."[25] Marvin's last statement was equally true of his personal life. As he told Nelson George in 1983, "I have been apathetic, because I know the end is near. Sometimes I feel like going off and taking a vacation and enjoying the last ten or fifteen years and forgetting about my message, which I feel is in a form of being a true messenger of God."[26] Marvin also reignited the romantic flame with his ex-wives, both of whom attended his CBS celebration.

Marvin eventually left Marilyn Freeman's West Lost Angeles apartment and shuttled between rented homes in Bel Air and

Palm Springs. His extravagant coke use forced him to surrender those properties and head to his sister Zeola's (Sweetsie) apartment. He eventually retreated to his parents' home on Grammercy Place, a sure recipe for disaster. Marvin hit the road one last time to exploit the success of his latest album. Marvin had waited too long after the album had peaked to tour. Still, he was enthusiastically received in many cities. His reluctance to perform live had only increased with his growing drug use and the paranoia and self-destruction it encouraged. According to one of his musicians, "there was more coke on that tour than on any tour in the history of entertainment." Marvin was "smoking it, even eating it."[27] Starting in mid-April—nearly two weeks after the last birthday he'd live to see—Marvin's 1983 "Midnight Love Tour" kicked off in California. It rambled across the country and back. A viral infection and exhaustion forced him to postpone two shows in Florida and Tennessee.[28]

Marvin's engagement in May at Radio City Music Hall was his most storied stop. Perhaps his most troubling visit happened in July in Boston. Marvin announced that he had hired legendary attorney F. Lee Bailey to launch an investigation into why someone had attempted to poison him. Marvin was interviewed by Janet Langhart, who was then lifestyle editor of Boston's WNEV-TV. "I feel that there has been a conspiracy to poison me and fortunately, I think, early enough we've discovered the conspiracy," Marvin told Langhart. "And I don't think I'm going to die from poison."[29] Marvin's bodyguard-cum-manager Andre White said that the Atlanta Poison Control Center had detected the poison in Gaye's system. The unnamed poison was found in Gaye's bloodstream during an examination and was allegedly given to him inside prescription medicine. White said that it was "slow-acting [poison] that's supposed to work over a period of three to four months. It's supposed to attack his voice and his brain cells and render him insane."[30] Marvin told *Jet* magazine that if "Dick Gregory didn't come and give me his formula to counteract the poison I had been administered, the doctor said I would probably be dead now, and that's the gospel truth."[31] Since nothing ever came of the investigation, it is hard to determine if the threat was legitimate. Perhaps it was another delusion that descended on Marvin from the haze of herb smoke and cocaine powder that engulfed him.

What is certain is that Marvin's paranoia deepened. "There was always something, and he was a little paranoid there at the end," Marvin's loyal friend Dave Simmons says in keen understatement. "When he would go onstage, Frankie and I had to stand onstage with him. [In his mind] there was always an assassin around the next turn. He always thought someone out there was trying to kill him. Frankie and I tried to tell him, 'Man, everybody loves you. Nobody's trying to kill you.'" Kitty Sears, Marvin's personal assistant in the last year of his life, witnessed Gaye's paranoid fantasies. "Marvin came down the steps [of his home] in his burgundy robe, and he fired me," Sears recalls. "But that was drugs. He was saying I wasn't loyal to him anymore and that I was going to work for somebody else. He talked to me so bad. I had tears coming down my eyes. And I went outside and I stood on the porch, and just as quickly he changed and said, 'I'm sorry Kitty, I didn't mean it.' Then he said, 'There they go, there they go. See them?' And I said, 'There's nobody there.'" Louvain Demps thinks that Marvin's paranoia was driven as much by guilt and the burden of the past as by drugs. "When you don't get things straightened up, you've got a lot of baggage to carry in your life," Demps says. "Whether you live to be 50 or 150, if you don't go back to straighten that stuff up…just imagine, one sin after another. It's like every year wearing an overcoat on top of the one you already have. And you never remove them. It's layer upon layer upon layer. So no wonder the guy was paranoid. He never got rid of the stuff."

Marvin's feelings of being unloved and unhappy increased as well. "I don't think Marvin realized how much he was loved," says Irene Gaye. "Or how sexy everybody really thought he was. Because I remember the Christmas before he passed, I took him his Christmas dinner, and there was a tear running down his face. And I aid, 'Marvin, why are you crying on Christmas?' And he said, 'Because I'm all alone. And nobody loves me.'" Janis remembers a scene that poignantly captures Marvin's free-floating sadness. "He was a miserable human being so much of the time," Janis said in a radio interview. "He was so unhappy. And I remember when my daughter was born, and this was in '74, and I had met him in '73, my mom said that she was sitting, talking to him in the waiting room. And he looked so sad, he looked so unhappy. She looked at him and she said, 'What's wrong? What's bothering you?' And he had his head in his hands, and he said, 'I'm just so unhappy.' She said, 'Why? You have everything that most men could want. You have a woman who loves you. You've just had a beautiful child. You have success. You're good looking. People love you. You have it all. What is it?' And he could not tell her. He said, 'I just don't know.' He wasn't happy on this planet. I know that."[32] Pete Moore of the Miracles agrees. He says one word best describes Marvin's soul in the midst of his multiple crises, failed marriages and career struggles: "tormented."

When Marvin came off the road in mid-August, he returned to his parents' home. He became more reclusive and depressed, just like his father. With Marvin's return came drug traffic and curious characters who rattled Rev. Gay's roost. "He was wondering why all these people were banging on the door at every time of day and night," says Irene Gaye. "And then there would be the girls in the garden [hollering] 'Marvin,' at two o'clock in the morning." Their proximity only heightened the enmity between furious father and sulking son. Marvin sank further into his depressive anarchy while Rev. Gay downed 100% vodka and swallowed valium. Both of them were trapped in a chemical and emotional maelstrom that would soon sweep them in its deadly trail. Marvin lost all sense of healthy inhibition when he did drugs in front of his mother. Alberta's relationship to her husband had greatly deteriorated since he sold the Washington home without sharing the proceeds with her. That made Marvin more desperately angry with his father than ever before.[33] It sparked negative memories from a childhood of abuse that left deep scars on his psyche.

As Louvain Demps told me, Marvin knew that his behavior was self-destructive. But he persisted in his habits so he could numb his suffering. "Even if you ask drug addicts [about their behavior] they know it's wrong," Demps says. "But it's something you depend on. Marvin was actually very complex. You know, as you're growing up you have little fears, little hopes, little dreams, little desires, and people around you can help make the difference in your life. And there are some things you see that you don't like. But if you don't get them out they grow up with you. And the things that went wrong, I think Marvin hid deep in his heart. Then as he got older, and as people and things were disappointments to him, I think those things just made him seek relief [through drugs]. I think he was covering up a mountain of wounds."

The wounds Marvin sought to cover were deep and painful. They were often inflicted by the belt of his father. Rev. Gay seemed to harbor a special hate for Marvin almost from the time he was born. Marvin's mother Alberta gave Marvin great love and attention. This reinforced Rev. Gay's deep insecurities and spurred him to whip Marvin even more.[34] Rev. Gay was locked in bitter competition with his namesake. Instead of bathing his head in the oil of pride, Rev. Gay poured venomous criticism on Marvin's brow. He withheld affirmation of his son in ingeniously destructive fashion. The Gay family was repeating the oedipal struggle. The deadly outcome for Marvin suggests a subversion of Freud's Oedipus complex. Freud held that the young child is erotically attached to the parent of the opposite sex and hostile to the parent of the same sex. Later, the child renounces sexual interest in the parent of the opposite sex and identifies with the parent of the same sex. Given Rev. Gay's abortive hostility, Marvin had a very strong love for his mother his entire life. In that sense, he failed to detach himself from his mother. He certainly didn't identify with his father. Indeed Afroedipalism often rewrites the narrative of familial sexual competition by ritualizing the violent assault on black sons (and daughters) as the rite of passage to adulthood.

For the Gay children, the rules of Afroedipal competition rebuffed any attempt to displace Father—as Rev. Gay demanded his brood call him—or to claim Mother as a protecting maternal figure. Mother was intimidated by the prospect of physical abuse as well. Hence, her authority derived from her husband's. Without his permission, Mother usually failed in her efforts to shield her children from Father's brutal discipline. The juvenilization of Mother (always the result, if not the intent, of male domestic violence) made her a co-sufferer with her children. This only increased her empathy and love for her children—and theirs for her. Thus, Rev. Gay brought his wife and children closer together in his vile effort to separate them. This deepened his resentment and fed his fury even more.

Father's punishments, like many forms of familial abuse, had a pronounced sexual dimension. Father often had his children strip naked and lay prostrate on their beds. They gripped the bedpost with both hands to receive his whippings. The sexualization of discipline imposed homoerotic meaning on his whippings of Marvin and Frankie. For Jeanne and "Sweetsie" it reasserted the brutality of patriarchal treatments of the female body. Like the paddling administered by male principals in school, the symbolic effect of Father standing over and behind his children to deliver blows in a percussive rhythm re-enacted ancient sadomasochistic rituals. As zoologist Desmond Morris writes:

> [T]he adoption of the female sexual rump-presentation pos-
> ture as an appeasement gesture...is largely confined now to a
> form of schoolboy punishment, with rhythmic whipping
> replacing the pelvic thrusts of the dominant male...
> [S]choolmasters...were performing an ancient primate form
> of ritual copulation with their pupils. They could just as well
> inflict pain on their victims without forcing them to adopt
> the bent-over submissive posture. (It is significant that
> schoolgirls are rarely, if ever, beaten this way—the sexual ori-
> gins of the act would then become obvious)."[35]

Father whipped all four of his children for bed-wetting. Thus, their punishment was further sexualized. The lack of control of their genitalia—a product of their anxiety over Father's beatings—brought them greater pain. It was a coercive sexualized masochism enacted for the pleasure of their domineering Father. According to Marvin's older sister Jeanne Gay, the children's bed-wetting proved the fear and nervousness of the household. Father beat the children until he saw welts rise on their bodies. Only then did he feel that they had learned their lesson.[36] Their skin became the screen onto which he projected his pedagogy of punishment and terror. Of all the children, Marvin flaunted Father's rules the most. He disappeared on Saturdays when they were to be in church. He used Father's hairbrush and left it dirty in a spot where he knew Father would see it. He wandered from school and showed up late at home. "From the time he was seven until he became a teenager, Marvin's life at home consisted of a series of brutal whippings," Jeanne Gay said.[37] If Marvin couldn't win Father's love by being a gifted child, he'd try to win his heart by defying his rule and by seeking attention through his rebellion. That tactic failed as well. It only got Marvin more beatings.

The sexualized brutality of the whippings was compounded by a feature of Father's aesthetic and perhaps erotic identity: his cross-dressing. Despite his Hebrew Pentecostal pedigree, with its rigidly repressed views of sexuality, Rev. Gay was a flamboyant and effeminate man. He liked to dress in women's clothing and makeup.[38] Father's sexual ambivalence and "male femaling"—males who adopt female identities in various ways and contexts with varying results—showed in his overtly feminine speech and body language.[39] Mother says that Father preferred soft clothing. He also liked to dress in her panties, shoes, gowns and nylon hose. Father also favored colorful silk blouses and occasionally straight-hair wigs.[40] Father would sometimes put waves in his hair. At other times he let it grow long and curled it under. Marvin often glimpsed Father in his "male femaled" form. Throughout Marvin's ghetto neighborhood, Father was referred to as "sissy." Questions arose about Father's sexuality: was he homosexual, bisexual or just weird?[41] Neither Marvin nor Mother knew for certain. But Father loved beautiful women with large buttocks and breasts. He is rumored to have had several girlfriends. He exploited his pastoral position to draw "sisters" at church to his bed.

What is clear is that Father's cross-dressing and "male femaling" tapped Marvin's sexual insecurities later in life. As he told David Ritz:

> I find the situation all the more difficult because, to tell you the truth, I have the same fascination with women's clothes. In my case, that has nothing to do with any attraction for men. Sexually, men don't interest me. But seeing myself as a woman is something that intrigues me. It's also something I fear. I indulge myself only at the most discreet and intimate moments. Afterward, I must bear the guilt and shame for weeks. After all, indulgence of the flesh is wicked, no mater what your kick. The hot stuff is lethal. I've never been able to stay away from the hot stuff."[42]

It is conceivable that Father's brutality was an attempt to expiate his guilt by projecting "sin" onto his children and harshly punishing them for their errors. The well-known parental saying that "this is going to hurt me more than it hurts you," made sense for Father in psychological and moral terms. Profound shame may have eaten at his psyche as a sexually ambivalent Pentecostal pastor. After all, he was responsible for the moral and spiritual welfare of his congregation. That may have provoked waves of self-recrimination that caused him to lash out at his family in physical and spiritual violence.

The children may have also been confused by Father's unstable sexuality. The Gay family's Afroedipal dynamics were intensified by Father's aesthetic and erotic mimicking of Mother's gender—Father, in a sense, was in sexual competition with Mother. The psychological development spurred by children identifying in erotic terms with the parent of the opposite sex was severely curtailed. The violence attached to Father's ambivalence—and the sexual overtones of his erotic and aesthetic choices—generated anxiety and insecurity. Father's behavior kept the children from seeing Mother as a refuge from terrorizing forms of masculine identity. Father's violent masculinity metastasized through his weakened household. He sought to absorb Mother's sex and gender. Thus their children were left with diminished psychic resources to explain their evolving sexual identities in reference to a healthy masculine model. (If Father had not been abusive, his cross-dressing may have opened up marvelous possibilities for rethinking sexual identity. But his sheer brutality only compounded his children's confusion).

Since Father's masculine femininity colonized Mother's maternal space, the children were doubly terrorized. Their troubles were linked to Father's confusion, from which there was no escape. And they may have internalized guilt—and perhaps even self-hate—for being the objects of his violence. They may have felt that their very existence was the reason for and reflection of Father's pain. When Father's belt lashed against their flesh, the children's resentment went far beyond his individual assault. Their suffering took on much larger meaning. Father's beatings not only called into question their self-worth, but also the way the world was ordered to either help or harm them. Every time he beat them, he may have made them feel as if God was beating them—or at least Father's God. Indeed, the fact that the Gay home doubled as their church for several years blurred the boundary between religious and personal identity for the Gay children. The cosmic and the common were inseparable.

Marvin's suffering was deepened even more at age 15 by a tragic event: his alleged sexual molestation by his uncle Howard. Uncle Howard later served a prison sentence for "indecent and immoral practices" with a boy.[43] I first learned of this terrifying story when I interviewed Los Angeles journalist Ron Brewington, who successfully campaigned to get a memorial star for Marvin Gaye on the Hollywood Walk of Fame. "The father was into cross-dressing," Brewington told me. "But more than that, the father's brother was a pedophile, and raped Marvin Gaye and raped Jeanne." "Raped Marvin Gaye?" I asked incredulously. "Yes, it's in the book," Ron replied. "It's called *Marvin Gaye: The Untold Chapter*, by Deborah Anderson.[44] And I asked her, 'Where did you get that information from?' She said Zeola related the story to her years later." After getting my hands on the hard-to-find book, I read the alleged story of the children's rape with great sadness.

According to Anderson, Father's brother, Howard, visited his brother and his family in Washington until he got back on his feet. One morning 15-year-old Marvin was in the bathroom brushing his teeth in preparation for school. Howard rapped on the door. Howard urgently needed to use the bathroom. Marvin quickly finished brushing his teeth and opened the door for his uncle. As Marvin attempted to leave, Howard begged him to stay and to close the door. Marvin complied. Howard said he had something important he wanted to discuss with his nephew. When Howard finished urinating, he demanded that Marvin approach him. Befuddled, Marvin moved toward his uncle and asked what he wanted. When Howard asked him to zip up his pants, Marvin retreated, telling his uncle to zip his pants himself. Howard replied that he needed help because his zipper was stuck. Just as Marvin extended his arm to help, Howard grabbed his hand and forced Marvin to touch his penis. When Marvin recoiled and asked his uncle what his problem was, Howard replied that it was just a game. Marvin insisted that "real men" didn't play such games.

Howard became angry. He intimidated Marvin by threatening to tell Father a lie that would bring Marvin more punishment. "Now, after the ass whippin' I heard him giving [you] last night, what do you think will happen to you?" Howard demanded. Howard let his pants drop to the floor, and forced a fearful Marvin to fondle his penis. Howard instructed Marvin to loosen his pajama pants so they could have "some fun." The young Marvin was momentarily frightened and paralyzed, realizing that Father would never take his word over Howard's. Marvin complied with his uncle's wish. Howard pulled down Marvin's pants as he directed his nephew to turn around and hold on to the sink. Howard entered Marvin from behind in a violent act of rape. Marvin questioned his manhood and wondered if he was gay. After his uncle finished his brutal act—the same act of rape he had allegedly performed on Jeanne—Howard told Marvin that if he let on to anyone he'd fabricate stories that would provoke Father's wrath. Howard made it plain to Marvin that he could assault him at will before leaving the bathroom. Marvin became ill and vomited in the sink.[45]

If this story is true it sheds further light on the sexual fears and insecurities that dogged Marvin as an adult. It may also help explain Marvin's attempt to medicate his misery through dangerous quantities of drugs. Many of Marvin's fans will rightly view his rape by a relative as an unspeakable horror. But many of them will not necessarily think that the brutal whippings Marvin received were equally devastating. To understand Marvin's domestically terrorized childhood, we must acknowledge how corporal punishment has been seen as a legitimate and desirable practice in American culture and black life.

It is unfortunate, perhaps even tragic, that corporal punishment is still viewed as an acceptable means to discipline children at home or in school. Corporal punishment refers to the intentional application of physical pain to modify behavior—the same kind of behavior modification applied in the extreme by Father.[46] For thousands of years, legal doctrines and religious beliefs have been used to justify corporal punishment of children.[47] Corporal punishment has been used to discipline children and youth in the United States since colonial times.[48] Things changed slightly in 1972, when the American Civil Liberties Union (ACLU) and the American Orthopsychiatry Association hosted a conference on the subject. At the time, only Massachusetts and New Jersey legally banned corporal punishment in its schools.

Two years later, the American Psychological Association passed a formal resolution calling for the abolition of corporal punishment in the nation's schools. Later in the decade, a report sponsored by the National Education Association denounced corporal punishment and argued that it should be banned. In 1987, the National Coalition to Abolish Corporal Punishment was formed to oppose the corporal punishment of children and young people in American schools. Europe (with the exception of England), Israel, and Japan, among other countries, already forbid the practice.[49] And Sweden, Norway, Denmark, and Finland have banned parents from administering corporal punishment as well.[50]

Twenty-seven states in America have legally banned corporal punishment in schools.[51] The nation's capital has followed suit. In 23 states, however, corporal punishment continues, accounting for the nearly three million cases of physical punishment doled out each year,[52] with nearly 20,000 students each year requiring medical treatment.[53]

To be sure, there is strong general support in the population for corporal punishment. Over the years, polls have indicated that the vast majority of children in America are occasionally spanked at home by their parents, who in turn support corporal punishment in schools.[54]

Still, there are unmistakable patterns of opposition and support for corporal punishment. Those who oppose corporal punishment are more likely female, highly educated and located outside of the South.[55]

On the other hand, Southerners and fundamentalist or conservative Christians are more likely than others to support corporal punishment.[56] Religion plays an especially important role because it fosters conservative values and reflects traditional views on the parent–child relationship. Conservative and fundamentalist beliefs buttress theological support for corporal punishment. Beliefs in Biblical literalism, the evil character of human nature, and the punishment of sinners, lead many fundamentalist and conservative Christians to support corporal punishment. If one believes that human beings are evil if they lack divine truth, then corporal punishment is a logical extension of the attempt to reform human behavior. Further, if one maintains that sinners are punished for their sins, then corporal punishment is viewed as the justifiable administration of pain for the purpose of correction. It is clear that Rev. Gay's brutality was motivated by such beliefs.

The advocates of corporal punishment contend that children are "better-controlled, learn appropriate appreciation for authority, develop better social skills, as well as improved moral character, and learn to better discipline themselves."[57] Supporters of corporal punishment in school maintain that the lack of classroom order leads to chaos. Without a way to preserve academic control, these advocates argue, teacher security will be compromised, an especially sensitive point in light of the recent spate of school shootings. Finally, advocates of corporal punishment cite the support of a majority of physicians and pediatricians in upholding the value of corporal punishment.[58]

These arguments, however, overlook several points. Corporal punishment has proved to be ineffective in correcting student misbehavior and has negative effects on the physical and mental health of its victims.[59] Physical punishment has not been shown to enhance moral character, increase respect for authority figures, preserve teacher control, or increase teacher safety.[60] There is no increase in violence in schools that reject corporal punishment as a viable disciplinary tool. And contrary to its advocates' claims, corporal punishment in schools is not always used as a last resort. Besides, many parents spank or beat their children out of anger and frustration, obscuring whatever lesson they are trying to impart. The most powerful lesson they may be passing along is that violence is appropriate behavior. There are better techniques than corporal punishment to change children's behavior. These include a positive learning environment where strong parent–child relations are encouraged; a nonviolent strategy to reinforce systematic teaching of desired behaviors; and techniques and strategies of positive reinforcement that highlight and reward appropriate behavior.[61]

It is not surprising, though surely disappointing, that blacks look more favorably on corporal punishment in the home and school than do other groups.[62] In that sense, Rev. Gay was in lockstep with the majority of black households. In a recent Africana.com poll, 59% of blacks said they believed that parents should spank their children.[63] For 25.9% of the black respondents, spanking should only occur under extreme circumstances. As Harvard Medical School professor Alvin Poussaint points out, blacks resort to corporal punishment 20–30% more than the general population.[64] Positive, even humorous, references to black corporal punishment abound, from the pulpit to the comedy stage. Black preachers extol the virtues of often violent corporal punishment. Black comics go to great lengths to draw the humor from graphic descriptions of ass-whipping. And black congregations and audiences laugh uncontrollably at these narratives because they reflect wide-spread cultural practice.

Black support for corporal punishment extends to the public sphere. Black folk strongly support paddling and other physical punishment in schools, despite the disproportionate targeting of black children. In the 23 states that still practice corporal punishment, black students are punished at twice the rate of their makeup in the population. Black students make up 17% of students, and yet they receive 37% of paddlings.[65] And black folk show greater support for corporal punishment for the public misbehavior of children than does the general population. Admittedly, this may stem from the fact that black children who misbehave in public are most likely viewed, not as "bad" children, but as bad "black" children.[66]

Indeed, the racial context of black corporal punishment cannot be overlooked. Those who justify black corporal punishment often point to life under Jim Crow when a wrong move or a threatening gesture from a black child might lead to his or her death. If a black child spoke in an uppity fashion or behaved in a rude manner—or simply in a manner that whites found offensive—he or she might find themselves, like Emmett Till, tossed to the bottom of a river. That racial context has also been used to justify the failure of black parents to explain rules of conduct to their children. Instead, they quickly resort to physical discipline. Black children who refused to obey were administered a swift measure of corporal punishment. Such justifications may have made more sense under Jim Crow—although that can't explain the extent and degree of black parental harshness, especially the kind evinced by Rev. Gay. But no such justifications are presently compelling. While it is true that the prospect of police misconduct toward black children calls for disciplined youth, nonviolent instruction in appropriate behavior is likely more effective than corporal punishment. It may even be argued that corporal punishment makes black youth more inclined to resort to violence to resolve disputes. After all, that is the behavior being modeled in millions of black homes.

The black past has often been critically examined as we attempt to confront the pains of our present circumstances. We look at slavery to determine its consequences on contemporary society and black behavior.[67] Black thinkers probe the psychological effects of "post-traumatic slavery syndrome."[68] And yet we have too often failed to link black practices of corporal punishment to slavery. The brutal lash of the slave master against black flesh for rebellious behavior is often ritually re-enacted in the context of black families. While we must refrain from overstatement of direct correlations between our slave past and our current predicaments—the discussion of corporal punishment above establishes its wide societal practice—there is also the need to probe the lingering affects of past traumas on black life and behavior. As the black psychologists Grier and Cobb stated in their famous book, *Black Rage*: "Beating in child-rearing actually has its psychological roots in slavery and even yet black parents will feel that, just as they have suffered beatings as children, so it is right that their children be so treated."[69] The psychic trauma of slavery that we have collectively attempted to escape is drawn on—and out—when we extend this brutal ritual to our children. Each time we reengage its visceral destructions, the pathology of corporal punishment inflicts fresh injury on old wounds. It is unavoidable that we view corporal punishment's long trajectory in the light of its violent use to control black bodies and to coerce their compliance to white rule. The symbolic displacement of the white plantation owner with black parents—especially the brutalizing black father—is a tragic image in the iconography of collective black self-hatred and internalized racism.

The brutalizing black father like Rev. Gay—and this does not add to the unjust demonizing of black fathers, but seeks to name the specific domestic uses and social locations of a mythologized male authority figure invested with powers to punish—is a staple of Afroedipalism and has often terrorized black families. Often brutalized himself—by older black men and fathers, as Rev. Gay was, or by the white society that makes his brutality necessary and convenient, even useful, perhaps— his domestic terrorism has not made him, amazingly enough, an unloved character within black culture. Black folk understand that often we do to each other what has been done to us. In fact, the brutalizing black father has often been shrouded in subversive adulation, since his praise largely undercuts a dynamic and strategic analysis of his destructive presence. When black writers have been brave enough to confront or portray his volatile outlines—say Toni Morrison or Alice Walker—they are roundly dismissed, without irony, as traitors to both black culture and to the black male in particular. But what is often defended in these cases is not edifying black masculinity, but a blasphemous black masculinity—*blasculinity* if you will—that trades on race loyalty to protect its deeply disloyal gestures. After all, terrorizing black children and women is the most abjectly unfaithful act of all. At bottom, it is an act of un-kinning, of violently unmaking the black family and dismantling its binding relations one beaten body at a time. And let it be clear: the figure of the brutalizing black father is capable of inhabiting the bodies of otherwise sane and spiritual men. The brutalizing black father is a rhetorical and intellectual temptation to familial omnipotence, of assuming the pose of benighted protector-as-punisher by any meanness necessary.

But when, like Rev. Gay, the brutalizing black father is also religious—which often means an exemption from moral self-examination, and instead, a relentless self-justification—the mix is often lethal. Scripture is heaped on scurrilous behavior to give it theological authority. If fundamentalist Protestants are more likely than others to engage corporal punishment, then a religious motivation to brutality yoked to the racial traumas of black life are well nigh celestial in their intensity—and perhaps their perversity. There's nothing like drafting God to do your dirty work, or failing that, doing your dirty work in the name of God, as was the case with Rev. Gay. Either tack depends on religiously misreading the Word.

Perhaps the most salient, and undoubtedly well-known, theological justification for corporal punishment is the maxim, "Spare the rod and spoil the child," often quoted as scripture. In truth, the line is from "Hudibras," a mock epic poem ridiculing the Puritans written in 1664 by English poet and satirist Samuel Butler. "Love is a boy, by poets styl'd/Then spare the rod and spoil the child." Of course, there is sufficient Biblical justification for corporal punishment.[70] But it is worth noting that the Bible verse that comes closest to Butler's sentiment is drawn from Proverbs 13:24, "He who spares the rod hates his son, but he who loves him is careful to discipline him."[71] In Hebrew, the word translated as "rod" is the same word found in Psalms 23:4, "thy rod and thy staff they comfort me."[72] Contrary to common belief, the shepherd's rod was used to guide the sheep—not to beat them.[73] It makes little sense that such a rod would be used to hurt children either, an interpretation surely lost on Rev. Gay.

Furthermore, notions of correction have been erroneously collapsed into a conception of punishment. Disciplining children is a critical function of parenting. It requires a different set of skills than those needed for corporal punishment. Discipline and punishment are not synonyms, as Rev. Gay and millions of others mistakenly believe. Discipline derives from the Latin word *discipuli*, which means "student" or "disciple."[74] The word suggests a teacher–student relationship, or one between a Rabbi–disciple. The point is to inculcate values through teaching, not hitting, spanking or other violent or abusive methods. The objective is to instruct children about loving, healthy and respectful relationships.[75] "Punishment" comes from the Greek word *poine*, and the Latin derivative *poena*, which means revenge. *Poine* and *poena* form the root words of pain, penalty, penitentiary and penance. Punishment is vastly different from discipline; it suggests inflicting pain as a form of revenge.[76] The relationship conjured by punishment is one of punisher and victim. The objective of punishment is compliance and control.[77] By remaking God in the image of a punishing "Father," we have often tried to sanctify our indefensible practices and turn a loving God into a "divine child abuser."[78] We have also tried to convince our children to accept our misbegotten visions of God as the lens through which they learn to punish themselves in the belief that they are defective or evil and that violence is normal and supremely useful.

The manner in which Marvin Gaye warred with himself—with his sexual and spiritual and moral identity—was largely the legacy of his father's religious views and vicious behavior.

Rev. Gay was the archetypal brutalizing black father whose love Marvin desperately sought his entire life. The physical and sexual abuse Marvin suffered as a youth stirred up demons that caused him abuse as an adult: drugs, paranoia, sexual insecurities, unstable relations with women, depression and suicidal impulses. Ironically, the ravages of post-traumatic slavery syndrome on Father—Marvin's first and most influential teacher—may have produced in Marvin what is termed Educationally Induced Post-Traumatic Stress Disorder (EIPSD).[79] The symptoms hold for any youth who suffered the extensive forms of physical abuse Marvin endured. They include difficulty sleeping, fatigue, feelings of sadness and worthlessness, suicidal thoughts, anxiety episodes, increased anger with feelings of resentment and outbursts of aggression, deteriorating peer relationships, difficulty with concentration, antisocial behavior, intense dislike of authority, and other evidence of negative high-risk behavior.[80] This fits Marvin to a tee.

It is too bad that Marvin was incapable of seeking out therapy. "When you have that kind of artistic temperament and sensibility, it's very hard to make your way in the world," Rona Elliott told me. "He wasn't Jewish. He wasn't going to go to a psychiatrist and say, 'My father dressed up this way, and my mother did this and that.' That's not the culture he came up in. So there wasn't a whole support system to take care of him." Trapped by his religious resistance to therapy—"all I need is God" is the mantra of many religious folk—Marvin cut himself off from a potential source of psychological insight that might have helped him to cope. Ironically, the source of some of his suffering was the religious worldview that viewed therapy skeptically. Marvin told David Ritz that he looked up the word schizophrenic when he was told it applied to him. "It's not just having a split personality," Marvin said. "It's a sickness that scrambles your feelings until you lose all emotional balance. That balance, especially in my case, is very delicate. I found myself uncertain of whether I could carry on. I needed rest."[81] When Ritz asked Marvin if he saw a therapist, he scoffed at the notion and eloquently revealed an attitude held by many black Christians.

> "Are you kidding?" he answered with a laugh. "What am I going to tell a stranger? And what's a stranger going to tell me? *Never!* Besides, the cure is already inside us. All we have to do is bring it out. All answers are contained within. God is within each of us. If we stop long enough to listen to the rhythm of our heartbeat, that's the rhythm of God's voice. After leaving Washington, I've never regularly attended church, but neither did I ever leave the church. The church never left my heart. I had religion, so why did I need head doctors? No, I didn't need to go to cocktail parties and talk about my psychoanalysis; I didn't need no shrink. It was a matter of changing styles."[82]

It may have been too much of a cliché for Marvin to struggle in a course of psychological therapy with the shadow his father cast on his life. And yet Father's presence dominated his life as much by his withheld affection—and his emotional absence—as by his negative input. But Father did his greatest damage by playing the brutalizing black father to the hilt, to the very end of Marvin's life. On the Sunday morning of April 1, 1984, the day before his 45th birthday, Marvin was sitting in his room, disheveled, sore, and depressed. The day before, he had been picked up in a car by a woman who recognized him as he wandered on the freeway next to his parents' home. Since he wanted to go to the Hollywood Park racetrack, the woman took him there to walk around for a couple of hours before she drove him home.

The next day, April Fool's day, Irene Gaye brought Mother her breakfast. Because she lived with Frankie and their daughter in the small apartment over the Gay's garage, the grits, eggs, and sausage were still hot. But Mother declined. "Go ahead, just give it to Marvin," Irene recalls Mother saying. "I'll eat later." And Father heard her say that. And I think that made him mad. He said, "Why give it to Marvin? Why not me? I'm the head of the household. Shouldn't I be served first?" Of course, Marvin had been taking care of the family for twenty years. Father hadn't worked in all that time. For the most part, Father stayed in his own room, drunk, descending into jealous rages because Mother showered Marvin with affection and attention. Mother's bedroom was between Marvin's and Father's, joined by connecting doors, a perfect metaphor of her situation in life.

When Irene took the breakfast to Marvin, he was glum. "He was so depressed," she says. "*So* depressed. I wish I knew then what I know now, just so I could have helped him more. I feel really bad." After serving Father his breakfast, Irene returned to her apartment. In the late morning, she was startled.

"I was in the kitchen, which was across from Marvin's room," Irene says. "I had just cleaned up when I heard the gunshot. So I said, 'Frankie, I think I heard gunshots.' He said, 'Oh, it's probably a car on the freeway.' And then, the next thing I knew, Mother was at the bottom of the steps, crying." Frankie put on his shoes and followed Irene down the stairs. When she opened the gate, Mother collapsed in Irene's arms. She was trying to tell her that Father shot Marvin. "But I thought she was saying that she'd been shot," Irene says. "And then when I was able to sit her down on the bench outside the gate and talk to her, we discovered that Father had shot Marvin." It was ironic that Father had shot Marvin with the very gun Marvin had given him a few months ago so he could feel safer. Marvin figured if Father had a gun, then whoever was pursuing him in his paranoid delusions would be scared off. Frankie didn't know if Father had gone beserk, and if he was aiming to shoot other family members as well. But he went into the house and up the stairs and found Marvin crumpled on the floor of his room next to his bed.

In the meantime, Irene remained outside until the paramedics showed up. They balked at entering the home until they could be assured that it was safe to go in. "They refused to go in until the gun and the person who fired it were outside," Irene says. "So I got Father, who was sitting on his bed, to go down and sit outside on the porch. And then he didn't know what he did with the gun. So I had to look for it. I was looking in all of these drawers and got exasperated. Then I started looking in the covers and there it was under his pillow. So when I took the gun down, the paramedics had me walk to the middle of the grass and put it down. And then they went in."

Irene accompanied the paramedics and led them to Marvin's room. When they got in the house, they asked her if she knew the victim's name.

"Marvin Gaye," she responded.

"Oh my God, don't tell me it's *the* Marvin Gaye!" the black man pleaded.

"Yes, it is."

"Oh, God," the paramedic exclaimed before he broke into tears.

Irene says that Marvin was still alive when they got to him, and that Frankie had had a brief conversation with his fatally wounded brother.

There is a great deal of confusion surrounding what lead Father to shoot Marvin. But fortunately Mother, the only witness, made a statement to the Los Angeles police.[83]

"It must have been around 11:30 a.m. or 12:00," Mother said. "I was in Marvin's room sitting on the foot of his bed talking with him. My husband came walking through my bathroom and asked me where he could find this insurance letter. I couldn't hear him very well, so Marvin asked him to come into the room where we were." When her husband refused, Marvin got angry.

"If you don't come in now, don't you ever come in my room again," Marvin angrily declared. At that point, Father joined them in the room. Marvin told him to get out and got up from his bed and walked over to Father and pushed him back.

"Marvin pushed him a couple of times," Mother said. "My husband turned and walked back to his bedroom. Marvin followed him yelling little cuss words at him." Then Marvin threatened Father.

"I'll beat you up," he said. Father and Marvin went into Rev. Gay's bedroom, with Mother following behind. She says she didn't see what happened in the bedroom, but she heard her husband's voice.

"He's kicking me," Father said. "I don't have to take that."

When Mother entered the room, Father was on the floor and Marvin was standing a short distance away. Mother took Marvin by the arm and led him back to his bedroom. Mother sat Marvin on the foot of his bed.

"Mother, I'm going to get my things and get out of this house," Marvin said. "Father hates me and I'm never coming back."

Mother thought that Marvin was taking drugs because he flew off the handle so quickly.

"Marvin used cocaine at times," Mother told the police. "When he used it, he would fly off real quick. My husband drinks every day. I think he was drinking today. But I didn't see him. I was standing about eight feet away from Marvin when my husband came to the door of the bedroom with his pistol. It's a silver colored revolver. He's had it about a year. He, my husband, was always quick to talk about shooting people. My husband didn't say anything he just pointed the gun at Marvin. I think the gun was in the right hand. I screamed, but it was very quick. He, my husband, shot and Marvin screamed. I tried to run. Marvin slid down to the floor after the first shot. Then my husband fired two more times. I ran out of the house and ran to my son's house next door. I told him to call the cops and the paramedics. My son Frankie and his wife called the police then went over."[84]

Dave Simmons, Marvin's friend, says he's convinced that the events of that day went just as Marvin planned them.

"I went over to the house after Marvin's death," Simmons says. "Frankie was in Europe. I talked to the old man, and he told me that Marvin had beaten him up, and actually left the room and told him he was going to come back and beat him some more. I'll always believe Marvin was committing suicide. When you give somebody a gun, and then you beat him and you tell him, 'Well, hold on, rest up, I'll be back to beat you again in a little while.' That's suicidal. And the old man told me, 'I just couldn't take another whipping. I just wasn't going to take another beating.' And you know, if you're mad with someone, what better way to really put a burden on him than to have your death on their conscience?" When I asked Simmons if that wasn't the ultimate passive-aggressive move, he concurred. "Oh, yeah, Marvin's sharp as nails," Simmons told me. "Too sharp. I can easily understand him doing something like that."

In his posthumously published memoir, Frankie Gaye, who died in 2001, recounted for the first time the brief conversation he had with Marvin before he died.[85] As he held Marvin in his arms, he says Marvin spoke to him.

"I got what I wanted," Marvin said.

"Don't talk like that," Frankie told Marvin. Frankie writes that Marvin must have been high on coke when Father shot him, and that the drug was influencing his conversation.

"No," Marvin uttered. "I couldn't do it myself, so I made him do it."

"Oh Marvin," Frankie cried, holding his head close to Marvin's, "it didn't have to be this way."

"It's good," Marvin told him. "I ran my race. There's no more left in me."[86]

In light of Simmons's and Frankie's comments, irony abounds: Father received a small measure of the punishment he viciously meted out; Marvin died in a fight with Father over Mother; Marvin had become like Father in his abuse of the father who had abused him; and Father shot Marvin with a gun Marvin gave him to help protect him.

In the Afroedipal drama that was set in motion with Marvin's birth in 1939, it appears inevitable that he would meet his end at his father's hand in his own bedroom—the site of so much pain and suffering for him in his formative years. It was also the scene of the realization of a violent line often repeated by black parents: "I brought you in this world, and I will take you out." Of course, in traditional oedipal script, and in Greek mythology, the son displaces, or removes, or slays the father. But in Afroedipal narrative—at least the one written in Marvin's handwriting above Father's signature—the son kills through self-destruction. This is the vicious doubling back performed in Afroedipal myth: Marvin murders his father by getting his father to murder him. Thus, he achieved suicide by proxy—a practice strictly forbidden in his still active religious imagination, one shaped by his father's beliefs—and forced it on the man who refused to love him back in the way Marvin wanted, in the way he needed. So Marvin extracted from Father a lethal act of generosity in the vocabulary he understood best: violent destruction. Marvin depended on Father to love him in the only way he could, in the way he had been showing to Marvin his entire life—to hate him to death. Thus, Marvin was able to get revenge on Father by forcing him to kill him and to live with the consequences. In death, Marvin had achieved posthumous Afroedipal fulfillment as well: he got Mother to leave Father, something she could never do while

Marvin lived. Whether he did any of this intentionally is almost irrelevant. The fact is that Marvin Gaye—a man chased by demons who chased away the demons of millions of others with his heavenly sound and divine art—was now free from a father who gave him life but not its meaning, and a world in which his soul was too weary to remain.

"Trouble Man"
From the Prince of Motown to the Pied Piper of R & B

In December 1978, Marvin Gaye released *Here, My Dear* an overlooked masterpiece. The album was Gaye's shamelessly one-sided account of his marriage and divorce from his first wife, Anna Ruby Gordy Gaye, the older sister of Motown founder Berry Gordy. The record is remarkable on many levels, not the least being the fashion in which it was crafted: as the bounty of divorce for the departed Anna, to whom Marvin agreed to pay $600,000 by giving her the $305,000 advance on his next album, with the remaining $295,000 to be drawn from earnings on the same album.

"That's insane!" Gary Harris comments in awe at the sheer magnitude of Marvin's irresistible hubris. "The way *Here, My Dear* came about as a result of a court decision, where he decides he wants to, instead of paying money, make a record and give all the proceeds to the wife he's divorcing, who is the label head's sister! That's just so anti-authoritarian, and so brilliant. It's a singular case, and in a lot of ways the best record he ever made. On top of all that, he really hit it out of the park creatively, and he had so many of what we'd consider the wrong reasons for doing it, in terms of the politics of the business that you go along to get along. You're gonna shit on the record company president, and he's your brother-in-law? And you're going to do it in a public way? And your artwork is going to be reflective of the [divorce] game, with the Monopoly board, with the music and this and that on his side of the board, with the piano and the tape deck. And she's got the house and the money and I think a diamond bracelet—you can see her hand. And in his hand is the record, and he's handing her that. I mean, how does he get that record through the system? What were the machinations and the process? What was he kicking to be able to tell Berry, 'Look, this is what I'm doing.' Or even go to the judge and say, 'This is what I'm doing.' And then have everybody agree with him, and then like it enough to put it out and promote it!"

Despite Marvin's efforts, *Here, My Dear* was a commercial failure, not because it lacked ideas and sophisticated music, but, perhaps, because it possessed them in abundance. I think *Here, My Dear* was simply too sophisticated, too boldly honest, too remarkably insightful—and too close to the emotional quick to succeed commercially. On "I Met a Little Girl," Gaye appeals to his past: musically, through sweet fifties harmonies, and personally as he narrates meeting Anna, falling in love with her, and the relationship's demise. On "When Did You Stop Loving Me, When Did I Stop Loving You," which appears again as an instrumental and a reprise, Marvin uses a Latin-tinged mellow groove to probe for more than six minutes the philosophical question of love's origin and its end, both passing imperceptibly into existence, and into each other, as Marvin's multiple falsettos lash at the song's rhythms, and Anna: "You said bad things and you lied." On "Anger," Marvin mounts a funky shuffle of percussion and bass to declare the defining vices of a fundamental human passion: "Anger...can make you old...can make you sick...destroys your soul." The songs cross every genre— "Anna's Song" is a rhythmically complex patterning of soul-jazz that conjures Coltrane's ballads, while "Funky Space Reincarnation" is disco-funk that dreams of a raceless musical universe. And "Here, My Dear" is a poignant doo-wop love fugue transposed to detail Marvin's sorrowful joys and sad nostalgia in the aftermath of their breakup.

The *New York Times*' Robert Palmer, one of the few critics at the time to appreciate Gaye's stellar achievement, contended that the album is "too rich, too demanding," and that it "is an inventory of the whole expressive range of black popular music at the end of the seventies, a testing of limits, and an affirmation of musical values."[1] Palmer was alert to how Gaye fits into a black musical tradition whose best artists have drawn portraits of personal pain that also limned the suffering of those who embraced their work. Palmer wrote that while some listeners and critics "may have trouble equating self-indulgence with innovation and excellence," they should remember that much of the greatest black popular music has "has been a triumph of what critics call manner over what they call matter."[2] Palmer elaborates, and also suggests something of the self-critical impulse that, together with his mournful self-pity, animated Gaye's best work.

Some of the finest blues recordings—the most rhythmically incisive, the most movingly sung, the most resonant in cul-

tural meanings—used shopworn texts and double-entendres
and celebrated the singer's sexual prowess in the most vain-
glorious terms. Billie Holiday frequently worked her vocal
magic on Tin Pan Alley confections that were almost
entirely devoid of redeeming value on their own. Mr. Gaye's
Here, My Dear has something to do with both these situa-
tions. When their lyrics are trite, one tends to forgive it
because the music and singing are superb. And even though
self-serving recrimination seems to be a shallow value, it
does have the virtue of honesty. How many people have felt
the way Mr. Gaye seems to have felt after being spurned by a
lover? And how many have been able to turn those feelings
into two records full of striking music?[3]

While Marvin was one of the most excruciatingly honest
artists ever—he shared with the public his fears and insecurities, his hopes and aspirations, his loves and hates—he withheld information as well. The reason may be found on "When
Did I Stop Loving You, When Did You Stop Loving Me," as
Marvin recalls "memories of the things we did, some we're
proud of, some we hid." On "Here, My Dear," Marvin chided
Anna because "you don't have the right to use a son of mine to
keep me in line," as he confesses, "one thing I can't do without
is the boy God gave both of us." In 1965, early in the year,
Anna became pregnant—or so it appeared. Louvain Demps,
the Andantes singer, knew it was impossible. "My mom knew
Anna," Demps informs me. "All the Gordy women were glam-
orous women. They were foxy ladies! She met Anna in a night-
club. My mom told me that she was unable to bear children. I
never said a word to anybody about it. And when they were

having a baby, it was like she actually went through a transformation. She actually put on a lot of weight and she actually did look pregnant." Some in Motown's and Marvin's inner circle knew that Anna adopted the baby. Some even found out later that the baby's mother was really Anna's niece, Denise Gordy, the 15-year-old daughter of Anna's brother George. Marvin admitted to his biographer David Ritz that the baby was adopted without discussing his birth parents.[4] Neither did Marvin tell him that he was the baby's biological father.[5] It was understandable: Marvin had made love to a minor, apparently with the consent of all involved. Still, Denise was under the age of legal consent for sexual relations, and Marvin might have gone to jail for statutory rape.

"You know what I thought about?" says Demps. "It's almost like Abraham and Sarah and their servant Hagar. And she said, 'Take the lady and have a baby.' But then, afterwards, she regretted it. And I think that was a demon that rose up in her. I don't think it happened without her permission. If Anna gave permission, can you imagine? Just switch roles. You're a guy, and you told your best buddy, 'Okay, here's my wife.' You know what I'm saying? And then you have to look at that every day. Not the baby, per se. 'Hell hath no fury like a woman scorned.' And though he loved Anna, I think that was a bad call. I think that created another monster."

The story of Marvin's secret fathering of a son with an underage relative by marriage—and his public relationship with a high-school girl whom he got pregnant four months after meeting her—unavoidably brings to mind a gifted contemporary artist who, like Gaye, has struggled with the tensions between sexuality and spirituality, and who has been accused of having dalliances with underage girls: R. Kelly, the self-proclaimed "pied piper of R & B." Kelly married the late pop chanteuse Aaliyah—whose debut album, *Age Ain't Nothing But a Number*, he produced in 1994—when she was fifteen. The marriage was quickly annulled when her parents discovered she had lied to obtain a marriage license in Kelly's home state of Illinois. In 2000, allegations surfaced that Kelly had had sex with two women when they were minors and students at Kelly's alma mater, Kenwood Academy in Chicago's Hyde Park. The singer settled a suit in 1998 with yet another accuser. Then, in June 2002, Kelly was indicted in Illinois on 21 counts of child pornography. In January 2003, an additional 12 counts followed in Florida in relation to the initial investigation. At the center of Kelly's charges is a videotape that allegedly captures the singer having sex with girls as young as thirteen, and the possession of child pornography.

Kelly's case has been used to suggest a number of competing, contradictory theses. One is that he has sought cover behind his celebrity status in deflecting criticism of his nefarious activities. Another is that the race of his alleged victims—all black—proves that black girls don't rate nearly as highly on the nation's legal totem pole as white girls, as seen in some of the recent stories plastered all over the press involving white teens who were horrifically abducted and raped, but eventually returned home. Still others say that because Kelly's latest album, *Chocolate Factory*, has sold more than 2.5 million copies, his fans have subordinated concern for vulnerable young girls and have instead rallied to an artist who portrays himself as the victim. His advocates have said that Kelly is a besieged genius whose good deeds and great art shouldn't be overlooked in the midst of his troubles, and that he deserves his day in court—not the court of public opinion.

All of these things, and more, may be true. Indeed, they prove how it is most likely that truth results from simultaneously holding in mind two conflicting propositions that don't conveniently give way to black and white choices. If R. Kelly is guilty of the criminal offenses with which he has been charged, he should suffer the consequences. Of course, if the allegations against him are true, he should also be afforded the opportunity to seek therapy to confront the demons and choices that shape his behavior. This doesn't absolve Kelly of culpability for his possible actions. Neither does it seek to undermine concern and profound empathy for the young girls whose lives will have been tragically marked by these encounters.

Still, one can't help believe that there is a larger story here, a bigger pathology, that the scapegoating of R. Kelly avoids: that the black community has to face up to vicious patterns of young girls being sexually exploited by black men. Most teenage black mothers are impregnated by men who are older than they are, sometimes considerably older. The relative silence of blacks in the face of an epidemic of exploitation of young black girls only reinforces their second-class status—a status, painfully enough, that accords with their treatment in a broader white society that cares little for their lives.

If the focus on R. Kelly leads to him being treated as a symbol of such exploitative practices, and thus, of the need to rid our community of their presence, one might applaud such efforts. For the most part, however, Kelly is being made morally singular; his alleged transgressions are said to grow from a sickness all his own, or at least, one that he shares with other pedophiles.

The harder truth for black folk is to confront the prospect that it's not only pedophiles who exploit teen girls. Rather, it is black men, sometimes of prominent community standing, at other times ordinary figures, who routinely prey on vulnerable black girls with little outrage from the masses. The temptation is to seize on Kelly as an example of *his* problem alone, and not *ours* as a community. Black communities support abominably sexist beliefs about the low social status of black girls. To let ourselves off the hook by taking moral self-satisfaction in purging our community of R. Kelly is to claim false victory. Moreover, it distracts attention from the larger, more difficult mandate: to point fingers at figures in our own lives who have helped to perpetuate a culture that victimizes black females. Of course, it is not a case of either/or: we must stop pedophiles individually and pay attention to a culture of subtle *pedophobia* that ignores the devastating impact on children's lives of the practices we have learned to take for granted in our communities.

R. Kelly's trouble also reflects how we have tended to target younger blacks with a venomous focus we are unwilling to apply to older figures. For instance, James Brown's troubles with domestic violence are well-known, and yet there has not been a steady outcry for his public shaming. And Marvin Gaye, according to his mother, had become a "monster" because he had taken to beating his girlfriends near the end of his life. I am surely not arguing that we should ostracize either of these figures from black moral community; I am suggesting that we make critiques of domestic abuse and the logic of black patriarchy that sustains it. I realize that we must acknowledge the unique genius of Brown and Gaye, even as we make a concerted effort to attack the root of assaults on black women. No one,

including musical geniuses, must be exempt from moral criticism. Neither should they be conveniently used by the rest of us
to avoid the problems they reflect—and learned—in our community. We must not have a generational double standard: we
overlook the transgressions of our fathers but mercilessly attack
the sins of our sons.

Critic Mark Anthony Neal acknowledges the double standard and places it in historical context. Neal argues that "Kelly
is a product of an era when the private and the intimate in
black life" has come into full public view, something that had
already begun when "Gaye, Major Harris, and Minnie
Ripperton recorded songs with feigned orgasms in the background."[6] As a result, Kelly shares with the public "not only his
perceived sexual exploits, but the demons that have haunted
him as a young black man coming of age" in the midst of massive global media.[7] As Neal says:

> For all of the political significance and cultural weight
> attached to figures like Jack Johnson, Jesse Owens, Joe Louis,
> Sammy Davis, Jr., Jackie Robinson, Wilt Chamberlain, and
> Nat King Cole, none of them—with the exception of
> [Muhammad] Ali—lived in the constant media glare that
> even second-rate rappers and third-string point guards face
> today. This doesn't excuse [Allen] Iverson with a gun or
> Kelly with under-age girls, but places their indiscretions in a
> broader context than 'what's wrong with the hip-hop genera-
> tion?'…[M]y point is not to compare 'sins' but to highlight
> how contemporary culture's coverage of those sins unfairly
> depicts the sins of the 'sons' (and daughters) as worse than
> those of the 'father' (and mother). R. Kelly is no Marvin

Gaye, nor should he be. But R. Kelly is a Soul Man, who seemingly for lack of any other recourse, has chosen to share his demons with us through his music as so many tortured Soul Men of the past have."[8]

R. Kelly has been crying out for help for quite a while. He has been begging the black bourgeois establishment to come to his aid, whether they were in church or in other helpful spots in the community. R. Kelly is a genius who more than any other artist of his generation has tapped the vein of agitation between sex and spirit that gives his art a vitality, and a troubling gravitas, perhaps even a disturbing pathos, that is absent in the work of most of his peers. And he has understood more than any of his colleagues the need to excavate and extend the history of black music. His *Chocolate Factory* is a stunning archive and exploration of black musical styles and genres over the last half century. Unsurprisingly, it alludes brilliantly to Marvin Gaye.

From the beginning of his career, R. Kelly has been sensitive to the musical legacy he inherited. More than a decade ago, a gaggle of new jack singers, influenced by the Gap Band's Charlie Wilson, erotically amplified his smoldering synthesis of pop music and churchy fervor. First, it was Guy's brilliant lead singer, Aaron Hall, who seemed destined to inherit the mantle of Wilson's sophisticated art. And later, it was the R & B group Public Announcement's guiding spirit, R. Kelly, who appeared to have a claim to Wilson's vocal pedigree—and as it would soon become apparent, those of Ronald Isley, Sam Cooke and Marvin Gaye. But while Hall's career bogged down in lackluster performances and mediocre material—unfortunately, he has virtually disappeared—Kelly has bumped off naysayers and ground credibility from the stones of doubt cast at his talent. With 1991's *Born Into the '90s* and 1994's *12 Play*, as well as his work for acts from Changing Faces to Michael Jackson, Kelly proved he could shape memorable pop melodies around liquid grooves and lively harmonies. And within all that, Kelly's songs—pushed along by gritty themes and hip-hop chutzpah—retained their street identity. With the multi-platinum *12 Play*, Kelly heightened the stakes of his carnal cravings—mastering the female form became his magnificent obsession, in lyrics *and* in life. Kelly's explicit sexual desires transgressed a dangerous boundary when they allegedly found fulfillment in teen protégée Aaliyah.

The controversy and pain of Kelly's past caught up with him on his third, self-titled album *R. Kelly*. Like Marvin Gaye (whose secular spirituality bathes this project) before him, Kelly reshapes his personal turmoil to artistic benefit. It's worth taking a look at the album as a sign of how he's tried to fuse sexuality and spirituality, elevate eroticism, confront his demons—and make good music in the process. He opens and closes the album with dramatic testimonials: On "Intro—The Sermon," Kelly vents his frustrations at living under a "magnifying glass." The organ-drenched homily pulsates with his overdubbed call-and-responses. It's as if he trusts only his voice to validate his suffering. But if the spark of testimony is confession, Kelly shows that testimony can be genius when it is defiant. He deliciously enlivens this paradox by admonishing his critics to judge themselves even as he refuses to repent for his own erotic escapades. He *still* doesn't see anything wrong, as his earlier song proclaimed, "with a little bump and grind."

It's fitting, then, when Kelly follows this introduction with

"Hump Bounce," a sly reminder that dancing on the floor and dancing in the sheets are separated more by opportunity than intent. The track's churning groove is airbrushed by female harmonies and built on a James Brown riff lifted from (where else?) "The Payback." But it's telling that Kelly refrains from using a sledgehammer where a metaphor might do. Now, unlike on *12 Play*, when he wants to indulge his erotic appetite, he rediscovers the neglected delights of seduction. On the mellow "You Remind Me of Something," Kelly searches for just the right image of his beloved in an amateurish but auspicious detour from simple sex. Perhaps it's the way this album revels in a seventies black pop aesthetic that bestows romantic resonance on Kelly's nocturnal ambitions. For instance, on "Down Low (Nobody Has to Know)," Kelly twists and shouts to the Isleys' influence on his art—as the legendary brothers themselves lend him their voices and hands. Ron Isley's yearning falsetto glides around Kelly's plaintive tenor—and Ernie Isley's sublimely psychedelic guitar licks—as they tenderly outline their obligation to embrace forbidden love.

"Thank God It's Friday" is sheer fun—a disco groove cobbled together from some rhythmic remains of the S.O.S. Band. Kelly takes an honest swing every time he steps up to the plate, even if he's about the business of putting his own authentic spin on a borrowed style. For example, "I Can't Sleep Baby (If I)"could have been written by Babyface. Kelly's vocals quiver with vulnerability as he faces his lover's departure. And on "(You to Be) Be Happy," Kelly burns a light inside the considerable shadow of the raunchy but irresistible late rapper Notorious B.I.G. By pinching a hypnotic beat here and a jazzy piano riff there—and by coaxing a PG performance from the MC—Kelly weaves a romantic tapestry from fragments of sounds that surface in the music of Mary J. Blige, B.I.G., and the latter's (former) wife, Faith.

But the heart of Kelly's vision—and songs with titles like "Heaven If You Hear Me" and "Religious Love" bear this out— beats in the love he has found in religious faith. Kelly's is not a sanctified sexiness like that of, say, Prince—though in live performance, Kelly is not above juxtaposing horniness and holiness, Pentecost and panties. But on the album's most powerful cut, "Trade In My Life," Kelly takes his sexuality to church, as searing organ chords and the full throttle of gospel hotshot Kirk Franklin's choir, sweep him from the pit of desolation. Kelly begins with a stunning a cappella prayer that God "look down on the ghetto" to save his children, a sentiment that is sweetly pressured by ethereal background harmonies that cut across Kelly's pleading voice. He ends with a shout of praise as the choir surges, joining him in thanking Jesus for being the head of his life. With this audacious jubilee, as with the entire album, it seemed that R. Kelly was truly coming into his own—that he was being reborn before our very ears.

On subsequent albums and songs, Kelly continued to struggle with his spirituality, even as he indulged his erotic ambitions. And his hunger for God remained clear, even if that hunger was challenged by the seductions of the flesh—just as with Marvin. But nowhere was his consciousness of the tension between his secular pursuits and spiritual prospects more poignantly expressed than on his song, "I Wish," when he says that "voices in my head be telling me to come to church, saying the Lord is the only way for you to stop the hurt," sharpened by the concluding couplet: "Instead of y'all throwing stones at me, somebody pray for me."

I went to visit R. Kelly at his Chocolate Factory studio in Chicago, to ask him about Marvin Gaye, and about his own life and music. Obviously we couldn't speak about his legal troubles—in fact, they almost prevented us from talking, but the singer ignored the advice of his counsel, and spoke with me at 1:30 a.m. one October morning in 2003. But we did have a wide-ranging conversation about Gaye's legacy, and about Kelly's spiritual conflicts and moral struggles. As we sat in his studio—the singer wore a doo-rag, sneakers, and a black tee shirt and jeans that were "super-sized" like the McDonald's fast food he loves—Kelly was remarkably forthright, perhaps even gently defiant, in his unapologetic embrace of the fusion of sex and soul even as he aspired to higher ground.

"One thing Marvin Gaye did that's still important to me and other [singers], and his fans around the world, is that he was not afraid to say what he felt," Kelly told me. "He was not afraid to sing from his heart. Back then, sometimes you had singers and artists that would sing what they thought radio would play. They thought about what people would think about them before they wrote a song. Well, Marvin Gaye speaks his mind, and he speaks it musically. Sort of like Ali: [Marvin] was one of the greatest to ever do it, if not the greatest, because of the fact that he speaks from his heart. And what comes from the heart is what reaches and touches the heart. His music talked, and when he was singing, the words became a sentence, and the sentence became a song, and the song became life. And when people hear Marvin Gaye, they say, 'I went through that same thing,' or somebody will say, 'I know somebody who went through the same thing.' Or somebody is going to do, 'Damn, I *want* to go through that same thing'—I'm talking about 'Sexual

Healing.' That's what Marvin Gaye was about, and that's what I'm trying to be about."

I couldn't help but notice that Kelly spoke at times of Marvin in the present tense, as if his music were still vital and alive to him, as if Marvin's spirit continued to hover in his musical mind. Kelly also says that Gaye was forthright about the troubles he endured.

"In the midst of talking about it he was actually crying out. And that's why people felt Marvin, because the world was crying, too, especially back then with the hate and prejudice. Marvin became not only a writer and a singer; he became a scientist of music. And if you're a scientist you're all about inventing and creating solutions. Some people invent problems, some people invent solutions. And Marvin, through his music, invented solutions. You've got people that flip the light on every day. But who created it? He was a scientist of music, one of the great creators of music on this earth, because just as the lights still flick on, people are still making love to his music, and still listening to his music, perhaps more than when he was alive. And that's the kind of mark you want to make before you get out of here. That's why Marvin is just as alive to me as Elvis is [to some people]."

Kelly's face is lit up; he's obviously enjoying speaking about Marvin. The passion is evident, and so is his obvious identification with Gaye. As we talk, there's a small entourage of folk in the room: musicians who are waiting for Kelly to remix a song for the female group JS; his publicist, who is waiting patiently to usher him away to tape a congratulations speech for an award he's receiving, and what appear to be dancers and singers. I think of how Kelly lives in the studio; he breathes work, as his list of production credits readily attest. In a way Marvin never could, Kelly has found refuge in the universe created by the studio. He is addicted to the studio as he constantly reshapes and refines his sonic identity through restless, relentless experimentation with songs, styles, and even other singers, like Ronald Isley, or Celine Dion. I ask Kelly what it is about Gaye's craft and lyrics that excite him musically.

"He's not selfish at all. He follows the *spirit* of the music; he respects the gift of the music. He loves God. Any man that cries out and tells you that they're a 'Trouble Man,' they're more qualified to get next to God than anybody, because they're not afraid to say that's what they need. They're not afraid to say they're going left, but they want to go right. Marvin was all about that. He wore that badge. And his music is married to his lyrics. If he hears his words first, and [then] the melody, then he's going to create the music that's going to be married to that. Not engaged; married, done deal. Marvin is married to everything you heard him do. The music married the lyrics, the lyrics married the music. If you took the lyrics away, you would still hear the words to the music. And his music was not just a song, it was a story. Even through his love ballads you can hear his cry. And that's what the passion comes from. His passion was incredible. His passion exceeded most people's passion because he *so* loved the world. And you could tell the love was in his voice, in his tone, even though sexuality was there at the same time. But he knew every note that he hit. He wanted people to feel him through that. How do I know this? Because I feel the same way!"

Kelly is animated, his hands flailing the air, his chiseled face grimacing in passionate declamation, his eyes full of the same fire that drove Marvin Gaye. It's fair to say that he was channeling Gaye by now, not in a perfunctory sense of acknowledging Gaye's genius or in remarking on his gifts, but because he feels the singer's same motivation so deeply in the pit of his stomach. So it makes sense that when I ask him to speak about what motivates singers like him and Marvin Gaye to expose their hearts—and hurts—to the public, he proved more than ready to respond, using not the royal "we" to refer to himself, but collapsing him and Marvin into a singular musical entity.

"Well, we got prophet in us. We are not just somebody who is at a studio trying to write a song and sell some music and make some money. We don't care if we eat or not with this. We don't care if we die or not with this, because that's how much we love it. That's how much we respect the gift. And when you respect something as much as I respect what I do, and Marvin obviously respected what he did, you're willing to die for it. You're no different than the firemen who went into the building on September 11th. We knew the consequences; we knew the possibilities of not coming out. And that's how deep you've got to be embedded in what you do, with the understanding that the depth of your struggle determines the height of your success. You have to be able to understand that before you can ever say you're trying to be a legend at anything. A great leader is a great follower, and how you remain a great leader is you have to remain a great follower, and Marvin was a follower of what he heard in his head. I follow what I hear in my head spiritually, and I humble myself totally."

Kelly's identification with Marvin makes it plain to me that he also understands that, like Gaye, he will make mistakes, and since they're both so public about their travails, I wonder how he confronts those failings—and his critics.

"I'm in love with people; I'm in love with the world. I don't care if you hate me or whatever you're doing, I'm in love with you, because my mom taught me and raised me that way. And God is pretty much instilled in me through my mom. So that's what I decided I'm going to do. I'm not going to hate nobody 'cause they hate me. Because I know better. And when you know better, you do better. You're going to have your mistakes; you're going to have your flaws, because we're not perfect. But through that you're going to shine through your music, because your faults feed your music, and your music feeds your passion, and your passion feeds your gift. And then when I come in here to write these songs, all that I've been through is going to come to me, to my fingers, to my heart, to the keyboard, out of the speaker, into somebody's ear, and then into their heart. You're talking about major surgery when Marvin played music. He opens them up and dissects them, and fixes whatever they were going through and closes them up. And now they're going to live."

Since I know Kelly is struggling to hold onto God—you can hear it all in his music, and in many ways, it's similar to Marvin's struggle to keep pursuing his spiritual quest in the midst of his mounting problems—I ask him about his own spirituality and what it does for him in the day to day battles with his flesh.

"When we go through something within ourselves and we cry for help, you pray, you can't rush God to help you. You can't tell God when to do it. You have to have the confidence in knowing who God is, and then just believe that it's going to happen. Sort of like when I figured I wanted to do music for the rest of my life. That didn't make me rich—my desires. Desires don't make you rich. Hard work makes you rich. And that's in anything. Even in the process of wanting to be a better person, you've got to struggle. Whether it's drinking, sex, smoking, weed, whoring, pimping, whatever you do. God ain't gonna fix you until He decides to fix you. Why? Because He's got a plan for you. And if He got a plan for you and you don't know the plan, then you really just got to trust Him to come through for you when He's going to come through for you. See, we're all soldiers, and we fight battles. When you're preparing for it, you ain't got to tell everybody, 'Yeah, I'm preparing to fight battles and be a great man.' No. You can hear it through the music if you got some sense about you."

Kelly looks me straight in my eyes; while he may trust that I've got some sense about me, he wants to make sure that I'm one of those who truly gets that he's referring to himself in his music.

"If you hear the cry, the struggle, the sadness, the sex, the God, 'I Believe I Can Fly,' 'The World's Greatest,' 'The Storm Is Over Now,' 'Ignition,' [all Kelly tunes], you hear them fighting."

He's talking about himself, but I'm not sure who the "them" is he's referring to. I keep listening, because it becomes evident that it's a cosmic clash on the battlefield of his soul.

"You ain't seen no knockout, so there's got to be a battle going on. Now you've got to sit back and place your bet. You can bet on the devil; you can bet on God. That's on you. But just know that the fight is happening."

Kelly looks sad but determined; he's revealing his own struggle in metaphoric terms, speaking in a third person voice about a first-person experience. And it is clearly pressing on his mind. That's when he switches back to the declarative, triumphant first-person voice.

"I believe in the fight. I believe I'm going to knock the hell out of the devil eventually. But even in a fight there's a process. There's a rest period, you get up and go back in, you sweat some more if you want to become stronger. But right now, I got a mission to do. I gotta put this music out here. And if you guys in here don't realize what battle you're in, you're going to get knocked out. I don't care what it is, because every level is another devil. No different than the Pac man. You get them $500 apples, here come the devil. You go to another level, and there's more apples on that level. And he's coming to eat you up on that level. You can never master the game."

I can tell that Kelly is striking close to home. He's perhaps revealing more than he intended, but he's preaching now and the Spirit has drug him into a place where he won't, simply can't be quiet. In the middle of asking him whether he sees that struggle in his own spirit, point blank, and that his music is but the testimonial of his internal demons, he cuts me off, not rudely, but in the rush of thoughts that need to spill on the table.

"That's what the great men like the Marvin Gayes, and the Donny Hathaways, the R. Kellys, the Michael Jacksons, and Martin Luther Kings, and Malcolm Xs, we believe in letting people know about our struggle."

I knew as soon as I heard those words that folk might read Kelly as being possessed of a delusion of grandeur, that how dare he compare his struggles, or those of artists, with those of world-class leaders. But in the moment, at the time, with the glare of the public in *all* of his business, I was sure that martyrdom couldn't feel that far off—even if it was a self-imposed necessity. But I also knew that older folk in my generation carp about young people not giving a hang about history. Well, like it or not, if we get young people to latch onto the narratives of struggle that informed us, we can't be mad at them for creatively applying them to their lives and using the older stories as a lens through which to perceive their struggles. The same folk are angry at the rap group Outkast for appropriating Rosa Parks's name to tell a story about engaging enlightened elders, when the wonder is that anybody in their generation even knew her name, much less was inspired to link her legacy in symbolic fashion to the hip-hop generation.

"That's why people love us, that's why my fans love me. Because I'm not afraid to say, 'Trade in my life.' I'm not afraid to say, 'Heaven, I Need a Hug.' (Two more Kelly songs). [Some people say] if you're a gospel singer then you can't do a love ballad. I don't believe in that. I believe in doing what you feel. And at the same time continuing to pray to God and ask him to make you a better person. And that's why the church is so screwed up now. That's why guys like me go to church and be like, 'If I wasn't keying in on who God is, I would say, man, I ain't trying to hear all that. I see everything going on in here, the same as I see going on in the street."

And then Kelly acknowledges that his troubles are real, that they are allegedly caught on tape, and that the folk who indict him have dirty hands as well.

"You all judging me in here, talking about, 'Hey, that's the guy on that nasty little video. First of all, you didn't see the video if you don't watch videos! So how could you even judge me? I'm street smart. Ain't nothing but street people in the church. [It's like asking] why do you go to the gas station? Because you need gas. Why are you going to church? Because you need God. Well then how are you going to judge me if you need God? I'm a simple person, and I think simple things. Because sense is simple."

We close our conversation by talking more of God and religious community, and how Kelly depends on believers to help him in his struggles against the evil around him—and at his door. I ask him what folk should do when they hear Marvin Gaye speaking about God as his friend, and then they hear him confess that he's addicted to drugs, as a way to get to his own sense of how people should respond to his troubles.

"People who love God will start praying for that man. He's a walking commercial. When I put out stuff like 'I Believe I Can Fly,' the real true God warriors are gonna start praying for me. And intervening for me. Because they know I got a monster at me."

The words strike me hard. A monster. Kelly knows it. He feels it. Marvin's mother said he had become a monster. Kelly understands the threat like Marvin understood it, even though I'm not suggesting that their visions of just what it is and how it should be fought are identical. What is true for Kelly, as it was for Marvin Gaye, is that he has come to grips with his finitude and is trying to work out his soul's salvation in the midst of his own self-inflicted wounds and those injuries imposed from outside. At the same time, like Marvin, he insists on charting his own path and defining his spirituality in a fashion that is undoubtedly unorthodox, and unacceptable, to the traditionally religious. Still, Kelly seized upon traditional religious categories to explain his life, and to forgive himself. In that way, he sounds very much like Marvin Gaye.

"I've worked out in my mind that I'm not born perfect. I've

worked out that I'm going to drink. I'm going to have sex. I'm going to smoke weed sometimes. Everybody has got his own devil. All kinds of devils and demons out there. I love women. That could be a problem, or it couldn't be a problem, depending on what God says. Not man. I don't listen to man. I love people, no matter what they do to me. Or say about me. I'm gonna love you brother. Why? In the midst of my struggle, with all my pain and hurting, I'm trying to be like Jesus. I found out that Jesus loves everybody. Call me strange. I don't care. I love God."

Discography

Albums

Numbers within square brackets are chart peak positions [R&B, Pop].

The Soulful Moods of Marvin Gaye
Tamla 221, 6/8/1961.

That Stubborn Kinda Fellow
Tamla 239, 1/31/1963.

Marvin Gaye Recorded Live on Stage
Tamla 242, 9/9/1963.

When I'm Alone I Cry
Tamla 251, 4/1/1964.

Together (Marvin Gaye & Mary Wells)
Motown 613, 4/15/1964. [-, 42]

Marvin Gaye's Greatest Hits
Tamla 252, 4/15/1964.

Hello Broadway
Tamla 259, 11/12/1964.

Side By Side (Marvin Gaye & Kim Weston)
Tamla 260, cancelled.

How Sweet It Is to Be Loved By You
Tamla 258, 1/21/1965. [4, 128]

A Tribute to The Great Nat King Cole
Tamla 261, 11/1/1965. [-,-]

The Moods Of Marvin Gaye
Tamla 266, 5/23/1966. [8, 118]

Take Two (Marvin Gaye & Kim Weston)
Tamla 270, 8/25/1966. [24, -]

United (Marvin Gaye & Tammi Terrell)
Tamla 277, 8/29/1967. [7, 69]

Marvin Gaye's Greatest Hits, Volume 2
Tamla 278, 9/10/1967. [-,-]

You're All I Need (Marvin Gaye & Tammi Terrell)
Tamla 284, 8/26/1968. [4, 60]

In the Groove (later issued as I Heard It Through the Grapevine)
Tamla 285, 8/26/1968. [2, 63]

M.P.G.
Tamla 292, 4/30/1969. [1, 33]

Marvin Gaye & His Girls
Tamla 293, 4/30/1969. [16, 18]

Easy (Marvin Gaye & Tammi Terrell)
Tamla 294, 9/16/1969. [-, 184]

That's the Way Love Is
Tamla 299, 1/8/1970. [17, 189]

Marvin Gaye & Tammi Terrell Greatest Hits
Tamla 302, 5/12/1970. [-,-]

Marvin Gaye Super Hits
Tamla 300, 9/22/1970. [-,-]

What's Going On
Tamla 310, 5/21/1971. [1, 6]

You're the Man
Tamla 316, cancelled. [-,-]

Trouble Man
Tamla 322, 12/8/1972. [3, 14]

Let's Get It On
Tamla 329, 8/28/1973. [1, 2]

Diana & Marvin (Marvin Gaye & Diana Ross)
Motown 803, 10/26/1973. [7, 26]

Marvin Gaye Live
Tamla 333, 6/19/1974. [1, 8]

I Want You
Tamla 342, 3/16/1976. [1, 4]

Marvin Gaye's Greatest Hits
Tamla 348S1, September 1976. [-,-]

Live at the London Palladium
Tamla 352, 3/15/1977. [1, 3]

Here, My Dear
Tamla 364, 12/15/1978. [4, 26]

Love Man
Tamla 369, cancelled.

In Our Lifetime
Tamla 374, 1/15/1981. [6, 32]

Midnight Love
Columbia 38197, October 1982. [1, 7]

Dream of a Lifetime
Columbia 39916, May 1985. [8, 41]

Romantically Yours
Columbia 40208, 1985. [-,-]

Every Great Motown Hit of Marvin Gaye
Motown 6058ML, September 1983. [-,-]

Motown Remembers Marvin Gaye
Motown 6172TL, March 1986. [-,-]

Marvin Gaye Anthology
Motown MCD06199MD2, August 1986 . [-,-]

The Very Best of Marvin Gaye
Motown 7/17/2001. [-,-]

What's Going On [Deluxe Edition]
Motown 2001. [-,-]

Let's Get It On [Deluxe Edition]
Motown 9/18/2001. [-,-]

I Want You [Deluxe Edition]
Motown 2003. [-,-]

Singles

Numbers within square brackets are chart peak positions [R&B, Pop].

Let Your Conscience Be Your Guide / Never Let You Go
Tamla 54041, 5/25/1961. [-, -]

Sandman / I'm Yours, You're Mine
Tamla 54055, 1/19/1962. [-, -]

Soldier's Plea / Taking My Time
Tamla 54063, 5/8/1962. [-, -]

Stubborn Kind of Fellow / It Hurt Me Too
Tamla 54068, 7/23/1962. [8, 46]

Hitch Hike / Hello There Angel
Tamla 54075, 12/19/1962. [12, 30]

Pride and Joy / One of These Days
Tamla 54079, 4/18/1963. [2, 10]

Can I Get a Witness / I'm Crazy 'Bout My Baby
Tamla 54087, 9/20/1963. [15, 22]

You're a Wonderful One / When I'm Alone I Cry
Tamla 54093, 2/20/1964. [-, 15]

Once Upon a Time / What's the Matter with You Baby
Motown 1057 (p/s), 4/14/1964. With Mary Wells [-, 19 / 17]

Try It Baby / If My Heart Could Sing
Tamla 54095 (p/s), 5/21/1964. [-, 15]

Baby Don't You Do It / Walk on the Wild Side
Tamla 54101 (p/s), 9/2/1964. [-, 27]

What Good Am I Without You / I Want You 'Round
Tamla 54104, 9/30/1964. With Kim Weston [-, 61]

How Sweet It Is (To Be Loved By You) / Forever
Tamla 54107, 11/4/1964. [-, 6]

I'll Be Doggone / You've Been a Long Time Coming
Tamla 54112, 2/26/1965. [1, 8]

Pretty Little Baby / Now That You've Won Me
Tamla 54117, 6/18/1965. [16, 25]

Ain't That Peculiar / She's Got to Be Real
Tamla 54122, 9/14/1965. [1, 8]

One More Heartache / When I Had Your Love
Tamla 54129, 1/31/1966. [4, 29]

Take This Heart Of Mine / Need Your Lovin' (Want You Back)
Tamla 54132, 5/2/1966. [16, 44]

Little Darling (I Need You) / Hey Diddle Diddle
Tamla 54138, 7/26/1966. [10, 47]

It Takes Two / It's Got to Be a Miracle
Tamla 54141, 12/2/1966. With Kim Weston [4, 14]

Ain't No Mountain High Enough / Give a Little Love
Tamla 54149, 4/20/1967. With Tammi Terrell [3, 19]

Your Unchanging Love / I'll Take Care of You
Tamla 54153, 6/12/1967. [7, 33]

Your Precious Love / Hold Me Oh My Darling
Tamla 54156, 8/22/1967. With Tammi Terrell [2, 5]

If I Could Build My Whole World Around You / If This World
Were Mine
Tamla 54161, 11/14/1967. With Tammi Terrell [2 / 27, 10 / 68]

You / Change What You Can
Tamla 54160, 12/21/1967. [7, 34]

Ain't Nothing Like the Real Thing / Little Ole Boy, Little Ole Girl
  Tamla 54163, 3/28/1968. With Tammi Terrell [1, 8]

You're All I Need to Get By / Two Can Have a Party
  Tamla 54169, 7/9/1968. With Tammi Terrell [1, 7]

Chained / At Last (I Found a Love)
  Tamla 54170, 8/20/1968. [8, 32]

His Eye Is on the Sparrow / Just a Closer Walk with Thee
  Motown 1128, 9/10/1968. B-side by Gladys Knight and the Pips [-, -]

Keep on Lovin' Me Honey / You Ain't Livin' Till You're Lovin'
  Tamla 54173, 9/24/1968. With Tammi Terrell [11, 24]

I Heard It Through the Grapevine / You're What's Happening (In the World Today)
  Tamla 54176, 11/30/1968. [1, 1]

Good Lovin' Ain't Easy to Come By / Satisfied Feeling
  Tamla 54179, 1/14/1969. With Tammi Terrell [11, 30]

Too Busy Thinking About My Baby / Wherever I Lay My Hat (That's My Home)
  Tamla 54181, 4/2/1969. [1, 4]

That's the Way Love Is / Gonna Keep on Tryin' 'Til I Win Your Love
  Tamla 54185, 8/4/1969. [2, 7]

What You Gave Me / How You Gonna Keep It
  Tamla 54187, 11/6/1969. With Tammi Terrell [6, 49]

How Can I Forget / Gonna Give Her All the Love I've Got
  Tamla 54190, 12/16/1969. (1) [18/-, 41/67]

The Onion Song / California Soul
  Tamla 54192, 3/20/70. With Tammi Terrell. (1) [18, 50]

The End of Our Road / Me and My Lonely Room
  Tamla 54195, 5/19/70. [7, 40]

What's Going On / God Is Love
  Tamla 54201, 1/21/1971. [1, 2]

Mercy Mercy Me (The Ecology) / Sad Tomorrows
Tamla 54207, 6/10/1971. [1, 4]

Inner City Blues (Make Me Wanna Holler) / Wholy Holy
Tamla 54209, 6/10/1971. [1, 9]

You're the Man - Pt. I / You're the Man - Pt. II
Tamla 54221, 4/26/1972. (1) [7, 50]

Trouble Man / Don't Mess with Mr. "T"
Tamla 54228, 11/21/1972. [4, 7]

I Want to Come Home Home for Christmas / Christmas in the City
Tamla 54229, cancelled.

Let's Get It On / I Wish It Would Rain
Tamla 54234, 6/15/1973. [1, 1]

You're a Special Part of Me / I Think I'm Falling in Love
Motown 1280, 9/13/1973. With Diana Ross [-, -]

Come Get to This / Distant Lover
Tamla 54241, 10/11/1973. [3, 21]

You Sure Love to Ball / Just to Keep You Satisfied
Tamla 54244, 1/2/1974. [13, 50]

My Mistake (Was to Love You) / Include Me in Your Life
Motown 1269, 1/17/1974. With Diana Ross [15, 19]

Don't Knock My Love / Just Say, Just Say
Motown 1296, 6/18/1974. With Diana Ross [25, 46]

Distant Lover [live edit] / Trouble Man
Tamla 54253 (p/s), 9/5/1974. (2) [12, 28]

I Want You / I Want You [instrumental]
Tamla 54264, 4/1/1976. (3) [1, 15]

After the Dance / Feel All My Love Inside
Tamla 54273, 7/15/1976. [14, 74]

Got to Give It Up - Pt. I / Got to Give It Up - Pt. II
Tamla 54280 (p/s), 3/15/1977. [1, 1]

Pops, We Love You / Pops, We Love You [instrumental]
Motown 1455, 12/28/1978. (4) [26, 59]

A Funky Space Reincarnation - Pt. I / A Funky Space
Reincarnation - Pt. II
  Tamla 54298, 1/11/1979. [23, 106]

Anger / Time to Get It Together
  Tamla 54300, 6/1979. Canadian release [-, -]

Ego Tripping Out / Ego Tripping Out [instrumental]
  Tamla 54305, 9/28/1979. [17, -]

Praise / Funk Me
  Tamla 54322, 2/6/1981. [18, 101]

Heavy Love Affair / Far Cry
  Tamla 54326, 4/20/1981. [61, -]

Sexual Healing / Sexual Healing [instrumental]
  Columbia 03302, 10/1982. [1, 3]

'Til Tomorrow / Rockin' After Midnight
  Columbia 03589, 1/1983. [31, -]

Joy / Turn on Some Music
  Columbia 03935, 5/1983. [78, -]

Sanctified Lady / Sanctified Lady [instrumental]
  Columbia 04861, 5/1985. [2, 101]

It's Madness / Ain't It Funny (How Things Turn Around)
  Columbia 05442, 5/1985. [55, -]

Just Like / More
  Columbia 05791, 11/1985. [-, -]

The World Is Rated X / No Greater Love
  Tamla 1836 (p/s), 5/1/1986. [-, -]

My Last Chance / Once Upon a Time
  Motown 2083, 11/1990. (With Mary Wells) [-, -]

5, 10, 15, 20 Years of Love /
  Motown 2086, cancelled. (5)

Notes

ONE: "Stubborn Kind of Fellow"

1. Jessie Ash Arndt, "D.A.R. to Converge On Capital Next Week," *Washington Post*, April 29, 1939, p. S10.
2. Louis M. Jiggitts, "The South's Problems," *The Washington Post*, April 2, 1939, p. 9.
3. Ibid.
4. Ibid.
5. Steve Turner, *Trouble Man: The Life and Death of Marvin Gaye* (Hopewell, N.J.: Ecco Press, 2000), p. 15.
6. Ibid., p. 21.
7. Ibid., p. 23
8. Ibid., p. 29
9. Ibid., p. 36
10. Ibid., p. 47
11. Nelson George, *Where Did Our Love Go? The Rise and Fall of the Motown Sound* (New York: St. Martin's Press, 1985); Berry Gordy, *To Be Loved: The Music, the Magic, the Memories of Motown* (New York: Warner Books, 1994); Gerald Early, *One Nation Under a Groove: Motown and American Culture* (Hopewell, N.J.: Ecco Press, 1995); Peter Benjaminson, *The Story of Motown* (New York: Grove Press, 1979); and J. Randy Taraborrelli, *Motown: Hot Wax, City Cool, and*

Solid Gold (New York: Doubleday, 1986); Gerald Posner, *Motown: Music, Money, Sex and Power* (New York: Random House, 2002).

12. David Ritz, *Divided Soul: The Life of Marvin Gaye* (New York: Da Capo Press, 1991 [1985]), p. 29–30.

13. Wilson & Alroy's Record Reviews, www.warr.org/marvin.html

14. Eugene Chadbourne, *All Music Guide to Soul: The Definitive Guide to R & B and Soul*, edited by Vladimir Bogdanov, et al (San Francisco: Backbeat Books 2003), p. 272.

15. Richie Unterberger, *All Music Guide to Soul.* Ibid.

16. Reuben Jackson, "Marvin Gaye's 'Vulnerable': Wistful Thinking," *The Washington Post*, Wednesday, June 4, 1997, D7; Ritz, p. 348.

17. Tom Moon, Review of *The Vulnerable Sessions*, *Rolling Stone*, March 6, 1997, p. 70.

18. Motown also bundled the seven songs from *Vulnerable* with six of Gaye's R & B love ballads, as *Love Songs: Bedroom Ballads*, released in 2002. Some critics thought it a touch schizophrenic, attempting to meld Gaye's nimble treatments of pop tunes with his energetic R & B explorations. But I think there is much to be gained from such sonic juxtaposition; if nothing else, the collection highlights the similar musical elements that make both popular and R & B songs "classics."

19. Reeves' view is backed up by a statement Marvin made to the British magazine, *Melody Maker*: "I love singing ballads and pop stuff but you have to keep the R & B people happy. I was schizophrenic in a sense. I knew what I wanted but I didn't know how to get it. I'm just going to try and give the public what they want now." Quoted in Turner, *Trouble Man*, p. 102.

20. To be fair, Berry Gordy resisted Marvin's desire to sing popular ballads, too, but for different reasons than those cited by Bradford concerning the white establishment. Gordy wanted material he could filter through his Motown machine, which meant R & B material. But to his credit, though he didn't encourage Marvin to sing ballads, he released his first album, which was ballads, and a few more albums of similar material. See Gordy, *To Be Loved*, p. 159.

21. I am not suggesting that Gaye had no interest in making hits and ruling the charts; he did. I'm suggesting that he wanted both: great art and commercial acceptance. See Ritz, *Divided Soul*, p. 73.

22. Turner, *Trouble Man*, p. 62.

23. Turner, *Trouble Man*, p. 63.

24. Turner, *Trouble Man*, p. 73.

25. Ibid.

26. Ritz, *Divided Soul*, p. 64.

27. Turner, *Trouble Man*, p. 86.

28. Ritz, *Divided Soul*, p. 64; Turner, *Trouble Man*, p. 86.

29. Berry Gordy, *To Be Loved*, p. 225.

30. Not everyone was sold on the teaming of Marvin and Tammi. In 1969, music critic Robert Christgau, in reviewing *Marvin Gaye and His Women*, conceded that "Marvin Gaye may be the most talented soul singer alive," but contended that "he has the misfortune of being tall, light and handsome, the perfect Motown-ee idol, and so his soft side, which ought to be checked, is instead accentuated. In the case of the duos he has formed with Mary Wells, Kim Weston and Tammi Wells, this is true even on singles. . . .If you are attentive, you can occasionally hear each woman break out for a bar or two before sinking beneath the strings. Tammi Terrell, the current entry, does this most frequently and effectively but, like her partner, she is careful never to go too far." (Robert Christgau, "Wholly and Solely About Soul," *New York Times*, June 22, 1969, p. D35). Christgau concludes that the album is a "sad document." Christgau is reviewing the album in the context of listening to other soul duets, including Peggy Scott and Jo Jo Benson, and Otis Redding and Carla Thomas. Understandably, the gritty roots of Southern soul make for more compelling examples of the soul duo than the northern gloss of the Motown machine. Still—his chauvinism about Gaye's "soft side" needing to be checked, aside—Christgau misses the genius of the pairing of Marvin and Tammi. It is Gaye's seductive vulnerability that provides a stirring counterpoint to the gruff machismo of too many male-centered narratives in R & B. And it is Tammi's purposeful restraint—as is true of Marvin—that adds vibrancy and energy to her skillful and delicate interpretations of the songs she sang with Gaye, especially on the Ashford and Simpson material.

31. Elaine Jesmer, *Number One With a Bullet* (New York: Farrar, Straus & Giroux, 1974).

32. John Pumilla, "Marvin Gaye & Tammi Terrell: Perfect Together," at www.tammiterrell.com/perfect_together.html

33. Turner, *Trouble Man*, p. 108.

34. Dave Marsh, in his *The Heart of Rock & Soul: The 1001 Greatest Singles Ever Made* (New York: Da Capo, 1991), names Marvin Gaye's version of "I Heard It Through The Grapevine" as the greatest single in rock history. Throughout the world, Gaye's genius on the recording is amply recognized in the high positions the song snagged on critics' lists: it ranked 2nd in *Berlin Media* (Germany), "The 100 Best Singles of All Time" (1998), as it did on Australian writer Peter Holmes' "100 Best Songs of All time" (*The Sun-Herald*, 2003); it ranked 3rd on Dave Marsh and Kevin Stein's *The 40 Best of the Top 40 Singles by Year* (1989); it ranked 4th in *The Rolling Stone's* "The 100 Best Singles of the Last 25 years" (1988) and in the UK based *Sound's* "The 100 Best Singles of All Time" (1986); it ranked 5th on the UK's *Mojo* list of "The 100 Greatest Singles of All Time" (1997); it ranked 6th on "The Top 100 Singles of All Time" list that appeared in the British *New Musical Express* (1976); and Germany's *Zounds* ranked it 10th on its list of "The Top 30 Songs of All Time + Top 10 by Decade" (1992).

35. Although the Isley Brother's lead singer Ronald Isley maintains that Motown took the song from his group (it was eventually sung by Smokey Robinson and the Miracles), to "date no corroborating tape evidence has been located in the company vaults." Ben Edmonds, *What's Going On? Marvin Gaye and the Last Days of the Motown Sound*, p. 29.

36. Robert Webb, "Rock & Pop: Story of the Song: I Heard It Through the Grapevine—Marvin Gaye, 1968," *The Independent* (*London*), p. 18; Turner, *Trouble Man*, pp. 101–102.

37. Ben Fong-Torres, "Honor Thy Brother-in-Law: A Visit With Marvin Gaye," *Rolling Stone*, April 27, 1972.

38. Tim Cahill, "The Spirit, The Flesh and Marvin Gaye," *Rolling Stone*, April 11, 1974, p. 42

TWO: "If This World Were Mine"

1. Heather Ann Thompson, *Whose Detroit? Politics, Labor, and Race in a Modern American City*, p. 3.

2. Donald Clarke, *The Rise and Fall of Popular Music* (New York: St. Martin's Press), p. 439.

3. Nelson George, *Where Did Our Love Go?*; Suzanne E. Smith, *Dancing in the Street: Motown and The Cultural Politics of Detroit* (Cambridge, Mass.: Harvard University Press, 2001); Berry Gordy, *To Be Loved*; Gerald Early, *One Nation Under a Groove*.

4. Smith, *Dancing in the Street*, p. 7.

5. One of the ways the behavior and style of Motown's artists was shaped was through attendance of the company's "charm school" run by Maxine Powell. See Ritz, pp. 88, 89; Turner, p. 79.

6. Smith, *Dancing in the Street*, p. 21.

7. Liner notes from Stokeley Carmichael, *Free Huey!* Black Forum BF452 (Detroit: Motown Record Corporation, 1970), quoted in Suzanne Smith, *Dancing in the Street*, p. 17.

8. Smith, *Dancing in the Street*, p. 231.

9. Ibid., pp. 215–16.

10. Joanna Demers, "Sampling the 1970s in Hip-Hop," *Popular Music*, Volume 22/1, 2003, p. 55.

11. Mark Anthony Neal, *What the Music Said*, p. 63; B. Lee Cooper, "Popular Music: An Untapped Resource for Teaching Contemporary Black History," *The Journal of Negro Education*, Volume 48, Issue 1 (Winter, 1979), pp. 20–36.

12. Smith, *Dancing in the Street*, p. 233.

13. Demers, p. 44. Also see Mark Anthony Neal, *What the Music Said*, p. 62.

14. Ritz, *Divided Soul*, p. 132.

15. Frankie Gaye, *Marvin Gaye, My Brother*, p. 67. Earlier, however, Frankie Gay contended that Marvin had never written him in Vietnam, hurting his feelings, according to David Ritz. "'The death and destruction I saw in Vietnam sickened me,' Frankie told me. 'The war seemed useless, wrong, and unjust. I relayed all this to Marvin and forgave him for never writing to me while I was over there. That had

266 NOTES TO CHAPTER TWO

hurt, because he was a big star and none of my buddies believed he was my brother. 'Wait,' I told them, 'he's going to write me back and prove it to you.' He never did.'" David Ritz, *Divided Soul*, p. 146.

16. There are conflicting accounts of how the song came about. Mel Farr says that he, Marvin, and Farr's fellow Detroit Lions teammate Lem Barney had gone to play golf, and afterward, to Marvin's house afterward. During their conversation, Farr says he said, "Hey, what's going on?" and that Marvin replied, "You know, that'd be a hip title for a song. I think I'll write it for the Originals." Marvin began playing the piano, and when they dropped by the next day, Farr says they told him, "That's not for the Originals, Marvin. That's for you." See David Ritz, *Divided Soul*, p. 146. Another version has Al Cleveland giving the song to Marvin, after writing it in Benson's apartment. Benson is said to have hit on the hook line one afternoon as he drived past Lake Michigan, and presumably asked, "What's going on?" See Turner, *Trouble Man*, p. 109. I have tried to stick as closely to the story told to me in my interview with Benson cited in the text.

17. Ben Fong-Torres, "Honor Thy Brother-In-Law: A Visit with Marvin Gaye," *Rolling Stone*, April 27, 1972.

18. Turner, *Trouble Man*, pp. 110–111. Also see Gordy, *To Be Loved*, pp. 302–303.

19. Cited in Ben Edmonds, *What's Going On?*, pp. 118, 211–212.

20. Marvin was disdainful of some of Norman Whitfield's earlier attempts at "message music," which he felt was as distasteful to him now as mindless pop he was being asked to perform. Gaye felt that Whitfield was being more trend conscious than desirous of circulating social protest. See Edmonds, *What's Going On*, pp. 146–147.

21. Cited in Ben Edmonds, *What's Going On*, pp. 146–147.

22. Ibid., p. 147.

23. Vince Aletti, review of *What's Going On* (Marvin Gaye), and *Where I'm Coming From* (Stevie Wonder), *Rolling Stone*, 1971, p. 44.

24. Stanley Crouch maintains that Marvin's phrasing on "What's Going On," especially the line "Mother, mother," links him to Louis Armstrong: "[Armstrong's] rhythmic feeling was so pervasive, it ends up going in all kinds of places. For instance, if you listen to the way Marvin Gaye phrases 'What's Going On' that comes from Louis

Armstrong. When he sings, 'Mother, mother...' all that, that's straight from Pops." Interview with Stanley Crouch, outtakes for *Jazz: A Film By Ken Burns*, at www.pbs.org/jazz/about/pdfs/Crouch/pdf.

25. Joanna Demers, "Sampling the 1970s in Hip-Hop," *Popular Music*, Volume 22/1, 2003, p. 45.

26. Robert Hilburn, "In Soul, Gaye Taught What Was Going On," *Los Angeles Times*, April 8, 1984, pp. 58–59.

27. Larry Starr and Christopher Waterman, *American Popular Music: From Minstrelsy to MTV* (New York: Oxford University Press, 2003), pp. 321, 324.

28. Martha Bayles, *Hole In Our Sole: The Loss of Beauty and Meaning in American Popular Music* (New York: The Free Press, 1994), p. 230.

29. Marvin Gaye, as quoted on *Marvin Gaye: We Miss You*, Bailey Broadcasting Services, Disc 1, Hour 1, Track 8: 4:07–5:17.

30. Claude Brown, *Manchild in the Promised Land*, (New York: The Macmillan Company, 1965), p. 7.

31. Howard Thurman, *Deep River and the Negro Spiritual Speaks of Life and Death* (New York: Harper & Brothers, 1945, 1955); Richard Newman, *Go Down, Moses: A Celebration of the African-American Spiritual* (New York: Clarkson Potter, 1998).

32. Mark Anthony Neal, *What The Music Said*, p. 63

33. Claude Levi-Strauss, *The Savage Mind*, (Chicago: University of Chicago Press, 1966) p.17. Levi-Strauss explains bricolage in the context of a discussion of the bricoleur : "The *bricoleur* is adept at performing a great number of diverse tasks; but unlike the engineer, he does not subordinate each of them to the availability of raw materials and tools, conceptualized and procured specifically for this project; his instrumental universe is closed, and the rule of his game is to make do with the means at hand." This stresses activity that is both rational and improvisatory. Bricolage involves construction through whatever happens to be "lying around."

34. Nelson George, "Up and Down and Up with Marvin Gaye," *The Rock Musician*, edited by Tony Scherman (New York: St. Martin's Press, 1994), p. 100.

35. For Coltrane's notion of "sheets of sound," see Ira Gitler, "Trane on the Track," *Downbeat*, October 16, 1958, pp. 16–17.

36. Ben Edmonds, *What's Going On*, p. 122.

37. Stanley Crouch, cited in Nelson George "The Power and the Glory" *Village Voice*. May 8, 1984, p. 57.

38. Mark Anthony Neal, *What the Music Said*, pp. 63, 64.

39 Melville Herskovits, *The Myth of the Negro Past*. (Boston: Beacon Press, 1958), p. 71.

40. Harry Weinger, liner notes, deluxe edition, *What's Going On*, 2001.

41. Demers, p. 45.

42. Brian Ward, *Just My Soul Responding: Rhythm and Blues, Black Consciousness, and Race Relations* (Berkeley: University of California Press, 1998), p. 299.

43. At the time of its release, a *New York Times* critic wrote that *Trouble Man* is "a new white-financed black film starring Robert Hooks, one of the founders of New York's Negro Ensemble Company, as a supremely self-assured Los Angeles private eye know simply as Mr. T…[A]lthough it's not a bad film, it represents such a peculiar collaboration of interests that it should be of concern to both black and white film sociologists. Also, it dramatizes such a wild confusion of values I'm not sure it wants to be described as cool or uppity." Vincent Canby, " 'Trouble Man' Arrives," *New York Times*, Nov. 2, 1972, p. 48. Given its virtual cultural disappearance—directed by the talented Ivan Dixon (the black "Hogan's Heroes" television star who also directed the pioneering film *Nothing But a Man*), the film is not available on videotape or DVD—it may take sociological investigation to determine its whereabouts.

44. Mark Anthony Neal, *What the Music Said*, p. 66; Vince Aletti, *Trouble Man* review, *Rolling Stone*, 1972.

45. Ritz, *Divided Soul*, p. 164.

46. Vince Aletti, *Trouble Man* review, *Rolling Stone*, February 15, 1973.

47. Ben Sidran, *Black Talk* (New York: Holt, Rinehart and Winston), 1971, p. 101.

48. Vince Aletti, *Trouble Man* review, *Rolling Stone*, February 15, 1973.

49. Mark Anthony Neal, *What the Music Said*, p. 67.

50. Ibid., pp. 67, 68.

51. Ritz, *Divided Soul*, pp. 106–107.

52. David Davis, "Red, Hot and Blue: Marvin Gaye's Soulful Anthem at the '83 All-Star Game Marked the Rise of a New NBA but Proved to be His Last Hurrah." *Los Angeles Magazine*, Feb. 2003.

53. Ritz, *Divided Soul*, p. 261.

54. Davis, Ibid.

55. "Marvin Gaye Challenges Singer to Battle of Soul Songs," *Sacramento Observer*, November 7, 1968.

THREE: "Somethin' Like Sanctified"

1. Ritz, *Divided Soul*, p. 178.

2. See Michelle Wallace, *Black Macho and the Myth of the Superwoman* (New York: Doubleday, 1979); bell hooks, *Ain't I a Woman?Black Women and Feminism* (Boston: South End Press, 1982); Patricia Hill Collins, *Black Feminist Thought: Knowledge, Consciousness and the Politics of Empowerment*, 2nd edition (New York: Routledge, 2000). Also see Brian Ward, *Just My Soul Responding*, p. 371.

3. Brian Ward, *Just My Soul Responding*, p. 371.

4. The exception can be found on his last, posthumous album, *Dream of a Lifetime*, which includes "Sanctified Lady" (originally "Sanctified Pussy"), "Savage in the Sack," and especially "Masochistic Beauty."

5. Brian Ward, *Just My Soul Responding*, p. 380.

6. "What is Hebrew Pentecostal?" found at www.houseofgod.org /hebrew_pentecostal.htm

7. Steve Turner, *Trouble Man*, p. 10.

8. Tim Cahill, "The Spirit, The Flesh and Marvin Gaye," *Rolling Stone*, April 11, 1974, p. 41.

9. Ibid.

10. Teresa L. Reed, *The Holy Profane: Religion in Black Popular Music* (Lexington: The University of Kentucky Press), 2003, p. 23.

11. Tim Cahill, "The Spirit, The Flesh and Marvin Gaye," *Rolling Stone*, April 11, 1974, p. 41.

12. Reed, p. 33.

13. Cahill, p. 43.

14. See Craig Werner, *A Change Is Gonna Come: Music, Race & Soul of America* (New York: Plume, 1998) p. 278.

15. Ibid.

16. Carlyle C. Douglas, "Marvin Gaye: After shunning concerts for five years, Motown's supersensitive superstar is back!" *Ebony*, November, 1974, p. 54.

17. Nelson George, "Up and Down and Up With Marvin Gaye," *The Rock Musician* (New York: St. Martin's Press, edited by Tony Scherman), 1994, p. 99.

18. Ibid.

19. Ibid., p. 62.

20. Martha Bayles, *Hole In Our Soul*, p. 271.

21. Orea Jones, "The Theology of 'Sexual Healing': Marvin Gaye," *Black Sacred Music* 3:2, Fall, 1989, p. 69.

22. Ibid.

23. Ibid., pp. 69–70.

24. Ibid., p. 70.

25. Ibid.

26. Ibid., p. 73.

27. Graham Cray, "Through Popular Music: 'Wholy Holy'?," in *Beholding The Glory: Incarnation through the Arts* (Grand Rapids, MI: Baker Books), 2000, pp. 123–124.

28. Ibid., p. 125.

29. Ibid, p. 125–126.

30. Ibid., p. 129.

31. Ibid., p. 131.

32. Ibid., pp. 131–132.

33. Ibid. p. 132.

34. Ibid.

35. Ibid, p. 134.

36. Ibid., p. 135

37. Ibid.

38. David Ritz, *Divided Soul*, p. 182.

39. Romans 3:23.

40. For instance, see Rosemary Radford-Reuther, *Sexism and God-*

Talk: Toward a Feminist Theology (Boston: Beacon Press,1983) and Elisabeth Schussler-Fiorenza *In Memory of Her: A Feminist Theological Reconstruction of Christian Origins* (New York: Crossroad/Herder & Herder, 1983).

41. As David Ritz writes, "Part of Marvin was too sophisticated to subscribe to the tenets of his father's Pentecostal church, but another part—a more powerful part—was never able to shake off those notions. Spiritually, *In Our Lifetime* represents the best of his old-time religion, the part of Pentecostal preaching that insists on unrelenting praise, on the expression of gratitude as a way of coping with a worrisome world." *Divided Soul*, p. 283.

42. Marvin Gaye, as quoted on *Marvin Gaye: We Miss You*, Bailey Broadcasting Services, Disc 2, Hour 2, Track 2: 6:02–7:46.

FOUR: "How Sweet It Is to Be Loved By You"

1. Martha Bayles, *Hole in Our Soul*, pp. 271–272.

2. Ritz, *Divided Soul* pp. 307–308.

3. Nathaniel Mackey, *Bedouin Hornbook*, Callaloo Fiction Series, vol. 2 (Lexington: University of Kentucky, 1986), 51–52, cited in Fred Moten, *In the Break: The Aesthetics of the Black Radical Tradition* (Minneapolis: University of Minnesota Press, 2003), pp. 193–194.

4. Ritz, p. 183.

5. Dave Marsh, *Midnight Love* review, *Rolling Stone*, January 20, 1983, p. 48.

6. Neal, *What the Music Said*, pp. 70–71.

7. Ritz, *Divided Soul*, p. 180.

8. Ibid.

9. Nelson George, "Up and Down and Up With Marvin Gaye," *The Rock Musician* (New York: St. Martin's Press, edited by Tony Scherman, 1994), p. 101.

10. Robert Palmer, "Marvin Gaye Is Back and Looking Up," *New York Times*, May 18, 1983, p. C19.

11. Ibid.

12. Steve Turner, *Trouble Man*, p. 134.

13. Interview with Harry Weinger, 2003.

14. Ritz, *Divided Soul*, p. 162.

15. Brian Ward, *Just My Soul Responding*, p. 368.

16. Paul Gambaccini, "You're a Special Part of Me," review, *Rolling Stone*, December 6, 1973, As David Ritz notes, there were tremendous clashes and tensions around the album—from Marvin wanting half of the producer royalties to getting his name first. He got neither. Plus, there was a conflict in style of recording, with Gaye looser—sipping wine and smoking joints—and Ross more formal. See Ritz, *Divided Soul*, pp. 170–171.

17. Donald Clarke, *The Rise and Fall of Popular Music* (New York: St. Martin's Press), 1995, pp. 444–445.

18. Quoted in Ben Edmonds, liner notes, Deluxe Edition, *Let's Get It On*.

19. Ibid.

20. Ibid.

21. Kimasi L. Browne, "Brenda Holloway: Los Angeles' Contribution to Motown" in *California Soul: Music of African–Americans in the West* (edited by Jacqueline Cogdell Dje Dje and Eddie S. Meadows) (Berkeley: University of California Press 1998), pp. 335–336.

22. George, *Where Did Our Love Go?*, p. 157.

23. Jesmer, *Number One With a Bullet*.

24. Ritz, *Divided Soul*, p. 111.

FIVE: "Come Live With Me, Angel"

1. Martin Duberman, *Stonewall* (New York: Plume, 1994).

2. Craig Werner, *A Change Is Gonna Come* (New York: Plume, 1998), p. 205.

3. Ibid., p. 206

4. Iain Chambers, *Urban Rhythms: Pop Music and Popular Culture* (New York: St. Martin's Press, 1985), p. 187.

5. See Richard Dyer, "In Defense of Disco," *Gay Left*, 8, London, cited in Iain Chambers, *Urban Rhythms: Pop Music and Popular Culture*

(New York: St. Martin's Press, 1985), p. 149.

6. Iain Chambers, *Urban Rhythms: Pop Music and Popular Culture* (New York: St. Martin's Press, 1985), p. 187; Brian Ward, *Just My Soul Responding*, p. 425.

7. Ward, p. 429.

8. Ritz, *Divided Soul*, p. 228.

9. Martin Johnson, "Wounded Soul, Healing Heart," *Wall Street Journal*, August 19, 2003, p. D5.

10. Vince Aletti, *I Want You* review, *Rolling Stone*, June 3, 1976.

11. Ibid.

12. Ibid.

13. Ibid.

14. Ibid.

15. Janis Gaye, as quoted on *Marvin Gaye: We Miss You*, Bailey Broadcasting Services, Disc 1, Hour 1, Track 1: 0:52–1:26.

16. Janice Malone, "The Scoop: Widow of Marvin Gaye Talks About Her Husband," *New York Voice Inc.* V. XXXVII; Number 15, p. 18.

17. Ibid.

18. Janis Gaye, as quoted on *Marvin Gaye: We Miss You*, Bailey Broadcasting Services, Disc 1, Hour 1, Track 1: 4:40–5:10

19. Malone, p. 18.

20. *Behind the Legend*. 2000 Eagle Rock Entertainment PLC.

21. Ibid.

22. Ritz, *Divided Soul*, p. 164.

23. Also, the song's politics of seduction match the technical means to express political and social realities on other fronts, as well as complex, polyvalent rhythmic structures and harmonic possibilities brought out in Gaye's music. As Fred Moten argues: "The same technical innovations used to offer up new prescriptive and descriptive social visions are deployed in the no less important work of seduction. Gaye's masterpiece 'Since I Had You' exemplifies this, disturbing or disrupting the lectured narrative of love abandoned and retrieved with the ecstatics of unadorned, irreducible and highly aestheticized phonic substance...The recording is the only possible site of this refusal to reduce the phonic substance and this reordering of aesthetic space. It marks and makes possible that resistance of the object—to

disappearance or interpretation—that constitutes the essence of performance. In the production of the recording, Gaye produces that new space whose essence is the ongoing call for the production of New Space, of a new world, by holding—which to say, suspending, embracing—time. My initial interest, therefore, is rhythmic, though the harmonic complexities of a technically facilitated counterpoint—in the very pressure that it puts on rhythm—is also at issue here. I want to show how the imposition of certain specific and repressive temporal regimes of labor—which Adorno characterized as 'the rhythm of the iron system'—are both echoed and disrupted in 'Since I Had You.'...Gaye out to be situated in an ongoing thematic investigation of the relation between the production of knowledge and the production of economic and aesthetic value, between production in the factory and production in the studio. 'Since I Had You' is indelibly marked with this soundwriting against standardization by way of the most intimate knowledge of worker discipline, a knowledge that is, as it were, cut into the groove of the record just as surely as the groove cuts against the very grain of the uniformity of the line." *In the Break: The Aesthetics of the Black Radical Tradition* (Minneapolis, MN: University of Minnesota Press, 2003), pp. 225–227.

24. Deborah Cameron, *Feminism and Linguistic Theory* (London: Macmillan), 1987, p. 77. Cited in Brian Ward, *Just My Soul Responding: Rhythm and Blues, Black Consciousness, and Race Relations* (Berkeley: University of California Press), 1998, p. 375.

25. Ritz, pp. 170–171.

SIX: "Father, Father, Father We Don't Need to Escalate"

1. Ritz, *Divided Soul*, p. 114.

2. Ben Fong-Torres, "Honor They Brother-in-Law: A Visit with Marvin Gaye," *Rolling Stone*, April 27, 1972.

3. Ritz, *Divided Soul*, p. 53.

4. John C. Flynn, *Cocaine* (New York: Birch Lane Press), 1991, pp. 82–83.

5. Ritz, *Divided Soul*, p. 114.

6. Ibid.

7. Ibid.

8. Ibid., pp. 36–37, 53, 95,183,198–199, 215, 217, 236, 266, 271, 317, 329.

9. Ibid., p. 225.

10. Ritz, *Divided Soul*, p. 225.

11. Carl Arrington, "Ailing, but never out, a troubled Marvin Gaye finds out what the doctor ordered: *Sexual Healing*," *People*, Jan. 24, 1983, p. 31.

12. *Jet*, April 16, 1984, p. 62.

13. Ibid.

14. Ibid.; Ritz, p. 264.

15. Ritz, p. 265.

16. Ibid., p. 266.

17. Ritz, p. 286.

18. *Jet*, Nov. 27, 1980, p. 62.

19. Ibid.

20. Nelson George, "Up and Down and Up with Marvin Gaye," in *The Rock Musician*, edited by Tony Scherman (New York: St. Martin's Press), 1994, pp. 95–96.

21. Ibid., pp. 285–286.

22 . While the line is found in Charles Portis's novel, *True Grit*, on which the film is based, it also showed up in David Mamet's 1997 film *The Spanish Prisoner*, when the character Ricky Jay (played by George Lang) says, "I put a thief in my mouth to steal my brains." But the true inspiration for Portis and Mamet is found in Shakespeare's *Othello* (Act II, Scene III), where Cassio says, "I remember a mass of things, but nothing distinctly; a quarrel, but nothing wherefore. O God, that men should put an enemy in their mouths to steal away their brains! That we should, with joy, pleasance, revel, and applause, transform ourselves into beasts!"

23. Interview with Kitty Sears, 2003.

24. *Jet*, December 13, 1982, p. 29.

25. Ibid.

26. George, p. 99.

27. Ibid., p. 319.

28. *Jet*, July 11, 1983, p. 56.

29. *Jet*, August 1, 1983, p. 61.

30. Ibid.

31. Ibid.

32. Janis Gaye, as quoted on *Marvin Gaye: We Miss You*, Bailey Broadcasting Services, Disc 2, Hour 2, Track 2: 11:46–12:44.

33. Ritz, p. 326.

34. Interestingly, Marvin felt similar feelings of jealousy and resentment for his son, Marvin Gaye, III. When asked why he named his son after him and his father, Marvin gave a revealing answer: "I was torn. I liked the tradition of naming my son after me, but I also didn't want to be reminded of my father. When Marvin arrived, I made the decision: Tradition had to be upheld. That's what we learned from the Old Testament. I was also determined to avoid the pitfalls of Father in raising my son. Some I did avoid. Others I didn't. A child is a great source of joy, though I didn't realize how much little Marvin would dominate his mother's attention. I could see why Father had been jealous of me. I felt jealousy rising up within me." Quoted in David Ritz, *Divided Soul*, p. 100. Later, at a concert he gave at New York's Copacabana in 1966, *Variety* reported that when Marvin's infant son was passed to a person at ringside for the entire audience to see, attention was diverted from Gaye for a good while. As Ritz writes: "The incident not only embarrassed Gaye but placed him at odds with his infant son, who'd stolen the spotlight, reminding Marvin of the intensely competitive, push-and-shove relationship he faced with his own father." Ritz, *Divided Soul*, p. 108.

35. Desmond Morris, *The Naked Ape: A Zoologist's Study of the Human Animal* (New York: McGraw Hill), 1967, pp. 167–178, cited in Sharon Shockley Lee, "Legitimated Violence in Schools: The Power Behind the Paddle," *Advancing Women in Leadership Journal*, Spring, 2003. Advancing Women Website, www.advancingwomen.com.

36. Ritz, *Divided Soul*, p. 12.

37. Ibid.

38. Turner, *Trouble Man*, p. 16.

39. Ritz, *Divided Soul*, p. 18; Richard Ekins, *Male Femaling: A*

Grounded Theory Approach to Cross-Dressing and Sex-Changing (New York: Routledge), 1997.

40. Turner, p. 19.

41. Ibid.; Ritz, p. 17.

42. Ritz, p. 18.

43. Turner, *Trouble Man*, p. 19.

44. Deborah Y. Anderson, *Marvin Gaye: The Untold Chapter* (Stone Mountain, GA: De 'Vonne Productions), 1997.

45. Ibid., pp. 83–84.

46. "Corporal Punishment in Schools: Position Paper of the Society for Adolescent Medicine," *Journal of Adolescent Health* 2003, May 2003, Vol. 32, No. 5, p. 385.

47. Ibid.

48. Ibid.

49. Ibid.

50. Ibid.

51. Ibid.

52. Ibid., p. 386. This includes the officially reported cases, which, in the 1980s, reached a high of 1.5 million cases, plus estimates of actual occurrences that went unreported. Some argue that the number today is much closer to 400,000, but that is an extremely conservative estimate, one that discounts unreported cases and ignores private and parochial school incidents. Whatever the number is, it remains unacceptably high.

53. Aida Croal, "Sparing the Rod: Black Attitudes on Spanking," *Africana.com*

54. Ibid.

55. Since women are more likely to be directly involved in child rearing than men, they are also more likely to see the vicious effects of corporal punishment on children. Also, for many females, the experience of having their lives shaped by masculine priorities, perhaps even patriarchal violence, discourages support for corporal punishment. For the highly educated, familiarity with child development and an appreciation for viable alternatives to spanking erode their support for corporal punishment. And living outside the Bible Belt—with its staunchly traditional views on gender and the family—lessens the

likelihood of support for corporal punishment.

56. Harold Grasmick, Bursik, & Kimpel. 1991. "Protestant Fundamentalism and Attitudes Toward Corporal Punishment of Children," *Violence & Victims*, 6(4), 283–298; Harold G. Grasmick, Morgan, & Kennedy. 1992. "Support for Corporal Punishment in the Schools: A Comparison of the Effects of Socioeconomic Status and Religion." *Social Science Quarterly*. 73(1): 177–187; Christopher G. Ellison and Darren E. Sherkat. 1993. "Conservative Protestantism and Support for Corporal Punishment." *American Sociological Review*. 58: 131–144. This is not a claim of exclusivity, but strength. Other groups that support corporal punishment include, unsurprisingly, the National Association of Secondary School Principals, and the American Federation of Teachers.

57. "Corporal Punishment in Schools: Position Paper of the Society for Adolescent Medicine," *Journal of Adolescent Health* 2003, May 2003, Vol. 32, No. 5, p. 387.

58. Ibid.

59. Ibid.

60. Ibid.

61. Ibid; "Giving Guidance On Child Discipline: Physical punishment works no better than other methods and has adverse effects." Editorial. *BMJ*, Saturday 29, January, 2000, p. 261.

62. Christopher G. Ellison and Darren E. Sherkat. 1993. "Conservative Protestantism and Support for Corporal Punishment." *American Sociological Review*. 58: 131–144; Clifton P. Flynn. 1994. "Regional Differences in Attitudes Toward Corporal Punishment." *Journal of Marriage and the Family*. 56: 314–324; Clifton P. Flynn. 1998. "To Spank or not to Spank: The Effect of Situation and Age of Child on Support for Corporal Punishment." *Journal of Family Violence*. 13(1): 21–37; Harold G. Grasmick, Morgan, & Kennedy. 1992. "Support for Corporal Punishment in the Schools: A Comparison of the Effects of Socioeconomic Status and Religion." *Social Science Quarterly*. 73(1): 177–187.

63. Aida Croal, "Sparing the Rod: Black Attitudes on Spanking," *Africana.com*.

64. Ibid.

65. "Abolish Corporal Punishment in America's Public Schools." Found at http://www.petitiononline.com/maka13/petition.html

66. Clifton P. Flynn. 1998. "To Spank or not to Spank: The Effect of Situation and Age of Child on Support for Corporal Punishment." *Journal of Family Violence*. 13(1): 21–37.

67. For one example, see the work of Orland Patterson, *Rituals of Blood: Consequences of Slavery In Two American Centuries* (New York: Basic Civitas Books, 1998).

68. Alvin Poussaint and Amy Alexander, *Lay My Burden Down: Unraveling Suicide and the Mental Health Crisis Among African-Americans* (Boston: Beacon Press, 2000).

69. William Grier and Price Cobbs, *Black Rage* (New York: Bantam Books, 1974), p. TK TK

70. See, for instance, Proverbs 13:24; 19:18; 22:15; 23:13; 23:14; and 28:15.

71. *Holy Bible: New International Version.*

72. Sharon Shockley Lee, "Legitimated Violence in Schools: The Power Behind the Paddle," *Advancing Women in Leadership Journal*, Spring, 2003, Advancing Women Website, www.advancingwomen.com

73. Gregory K. and Lisa Popcak, *Parenting With Grace: Catholic Parent's Guide to Raising (Almost) Perfect Kids* (Huntington, IN: Our Sunday Visitor, 2000), cited in Sharon Shockley Lee, "Legitimated Violence in Schools: The Power Behind the Paddle," *Advancing Women in Leadership Journal*, Spring, 2003, Advancing Women Website, www.advancingwomen.com

74. Sharon Shockley Lee, "Legitimated Violence in Schools: The Power Behind the Paddle," *Advancing Women in Leadership Journal*, Spring, 2003, Advancing Women Website, www.advancingwomen.com

75. Ibid.

76. Ibid.

77. Ibid.

78. Ibid.

79. "Corporal Punishment in Schools: Position Paper of the Society for Adolescent Medicine," *Journal of Adolescent Health* 2003, May

2003, Vol. 32, No. 5, p. 388.

80. Ibid.

81. David Ritz, *Divided Soul*, p. 131.

82. Ibid., pp. 131–132.

83. *Jet*, April 23, 1984, pp. 57–58.

84. Ibid.

85. Frankie Gaye with Fred E. Basten, *Marvin Gaye, My Brother* (San Francisco: Backbeat Books, 2003), p. 185.

86. Ibid.

AFTERWORD: "Trouble Man"

1. Robert Palmer, "Marvin Gaye Tests The Limits," *New York Times*, March 25, 1979, p. D20

2. Ibid.

3. Ibid.

4. David Ritz, *Divided Soul*, p. 100.

5. Steve Turner, *Trouble Man*, p. 82.

6. Mark Anthony Neal, "The Tortured Soul of Marvin Gaye and R. Kelly," *PopMatters.com*, November 3, 2003.

7. Ibid.

8. Ibid.

Index